A Way of Putting It

Sermons of Peter Atkinson

EDITED BY
MICHAEL W. BRIERLEY

Sacristy
Press

Sacristy Press
PO Box 612, Durham, DH1 9HT

www.sacristy.co.uk

First published in 2023 by Sacristy Press, Durham

Sacristy Limited, registered in England & Wales, number 7565667

British Library Cataloguing-in-Publication Data
A catalogue record for the book is available from the British Library.

ISBN 978-1-78959-273-3

Contents

Contributors

Peter Atkinson has been dean of Worcester since 2007. Having ministered in parishes in Clapham, Tatsfield and Bath, he was, from 1991 to 1994, principal of Chichester Theological College. Subsequently rector of Lavant, he then spent a decade as a residentiary canon of Chichester before his appointment to Worcester.

Michael Brierley is director of formation at Ripon College Cuddesdon, Oxford. Previously he served as priest-in-charge of Tavistock and Gulworthy in west Devon (2007–14), and as canon precentor of Worcester and worship adviser for the diocese of Worcester (2014–21).

Georgina Byrne is Anglican tutor at the Queen's Foundation for Ecumenical Theological Education, Birmingham. A director of ordinands and dean of women's ministry while a residentiary canon of Worcester from 2009 to 2021, she has also been, since 2017, a chaplain to the Sovereign.

Stephen Cottrell is the archbishop of York and primate of England. He was assistant director of pastoral studies at Chichester Theological College and priest-in-charge of Parklands (1988–93), missioner for the diocese of Wakefield (1993–2001), residentiary canon of Peterborough (2001–4), bishop of Reading (2004–10), and bishop of Chelmsford (2010–20).

John Inge has been bishop of Worcester since 2008. After an incumbency at Wallsend, north Tyneside (1990–6), he was a residentiary canon of Ely (and vice-dean from 1999) until 2003, when he was appointed bishop of Huntingdon. Since 2013, he has been lord high almoner to the Sovereign.

Foreword

John G. Inge

"Feed my sheep": that is the charge given to Peter by Jesus, the Good Shepherd, not once, not twice, but three times in the encounter between them following Jesus's resurrection from the dead.[1] Peter fulfilled that calling 50 days later, at Pentecost. Immediately after a rushing, mighty wind had descended on the disciples with tongues of flame, he faced a great crowd of people from across the known world and launched into a sermon so powerful that, despite their diversity of language, they all heard him speaking directly to them in words that they could understand. Peter set the life of Jesus in its historical context, the story of Israel; he proclaimed Jesus as Lord and messiah; he called for repentance; and he promised forgiveness of sins and the gift of the Holy Spirit. Within hours, 3,000 people had been baptized.[2]

Like most sermons, Peter's sermon was unique, never to be repeated. Nevertheless, it offers a pattern for preachers to follow. The preacher needs the Holy Spirit: every sermon originates in prayer. Then, as Peter shows, a sermon is "food". Jesus had said, "I am the bread of life [...] Whoever eats of this bread will live forever; and the bread that I will give for the life of the world is my flesh" and "One does not live by bread alone, but by every word that comes from the mouth of God."[3] So Peter feeds the flock with the Word of God.

Peter spoke in such a way that every individual felt spoken to personally. A good sermon empathizes and engages with its hearers; it speaks to their experience, their fears, joys, hopes, and faith. In doing

---

[1]   John 21:15–17.

[2]   Acts 2:1–42.

[3]   John 6:48,51 and (quoting Deuteronomy 8:3) Matthew 4:4.

so, it may include an element of challenge: a call to repentance involves facing up to things that need to be put right. At the same time, it reassures listeners of God's boundless forgiveness. "God was in Christ reconciling the world to himself."[4]

It will be clear to anyone who has heard Peter Atkinson preach that this is the pattern, set by his namesake, which he himself follows. Peter shows us Jesus. He does so through his own relationship to Jesus in personal devotion, and by careful, prayerful, scholarly attention to scripture. Peter knows his flock: he speaks in ways that address their faith, their hopes, and their fears. He can be challenging; not only to those who hear him speak, for he can also speak truth to power. As a historian, Peter often offers a broader perspective on life. Especially in times as troubled as these, this is a source of hope. A more profound hope still comes from the way in which Peter expresses his conviction that we live in God's time: this is God's story, the story of salvation. In these and other ways, our Peter, like his predecessor, fulfils a calling to feed all those who turn to Jesus, the living bread come down from heaven.

I have been privileged to hear Peter preach on many occasions, and I have invariably been encouraged and inspired. The most memorable occasion was the funeral requiem of my late wife, Denise, included in this volume.[5] His sermon moved a packed cathedral to tears and brought us hope through the faith and love that were so beautifully articulated within it. I shall always remain grateful to him for that, but just as much for the countless other sermons from which I have profited, including many to the very few of us at the early morning eucharist in Worcester Cathedral.

There is much more about Peter for which I am profoundly grateful: he is a wonderful person and an exceptional priest. I have been greatly enriched by his exemplary ministry and have hugely enjoyed his company as a colleague for 15 years. I give heartfelt thanks for him: his friendship and his faith, his wit and his wisdom, have been gifts beyond telling.

His sermons are among his gifts. I have been very well fed by them. Indeed, I have feasted on them, as have so many people over the years.

---

4   2 Corinthians 5:19.

5   Sermon no. 49, "Alleluia is our song".

I am delighted that, by reading this collection, others will be able to benefit from them, and I commend this book enthusiastically and wholeheartedly.

Preface

Michael W. Brierley

The ministry of Peter Atkinson in the Church of England has been highly respected by many people, in many settings, at many levels. This includes not only his public roles as principal of Chichester Theological College (1991–4), canon chancellor of Chichester (1997–2007), and dean of Worcester (2007–23), but also his quiet care as a prayerful priest, his dedicated service to a wide range of church boards and committees, and his pastoral work as a spiritual director and guide. Among the valued gifts that he has exercised across these contexts is his preaching, nurtured by a deep immersion in scripture, Christian tradition and literature; and it is the common esteem in which he is held as a preacher that renders this aspect of his labours an extremely suitable medium through which, on the occasion of his retirement, to honour his ministry (an idea first conceived during the pandemic lockdown of 2020 by the three residentiary canons who then served with him at Worcester Cathedral)—an ecclesiastical equivalent, perhaps, to a festschrift, except that readers might much prefer to read Peter's own words than others' words written under his influence and inspiration.

The publication of Peter Atkinson's sermons as a tribute to his talents as a preacher simultaneously provides an object lesson in the art and skill of preaching. It is not just that studying collected sermons by a single author allows the reader to appreciate the particular themes and insights of the preacher's understanding of the gospel; it is also that the sermons themselves become a model in the craft of sermon construction: how to engage with biblical texts, how to engage with a congregation, and how to engage with contemporary society and the wider world, all in flowing yet economic prose that combines hermeneutical acumen, gentle wit, and spiritual wisdom. The introduction and conclusion to this volume

("Manifesting the risen Christ" and "On the purpose of preachers and preaching") seek to draw out the implications from these sermons for effective preaching, as well as celebrate the preacher who delivered them.

> That was a way of putting it—not very satisfactory:
> A periphrastic study in a worn-out poetical fashion,
> Leaving one still with the intolerable wrestle
> With words and meanings.[1]

Peter Atkinson's own suggested title for this collection, *A Way of Putting It*, drawn from a line in T. S. Eliot's *Four Quartets*, is typical of his self-deprecatory style: his preaching is indeed just one (or "a") way of putting "it" (as in, things in general, or more specifically, Christian faith, with which, of course, for him, life in general is entirely intertwined), while those who rate Peter as a preacher would be far from regarding his "way of putting it" as "not very satisfactory", "periphrastic" or "worn out" (indeed, quite the reverse). Nonetheless, as the motif of "wrestling" in these sermons makes clear, Peter is (rightly) far from giving answers that are all nicely and neatly wrapped up, as though there were nothing else to say, and these sermons do well to leave readers tussling, if not "intolerably", with words and meanings.

The fact that there are 50 sermons in this selection indicates a way in which they can be used devotionally. Had there been 40, they could have been read through, one each day, for the period of Lent. Few, however, would regard digestion of these sermons as a penance. The provision of 50 suggests that they can be enjoyed for daily reading as a celebratory discipline during Eastertide: this would befit Peter Atkinson's own emphasis on the importance of merriment, reading for pleasure, and taking seriously the festive seasons of the liturgical year.

No attempt has been made here to be exhaustive in coverage, either in terms of the ecclesiastical calendar, or in terms of significant events in Church and society over recent decades, although readers will find reflections on key moments. The first 25 sermons loosely accompany

---

[1]   T. S. Eliot, "East Coker", in *Four Quartets* (*The Complete Poems and Plays of T. S. Eliot* [London: Faber and Faber, 1969], pp. 177–83 at 179).

the reader on a journey from the Advent note of judgement through
to the mystery of the Trinity, ending with a profoundly illuminating
analysis of John's Gospel through the lens of friendship. The second 25,
beginning on the note of friendship, introduce the reader to a number of
saintly friends, or friendly saints, who open out the horizon to the eternal
kingdom of God, in which "a great multitude that no one could count,
from every nation, from all tribes and peoples and languages, [stand]
before the throne and before the Lamb".[2]

Sermons speak in different ways to different people. Not infrequently,
it is phrases (even asides) that the preacher may not have regarded as
integral to their message which yet resonate most powerfully with those
who listen. Readers, similarly, will find that some of these texts appeal
more than others. At the very same time, some emphases within these
sermons persist and recur, enabling a glimpse into Peter Atkinson's
distinctive theology and spirituality. Wrestling and celebration, struggle
and joy, work and rest, moral demand and wry humour: these are Peter
Atkinson's way of putting it in sermons, but not only that—they are also
his way of putting the Christian gospel into practice. Peter Atkinson is
himself "a way of putting it", and for that (if I may speak on behalf of
very many others in and beyond the Church), thanks be to him, and
thanks be to God.

Cuddesdon
Feast of the Epiphany 2023

---

[2] Revelation 7:9.

Acknowledgements

Biblical quotations, unless otherwise referenced, are taken from the readings for the service at which the sermon was given, supplied in the first footnote to the text. Unless otherwise stated, they are from the New Revised Standard Version: Anglicized Edition, copyright © 1989, 1995 National Council of the Churches of Christ in the United States of America; used by permission; all rights reserved worldwide.

Abbreviations

AV   Authorized Version
BCP   *Book of Common Prayer*
RSV   Revised Standard Version

Manifesting the risen Christ

Michael W. Brierley and Georgina A. Byrne

Of books on preaching, there seems to be no end. In the last 15 years alone (since, in fact, Peter Atkinson has been dean of Worcester), at least 70 books have been published on the art of delivering sermons. Guides suggest how to use story, how to use imagination, how to be personal, how to be pastoral, how to be prophetic, how to be missional, how to handle difficult texts, how to end well, and so on. Both the writers of this introduction work in theological institutions in which, rightly, the craft of preaching is taught, studied, practised and learned with enthusiasm and passion.

While much ink has been printed on the matter, the essentials of Christian preaching seem to be quite simple. At its heart is scripture. The primary purpose of the sermon stems from its liturgical context: it exists to "unpack" the passages of the Bible which have preceded it in any given service, and to enable hearers to connect with them in ways which are illuminating and life-changing. There may be an occasional case for sermons that bear no relation to their scriptural surroundings, but they are rare. Herein lie the advantages of a lectionary: not only is a particular church connecting with the same passages that are being read and studied elsewhere in its denomination and indeed ecumenically, but the Church is also "sitting under" scripture. Scripture is provided; the Church is not selecting scripture according to its own whim, determining for itself that to which it will listen (beyond deciding which lectionary to use and how to use it). Scripture is given: it may or may not be congenial, and it is up to the preacher to wrestle with it, with and for the congregation, until illumination comes.

Hence the preacher begins with scripture and their own prayerful study of scripture, their own careful reading and re-reading of texts that are provided. Through continual reading of the scriptures well in advance of the sermon, through meditation on the chosen passages, through the use of commentaries, through whatever means, the preacher needs to alight on a core message or series of messages: a new dimension to the gospel, something creative about faith that has caught them, a novel insight, a fresh understanding of the world. Whatever else this is, it has to be something that is both authentic and interesting to the preacher: if it fails to excite the preacher, it will certainly fail to excite the congregation; if it is not *true* to the preacher, then its absence of integrity will soon enough come across to those who listen (hence why, always, preachers preach first and foremost to themselves). Here is the preacher's preparatory task: so to read, to keep reading, until something of interest about faith and the world emerges from the scriptures of the day.

After this initial stage, the preacher's task is threefold. First, notwithstanding the fact that the preacher's preparation should begin with (prayer and) scripture, the preacher's *preaching itself* should begin with the world. Sermons which begin with scripture, religion or the Church are invariably likely to miss deep connection with the congregation. The preacher is usually a religious professional, while those to whom she or he is preaching are generally not. The congregation typically lives in the world beyond the Church, and hence the life that needs transforming is more everyday than the narrow religious sphere which may take up but just an hour of the week. The Church exists to serve the world, not constantly to point to itself. Illustrations should ideally be "ordinary", "Monday to Saturday", as that is the realm in which people live and move and have their being, and which cries out, groans, for redemption. One tutor of preaching, Brian Castle, once suggested that if the opening six seconds of a sermon did not get alongside (indeed, grab) the congregation, then connection with the congregation was lost and could not be regained. A sermon needs to start where people are.

Second, the preacher must proceed to the scriptures which are the heart (but not the beginning) of the sermon. Here, new insight is revealed, the fresh aspect of the gospel unveiled. Here, the preacher shares with the congregation how she or he has found the scriptures of interest: what has intrigued, what has startled or surprised, what has touched or moved, what has energized or inspired. The preacher imparts how the scriptures have come alive for her or him, and how they can come alive, too, for those who hear. Other scriptures may be drawn in, connections with Christian tradition may be made. This is the kernel of the sermon, its core, its substance, its dynamic.

The preacher then, third, returns to the world, and shows how this understanding of the scriptures sheds light on the existential matter with which the sermon began: it may be an area of personal life, of individual psychology or spirituality; it may be an area of local life, a pressing aspect of community concern; it may be an area of national life, religious or "secular"; it may be an area of global application and relevance; it may touch on some or all of these. The connection has to be made: how the scriptures impact and change the world for the better. This third stage is sometimes the element of preaching that gets lost. One regular churchgoer used occasionally to pronounce to their family over Sunday lunch the verdict on the morning sermon, "Strong on exegesis, weak on application". It was a withering critique: without solid encouragement to consider how it applies to real life and the world beyond the Church, even the finest exegesis has not done its work. The object of the sermon is nothing less than (by means of the scriptures) the transformation of the world. If the preacher does not indicate how the world is re-created by the aspect of the Bible that has been uncovered, then the potential of the sermon remains unfulfilled. This is what is sometimes referred to as the "takeaway", the answer to the question "So what?" What are hearers going to do about their life, indeed the rest of their lives, as a result of listening to this sermon? How are they going to be *different*? It might be a disposition, a spiritual practice, an act of social justice, or all three: the crucial matter is what change the hearers will make in the light of what they have heard. The sermon needs to steer, ease or gear the congregation towards a possible answer or range of answers to this question.

The essence of preaching would thus seem to be quite simple, if demanding: the task of the preacher is so to read the scriptures until something of interest and excitement has been revealed to her or him; and then to start with the world, progress to the scriptures, and finally to bring the two together, indicating how the latter illuminates and alters the former. Donald Gray, preaching at St Margaret's, Westminster, on a Sunday in late June 1995, reflected on (the feast of) the birth of John the

Baptist. He spoke on the folly of human desire to be indispensable. It was existentially transformative: beginning with experience, unfolding scripture, and then demonstrating how the word changed the world. It was simple and profound.

In the Gospel according to Luke, on the morning of Easter Day, the risen Christ does not appear to disciples in the vicinity of the empty tomb, as he does in the Gospels of Matthew and John.[1] In Luke, Peter even "goes home" after the drama of the early hours. In Luke's Gospel alone, the risen Christ first appears in an altogether different way: "on the road". And there, the appearance occurs in three stages. First, Christ draws alongside two disciples who are discussing the things that have taken place in Jerusalem and do not recognize him; that is to say, the appearance of the risen Christ begins with current affairs, the matters of the moment, the things which are preoccupying and perplexing those who walk. Second, the risen Christ unpacks the scriptures: he interprets the scriptures (concerning himself) in such a way that the hearts of the two walkers "burn within" them, receiving fresh understanding. Third, the disciples' experience and the insight of scripture are so brought together that the disciples' eyes are opened and they are unable to contain themselves: despite the distance and despite the lateness of the hour, they return to Jerusalem to share how their world is transformed, only to find that their friends' world is transformed further too. It is a threefold pattern: starting with experience, continuing with scripture, and culminating in transformation.[2] In this way, the road to Emmaus is a model for every sermon, an indication of how the risen Christ becomes present in the act of preaching.

The sermons of Peter Atkinson have been appreciated by those who hear them precisely because, at their best, they follow this transformative scheme. They start with experience (often very entertainingly), accessibly shed light on the scriptures, and show how the world can accordingly be a different place. As two of his residentiary canons, we listened to, were engaged by and were caught up with his preaching in this way over

---

[1]   Luke 24:1–35.

[2]   See further, David S. Stancliffe, *God's Pattern: Shaping Our Worship, Ministry and Life* (London: SPCK, 2003).

many years, and we could not be more delighted that, on the occasion of his retirement as dean of Worcester, this selection of his sermons points to and honours his skill in enabling the risen Christ to be manifest and known.

Sermons

Peter G. Atkinson

1

Raids on the inarticulate[1]

Words, however carefully and lovingly we try to use them, are in the end poor instruments for expressing the mystery of God. In his *Four Quartets,* T. S. Eliot describes how words "strain, / Crack and sometimes break, under the burden".[2] They are, he writes, a "raid on the inarticulate / With shabby equipment always deteriorating".[3]

The difficulty has been well understood by Christian writers down the centuries. St Augustine spoke of all our talk about God as a knowing which is aware of what is unknowable; and this is a theme developed by spiritual writers in both the eastern and the western traditions of Christian thought.[4] One of the roots of this profound reticence—indeed (one could say) this deeply reverential *agnosticism* about God—which runs right through the Christian tradition, is the insistence in the Old Testament that God could not be adequately represented by an image; and therefore God *must* not be represented by any image, for fear of falling into idolatry. Where the religions of the surrounding peoples

---

1   Sermon preached at the eucharist in Chichester Cathedral on the Third Sunday of Easter, 7 May 2000. The readings were Acts 3:12–19; 1 John 3:1–7; Luke 24:36b–48.

2   T. S. Eliot, "Burnt Norton", in *Four Quartets* (*The Complete Poems and Plays of T. S. Eliot* [London: Faber and Faber, 1969], pp. 171–6 at 175).

3   T. S. Eliot, "East Coker", in *Four Quartets* (*Complete Poems and Plays*, pp. 177–83 at 182).

4   Augustine, *On Order* (2.47): "cuius nulla scientia est in anima nisi scire quomodo cum nesciat"; "God is known by the soul only to the extent that it knows how much it does not know" (as quoted by Eugene TeSelle, *Augustine the Theologian* [London: Burns & Oates, 1970], p. 81).

built themselves temples and set up images of their gods, the temple of
Israel contained no image. Emptiness, silence, negation were the only
appropriate indicators of the unseen and unseeable God.

Yet at the heart of the Christian faith there lies that which simultaneously
denies and affirms all this. At the heart of the Christian faith lies the claim
that the unseen God has made himself seen, the unimaginable God has
shown us his face, the unapproachable God has made himself present
in our world, and the inexpressible God has expressed himself. God has
done this in the person of Jesus Christ. "No one has ever seen God", writes
St John; "the only Son, who is in the bosom of the Father, he has made
him known"; and again, later on in St John's Gospel, when Philip says
to Jesus, "Lord, show us the Father, and we shall be satisfied", the reply
from Jesus is, "He who has seen me has seen the Father."[5]

However, this does *not* mean that God has made himself *obvious*.
"Seeing Jesus" is not obvious, and therefore seeing God through Jesus
is not obvious. This is a motif in all the stories of the resurrection, and
nowhere in the Gospels are we so reminded of the "intolerable wrestle /
With words and meanings" (Eliot again) as in these strange and puzzling
narratives.[6] The risen Lord is triumphantly present, yet it is a presence
which is far from obvious. St Luke tells the story of two disciples who
walk with the risen Jesus all the way from Jerusalem to Emmaus, deep
in conversation with him; they invite him into their home and sit him
down to supper; yet they do not grasp who he is until he takes bread and
breaks it. In that familiar action, there is a moment of recognition; and
yet, in the very moment of recognition, he is gone. The presence of the
risen Lord is one which cannot be held on to, pinned down, or possessed.
"*Noli me tangere*", says the risen Lord to Mary Magdalene: do not cling
to me, do not hold on to me.[7]

And yet the presence of the risen Lord is the reverse of insubstantial.
There is nothing shadowy, slippery, evasive about him; rather, suggest
the evangelists, the opposite. Here is one who is overwhelmingly present,
almost more present than the disciples themselves. St Luke captures

---

[5]   John 1:18; 14:8,9 (RSV).

[6]   "East Coker", p. 179.

[7]   John 20:17.

something of this in the Gospel reading that we have heard today: emphatically the risen Lord is no ghostly presence, no merely *spiritual* presence: "See my hands and my feet, that it is I myself; handle me, and see; for a spirit has not flesh and bones as you see that I have."[8] Here is one who is almost larger than life; compared to this robust presence, it is the disciples who seem to be shadowy and insubstantial.

St John has another way of suggesting the same larger-than-life reality of the risen Lord. He tells of Jesus appearing to Mary Magdalene in the garden, appearing to the disciples in the upper room and appearing again eight days later when St Thomas was with them; and again, in Chapter 21, the moving epilogue to the Gospel, he tells of Jesus appearing by the Sea of Galilee.[9] In each such episode, the scene ends with Jesus still on stage; he never *disappears*, he never *goes away*. The curtain always descends with him *there*; as if the evangelist would say to us that our moments of time come and go, but he is *present*; he is larger than our time; he is *uncontainable*. It reminds one of the icons of the Lord in the tradition of the eastern Church, where the Lord's figure always breaks the margin of the picture, is always slighter larger than the frame.

And yet perhaps the most puzzling, and the most suggestive, of all the resurrection narratives is that of St Mark. For some of the most ancient texts of St Mark's Gospel tell of the women coming to the tomb on Easter Sunday morning, and finding the tomb empty, and meeting an angel who announced that Christ was risen; and then, these manuscripts say, "they went out and fled from the tomb, for terror and amazement had seized them; and they said nothing to anyone, for they were afraid."[10] Just that. There are other manuscripts of St Mark in which more is said, in which the risen Lord appears, but it is in words which seem to have been drawn from the other Gospels. The unquestioned text ends as I have quoted, with fear striking the women, and sending them out not to proclaim the news, but silent, awe-struck, and afraid.

We cannot be certain that this was how St Mark meant to end. But whatever he meant to do, it was a magnificent and courageous note on

---

[8] Luke 24:39 (RSV).

[9] John 21:1–14.

[10] Mark 16:8.

which to end. The reality of God breaks into the mundane world: and shall we try and put it into words, shall we try and describe it, define it, pin it down in words and images? No, let us describe only the awe, the fear, the confusion that we feel when God makes himself known; let us leave the presence of the risen Lord unsaid, and all the more eloquent for that. Here indeed is a bold and daring "raid on the inarticulate".

So the four evangelists, in their different ways, proclaim the double truth that God has made himself known, and has done so emphatically in the resurrection of Jesus; and yet he remains larger than anything that we can capture in words; he eludes our every attempt adequately to express him; he defeats our definitions, and he destroys our images.

And is that the end of the story; is that all that we shall ever be able to say of God? Not at all: as we heard in the epistle this morning. "Beloved", writes St John in his first epistle, "we are God's children now; it does not yet appear what we shall be, but we know that when he appears we shall be like him, for we shall see him as he is."[11]

What is being said here?—that there is an *appearing* of Christ still to come. We haven't seen all that there is to see of Christ, and we haven't seen all that we shall see of Christ; there is in God's time a more complete revelation of the mystery of Christ. We sometimes call it the "second coming", which is a phrase not to be found in the New Testament; it is better expressed, as the New Testament largely does, as the *appearing* or the *revealing* of Christ. We cannot put a human timescale on such a thing—remember the risen Christ in St John's Gospel breaking out of the frame of the present moment. But we do know that when that final and complete revelation of Christ comes about, all God's children will be caught up into him and transformed by him. That is not, says St John, something that we can capture in words—"it does not *yet* appear what we shall be"—but what we *do* know is that *when* Christ appears then "we shall be like him for we shall see him as he is".

The resurrection of Jesus Christ is not just an event which took place a long time ago; it is, rather, an event which *breaks into* our time and transforms it; it is an event in history, yes; but it is also an event in the present moment; and an event which embraces the future too. It defeats

---

[11] 1 John 3:2 (RSV).

our sense of time, just as it defeats our attempts to capture it in words. In the resurrection of Jesus, we are brought into the presence of the eternal God, the God beyond all our imagining. And if that inspires us with awe, and even terror—as it did the first disciples—then remember, too, those words of St John with which the epistle reading opened: "See what love the Father has given us, that we should be called children of God."

2

Paul on Mars Hill[1]

In the first reading that we heard this morning from the Acts of the Apostles, Paul is in Athens. Paul and Silas had set out from Antioch to visit the Christian communities that Paul had established throughout Asia Minor in the course of an earlier journey. From there, Paul received an urgent summons to cross into Greece and extend his mission there. A very turbulent period followed, with arrest and imprisonment, and a narrow and exciting escape from being lynched, as Paul and Silas made their way from one place to another, without any very definite route in mind, except to preach the gospel in as many places as they could. Almost inevitably, they were drawn to Athens. They arrived by ship, putting in at the port of Piraeus, as you may have done if you have ever cruised in the Aegean. Walking from there into the heart of the city, Paul would have passed the Temple of Demeter, and further on, a famous statue of Poseidon, hurling his trident; then came statues of Athena (the patroness of the city), Zeus (the king of the gods), Apollo, Hermes, and many more. And having arrived in the heart of the city, he saw the Acropolis with its still magnificent collection of temples. Paul, we are told, was "provoked".

To him, as to anyone else of the time, these statues and temples were not "works of art"; he did not come to Athens as a tourist, nor would he have known what a tourist was. What he saw in front of him were the objects of *idolatry*, and he was provoked. Very soon, he had attracted the attention of the students of philosophy who thronged the city—the followers of the Epicurean and Stoic schools of thought. The upshot

---

[1]   Sermon preached at the eucharist in Worcester Cathedral on the Sixth Sunday of Easter, 27 April 2008. The readings were Acts 17:22–31; 1 Peter 3:13–22; John 14:15–21.

was that Paul was invited to give a full-scale address to the Court of the Areopagus, which was the council that regulated the religious life of the city (the Areopagus, the hill or field of Ares, the God of war, called in the older English translations "Mars Hill", stood opposite the Acropolis). Paul's speech to the Court of the Areopagus was what we heard in the first reading this morning, and it makes very interesting reading.

Paul, as we have already noticed, was "provoked" by the quantity of pagan religion in Athens with which he found himself surrounded in all these exquisitely beautiful buildings. So the temptation for us is to see Paul as a boorish fellow, a narrow-minded fundamentalist who has no sense of beauty. There he is, staring at the Parthenon, as you and I may have stared at it. Can't he see that it is just about the finest building in existence? But his speech to the Court of the Areopagus is not boorish. He strikes a very careful note. However "provoked" he may have been by the idolatry implicit in all the altars, shrines and temples of the Greek capital, he doesn't simply launch into an assault. Rather, in a majestic sweep of ideas, Paul gathers together the whole scope of human culture and learning, and in the light of the gospel, gives it a positive, though limited, place. He's not an uncultivated oaf; rather, he's asking himself where this magnificent heritage of philosophy and art and learning actually fits into the religion of Jesus Christ.

He begins with the *religion* of the Greeks. He acknowledges the place that religion has in their lives, and he looks for good in it. And among all the many shrines and deities of the Greek pantheon, he finds one point of access to the Christian faith: the altar of the Unknown God (there is evidence of shrines and altars dedicated to the unknown gods, as if, with so many named gods and goddesses, it was important that none should be forgotten or overlooked). Well, says Paul, you look to the unknown god, and I'll tell you who he is; and he might well have echoed St John—"No one has ever seen God: the only Son, who is in the bosom of the Father, he has made him known."[2] So even amid the mass of shrines and temples, altars and statues, there was a way to Christ: and Paul found it and followed it through.

---

[2] John 1:18 (RSV).

He moves from religion to *cosmology*: the study of the universe and its origins:

> The God who made the world and everything in it, he who is Lord of heaven and earth, does not live in shrines made by human hands, nor is he served by human hands, as though he needed anything, since he himself gives to all mortals life and breath and all things.

Here, Paul is dipping into the language of the very people whom he is addressing: the Epicurean and Stoic philosophers of the Court of the Areopagus.

From cosmology he moves on to *anthropology*, to human *geography* and to *history*; from the study of the universe to the study of humankind. "From one blood [God] made all nations to inhabit the whole earth, and he allotted the times of their existence and the boundaries of the places where they would live." And here again, there are pathways to the knowledge of God: "so that they would search for God, and perhaps grope for him and find him".

And finally, Paul moves to the world of *human culture, ideas,* and in particular to the *poetry* of the Greeks: "though indeed he is not far from each one of us. For 'In him we live and move and have our being'; as even some of your own poets have said, 'For we too are his offspring.'"

Other religions; science; history; literature: all of them are potential pathways to God. Up to this point, Paul's audience may well have listened attentively and sympathetically. But then he moves them on a stage further. The world of human culture gets us so far, but it is not enough. God has done a new thing; God has changed the world; and he has given humankind a new and effective pathway to himself, in the life and teaching, the dying and rising again of the man Jesus. At this point, there is a parting of the ways among his hearers: some mock, some are prepared to listen further, or maybe only to debate the matter inconclusively; some were converted (including one name that went down famously in Christian history, Dionysius the Areopagite).

The way in which we read Paul's speech on Mars Hill has always been a litmus test of Christian attitudes to human culture. For one

strong tradition of Christian thought, Paul was damning human culture
with faint praise; he makes use of it only to demonstrate its ultimate
ineffectiveness as a way to God; he brings it in as a sermon illustration
to engage the attention of his intellectual audience, but discards it the
moment that he gets on to the gospel. Some of the early Christian
fathers emphatically follow this route; and one such was the third-
century theologian, Tertullian. "What then hath Athens in common
with Jerusalem?" he shouted, meaning: "What has the world of human
culture to do with the Christian message?"[3] But others were prepared to
see in learning and culture, art and scholarship, a true pathway to God.
Justin Martyr, writing in the middle of the second century, probably in
Rome, developed the idea that Christianity is not only the fulfilment of
the Hebrew Old Testament but is also the fulfilment of Greek philosophy.
In all human searching for God, the presence of the *logos*, the Word, the
unseen Spirit of Christ himself, could be discerned.[4]

Which is the right reading of Paul's speech on Mars Hill? Tertullian
or Justin? Is Paul simply making use of human culture as an evangelistic
device, or is he genuinely giving us a true if limited pathway to God?
There is one passage in Paul's authentic writings which gives an indication
of what he really thought. Just once he falls again into the language of the
Stoic philosophers, which he may well have learnt in Tarsus, that centre
of Stoic thought; but here, it is no device, no tool, here Paul speaks from
the heart: "Finally, beloved", he writes to the Philippians in that most
affectionate of his epistles, "whatever is true, whatever is honourable,
whatever is just, whatever is pure, whatever is pleasing, whatever is
commendable, if there is any excellence and if there is anything worthy
of praise, think about these things."[5] The excellent and the beautiful as

---

[3]   Tertullian, *De Praescriptione Haereticorum* (7), in *Tertullian on the Testimony
      of the Soul and on the 'Prescription' of Heretics*, tr. T. Herbert Bindley (London:
      SPCK, 1914), p. 45.

[4]   Justin Martyr, *Second Apology* (13), in *The Writings of Justin Martyr and
      Athenagoras*, tr. Marcus Dods, George Reith and B. P. Pratten, Ante-Nicene
      Christian Library 2 (Edinburgh: T&T Clark, 1867), p. 83. The editor is
      grateful to Dr Matthew Schrecker for assistance with this reference.

[5]   Philippians 4:8.

images of God and pathways to him: it is not a note that Paul often strikes, but he strikes it here, and it is echoed in his speech on the hill of Mars. It is the clue that Justin picked up and developed in his idea that the whole world of human culture can be a true "old testament", an authentic preparation for the gospel.

At a time when all communities of faith must examine their hearts, and ask themselves how far they have contributed to human wellbeing, and how far to human conflict and division, Justin's generous hospitality to other faiths, other schools of thought, other cultures, reminds us of an important and often neglected aspect of our own tradition. The Unknown God that lies within all human quest for truth and meaning is implicitly Christ himself. That was the heart of Paul's message on Mars Hill, and the message that Justin picked up and developed. But this is not to relativize the place of Christ. As in Paul's speech, the point must come when the *implicit* Christ is made *explicit,* the Unknown God is named and known, and then decisions must be made, and ways may part. Some mock, some are ready to debate the matter further, and some become disciples. But if, like the Paul of Mars Hill, we are prepared to enter sympathetically into the whole range of human thought and learning, art and culture, tradition and belief, and be ready to see Christ there, in Athens as well as in Jerusalem, then perhaps we can do something to reclaim for all communities of faith a name for enlarging, and not diminishing, the human spirit.

3

God's good time[1]

He threw himself down on the rather rickety seat in the leafy
arbour [. . .] and proceeded to stare vacantly at the long ragged
leaves about his head and to listen to the birds. There was no man
who had a more hearty and enduring appetite for doing nothing.[2]

G. K. Chesterton's picture of Father Brown offers a healthy and necessary
corrective—even a subversion—of the activism of our times. We are
beset by clamouring claims that to do things more and more quickly is a
virtue in itself: that a car which can reach the speed limit from zero in so
many seconds is better than one which takes a second longer; and that
a photocopier which warms up in a minute lags far behind one which
takes but half that time. Every moment counts in our digital-clock-ridden
world; while the nation's favourite poem insists that the way to inherit
the earth is to

> fill the unforgiving minute
> With sixty seconds' worth of distance run.[3]

Time, we tend to think, is a commodity, a piece of private property:
"my time is my own", we say; "I've no time to spare"; "you're wasting my

---

[1]   Sermon preached at mattins in St Mary's, Bepton, West Sussex, on the Sunday
      before Lent, 5 March 2000.

[2]   G. K. Chesterton, *The Father Brown Stories*, 11th edn (London: Cassell &
      Co., 1969), pp. 642–3.

[3]   Rudyard Kipling, "If—", in *Rudyard Kipling's Verse* (London: Hodder &
      Stoughton, 1940), p. 576.

time"; "I won't take more of your time"; "there's no time left." If time is
a commodity, a property, then it can be bought and sold; everything
has its price, and we end up with Benjamin Franklin's advice to a young
tradesman, "Remember that Time is Money."[4]

Well, there's a common-sense truth in all of this, so far as it goes;
but if time is money, then to worship time, and to worship the saving of
time, is as dangerous as the worship of money and as soul-destroying
as the miser's hoard. Father Brown's "hearty and enduring appetite for
doing nothing" is not only subversive of the active spirit of the age; it is
spiritually liberating.

Of course, we can only appreciate Father Brown's point of view if
we remember that the famous detective was methodical, conscientious,
diligent, an early riser, and one who faithfully served a busy parish as
well as regularly solving such thefts and murders as baffled the official
constabulary; clearly he was one who managed time well and achieved
a great deal in it. His doing nothing was the opposite of idleness; it was
the leisure of one who knew when to stop. It was also, I suggest (or rather
his creator G. K. Chesterton is suggesting), the leisure of one who knew
that time was not their own. It was not his to choose to spend or save; to
spare or to begrudge; Father Brown gave his time freely because his time
was a gift from God, and he saw it in that light. This is the perspective of
the psalmist, for whom time is precious, not because it is his, but because
it is God's. "Man is like a thing of nought: his time passeth away like a
shadow"; "thou hast made my days as it were a span long"; "my time is in
thy hand."[5] From this perspective, all the time we have, as with everything
else we call our own, comes from God; it is not ours to waste, nor yet to
hoard; it is given to us to give away freely, just as God has freely given it
to us. In our more pious moments, we sometimes speak of "using all the
hours God sends", and again of "God's good time"—and there is truth as
well as piety in those expressions. In our more sacrilegious moments, we
speak of *killing* time. Sometimes, as we ponder the unrelenting passage

---

[4]   *The Papers of Benjamin Franklin*, vol. 3, ed. Leonard W. Labaree (New
       Haven: Yale University Press, 1961), p. 306.
[5]   Psalm 144:4; 39:6; 31:17 (BCP).

of time, we may be tempted to say with Isaac Watts (and the psalmist he quotes),

> Time, like an ever-rolling stream,
> bears all its sons away;
> they fly forgotten, as a dream
> dies at the opening day.[6]

And yet that very opening day—each opening day—should remind us of the God who gave it. In the words of the same poet, we shall then say,

> This is the day the Lord hath made,
> he calls the hours his own;[7]

Or, in the words of the ancient acclamation at the lighting of the candle on Easter Eve, "all time belongs to him, and all ages."[8]

If, then, all time belongs to God, and even the hours are his and not ours, what follows practically from such a point of view? First, clearly, we have to be generous in our expenditure of time, both in God's presence, and in the service of others. We cannot begrudge the time that we devote either to the love of God or to the love of our neighbour, for it is not ours to begrudge.

Second, and equally clearly, we must not waste time, for we are but the stewards of God's good time, and he holds us to account both for this and for all other gifts with which he has entrusted us. But if we shun idleness on the one hand, we shall also shun the modern worship of busyness on the other. The God whom we worship is one of whom the story is told that he made the world in six days of hard work, and then

---

6   Isaac Watts, "O God, our help in ages past" (*Ancient & Modern: Hymns and Songs for Refreshing Worship* [London: Hymns Ancient & Modern, 2013], no. 746); cf. Psalm 90:5.

7   Isaac Watts, "This is the day the Lord hath made", *Ancient & Modern*, no. 7.

8   *Lent, Holy Week, Easter: Services and Prayers* (London: Church House Publishing, Cambridge: Cambridge University Press, and London: SPCK, 1986), p. 229.

took the seventh day off and did nothing.[9] What is more, we are told, he wrote the hallowing of one day in seven into the Ten Commandments that his people might follow his example.[10] Father Brown's knowing when to do nothing, and to do it not guiltily but with an "enduring and hearty appetite", shows how well he had learned to observe the sabbatical rule. So the second practical implication of seeing time as God's time and not ours is the principle of rest, of rhythm, for which we use that very good word which reminds us of what God did at the end of his work of creation—*recreation*. Even God drew breath before he began again, and re-created himself during his day of rest.

There is, however, a still deeper lesson to learn from the fact that our time is in God's hands, and he calls the hours his own. If the hours belong to him, if each hour is God's hour, if *this* hour is God's hour, then *now* is the moment to listen to him, *now* is the moment to hear him, *now* is the moment to meet him. We are not waiting for Godot, endlessly expecting some moment that never comes; God comes to us in the present moment. This is a theme of much of Our Lord's teaching. In the parable of the sheep and the goats, we find that the day of judgement, the last day, is in fact today; the moment of God's judgement is every moment when we either turn to, or turn away from, the person in need.[11] Don't be for ever fearing and fretting over what may lie around the corner, Jesus is saying to us; *now* is the moment that counts. "Do not be anxious about tomorrow", he says, "for tomorrow will be anxious for itself. Let the day's own trouble be sufficient for the day."[12] This is not a recipe for irresponsibility, or for failing to prepare or plan properly for the future; but it is a refusal to let the future dictate the present, to let what might be come before what is; it is a readiness to listen to God now, in this the hour he calls his own, or what some spiritual writers have powerfully described as "the sacrament of the present moment".

If the sacrament of the present moment frees us from the future, it frees us also from the past; and this is the fourth and final practical

---

[9]   Genesis 2:2,3.

[10]   Exodus 20:8–11.

[11]   Matthew 25:31–46.

[12]   Matthew 6:34 (RSV).

implication of the theme that we have explored today. If we are not to fret over the future, no more are we to fret over the past. This is not to say that we put the past behind us, as if it doesn't matter. It is to say that we are not to be governed by the past, by our own pasts, by the errors and failures and hurt memories that we seem to drag with us day by day. The Christian doctrine of forgiveness is not that none of these things matters, but that they matter so much that God gives us a way to be free of them; he lets our past go, and he comes to recreate us in the present; he neither wipes out what has happened, nor rewrites our history, but in his infinite creativity he finds a way of healing the wounds of memory and setting us free to be with him now, in the present moment, in the hour he calls his own.

Yet if God is the Lord of the present moment, if God can come to us and make himself known to us at *any* time, if *all* times belong to him, why do we need special times which are given up to him, holy days and holy seasons, hours of prayer and times of reflection and retreat? These, of course, are not for God's benefit, but for ours. We need the spaces in our lives, the periods of repose and receptivity, the times when (like Father Brown) we purposively and with a hearty and enduring appetite do nothing, that we may *appropriate* God's gracious work of recreation (*re-creation*) in our lives.

> Finish then thy new creation:
> pure and spotless let us be;
> let us see thy great salvation
> perfectly restored in thee;
> changed from glory into glory
> till in heaven we take our place,
> till we cast our crowns before thee,
> lost in wonder, love, and praise.[13]

---

[13]   Charles Wesley, "Love divine, all loves excelling", *Ancient & Modern*, no. 721.

He did not answer her at all[1]

A woman comes to Jesus in dire need: she is a foreigner, a Canaanite, a native of the district of Phoenicia in Syria: and her daughter is deranged, possessed, "tormented by a demon". She begs Jesus to cure the girl, he alone can do it; but apparently he rebuffs her. He did not answer her a word. He had nothing to say to her. And when she persists, he gives her a very disturbing answer: "I was sent only to the lost sheep of the house of Israel," he says. "It is not fair to take the children's food and throw it to the dogs." Some answer! Is this the Jesus who says, "Come to me, all who labour and are heavy laden, and I will give you rest"?[2] Is this the Jesus who taught his disciples to pray for their enemies and to forgive those who did them wrong?[3] Is this the Jesus who told the parable of the Good Samaritan—with its specific point that human need takes no notice of racial barriers, and the response to human need must do the same?[4] Well, the contrast between the familiar Jesus of these Gospel passages and the unfamiliar Jesus in conversation with this foreign woman is so startling that perhaps we need to take a closer look into this story.

Jesus had a particular task: his task was to announce the kingdom of God. That is to say, his message was that the long-promised reign of God, so eagerly awaited by Israel for so many centuries, was here at last. Not that it turned out to be the sort of kingdom that most of

---

[1]   Sermon preached at the eucharist in St Michael's, Beaulieu-sur-Mer, France, on Sunday, 18 August 2002 (Proper 15). The readings were Isaiah 56:1,6–8; Romans 11:1–2a,29–32; Matthew 15:21–8.

[2]   Matthew 11:28.

[3]   Matthew 5:44; Mark 11:25.

[4]   Luke 10:25–37.

Israel was expecting, with its crucified king, its policy of forgiveness and reconciliation, and its refusal to engage in armed resistance against the enemies of Israel. But all the same, Jesus announced that the kingdom of God had come, for those with the eyes to see it and the faith to embrace it. This was a message first and foremost for the people of Israel. They were God's chosen people; they were the instrument by which God would establish his reign upon earth.

Now the Gentiles were not left out of the picture. The prophet Isaiah in our first reading spoke of the day when foreigners would "join themselves to the Lord" and flock to the mountain of God, and the house of the God of Israel would become a place of prayer for all peoples. The prophet Zechariah paints a vivid picture of ten men from the Gentile nations catching the sleeve of every Jew and saying, "Let us go with you, for we have heard that God is with you."[5] But that lay in the future; first, Israel must be awakened, and that was the initial task that Jesus set himself and set his immediate inner group of disciples, to awaken Israel to her ancient destiny, to turn them to the Lord, and to prepare them in heart and soul to be the place and the people among whom God would establish his reign. And this is why Jesus says here, and elsewhere in the Gospels, that he was sent "to the lost sheep of the house of Israel".

Now one who has a message of immense significance, whose time is short, who has already made enemies, must conserve themselves for their one great task. They cannot allow themselves to be diverted into other tasks, other concerns, however good or praiseworthy they may be. For Jesus, as we can plainly see throughout the Gospel story, there was the constant danger of being swamped by the crowds who flocked to hear him; there must, too, have been the constant temptation to his own natural compassion to turn himself into the wonder-working leader whom the crowds demanded. To turn his back on wonder-working for its own sake was one of the first temptations that he had to face, back in the wilderness at the beginning of his ministry. And all the time he was beset by people in need, in far greater numbers than he could ever deal with.

And so we find that after periods of intensive teaching and healing, and escalating controversy, Jesus withdraws from the pressure of the crowds;

---

5   Zechariah 8:23.

sometimes alone, and sometimes with his inner group of disciples; he goes (as we might say) into retreat: to pray, to prepare his disciples for what lies ahead of them, to renew in himself and in them the primary task and mission which God has laid on them. Sometimes they go to the desert, sometimes to the hills, sometimes to the garden of Gethsemane, and sometimes (as here) into foreign territory, where they may hope to spend a while unrecognized and undisturbed. St Mark's version of the story confirms this interpretation of what is going on: "He entered a house, and would not have anyone know it"—and yet, St Mark goes on, "he could not be hid".[6] The woman comes to him and begs him to attend to her daughter.

So Jesus is faced by a dilemma. One act of compassion now will bring at once the demand for a dozen, a hundred, more; it has happened so often in the past, and it will happen again; but if he begins to heal and cure in Phoenicia, he can only make himself the centre of a wonder-working cult among a people for whom his primary task of preaching the kingdom of God will mean nothing at all. His energies will be diverted from the one thing that he alone must do and he alone can do: to proclaim to Israel that the kingdom of God has come. Jesus clearly feels that he cannot take the risk; he must save himself for the kingdom; he has to be silent in the face of the woman's desperate appeal. "He did not answer her at all."

I wonder if you have seen that magnificent and heart-wrenching film *Schindler's List*? It tells the story, as you may know, of Oskar Schindler, the wealthy and frivolous owner of an armaments factory in wartime Germany, who in reality is giving employment to as many Jews as he dares, providing them with "essential worker" status, and so saving them from the concentration camps. This is a policy of immense personal risk to Schindler; and he can only give refuge to Jewish workers if they are indeed convincing factory workers. But then a young Jewish woman begs him to give employment to her frail and elderly parents, who will be far from convincing as factory workers. To give them work risks the whole enterprise, risks the lives not only of those two old people but the lives of all the Jews employed in the factory. Oskar Schindler is angry: how can he risk the lives of all of them by giving work to these

---

6   Mark 7:24 (RSV).

obviously unemployable old people? And if he gives way once, will not every factory worker demand that he gives jobs to their elderly parents and grandparents as well? Schindler is at first unbending; but the young woman is eloquent in her desperation; and in the next scene, we see the old couple being admitted at the factory gates.

Back to Phoenicia: Jesus tries to explain to the Canaanite woman. "I was sent to the lost sheep of the house of Israel", he says. But the woman is desperate; she falls at his feet. "Lord", she says, "help me." But Jesus is still focused on the task that God has given him: to announce God's kingdom to the people of Israel. They are the children of the house, he says, and the children must be fed first. My bread is for the children of Israel; and when the children are hungry, and rations are scarce, and time is short, then you don't throw the bread about in such a way as the dogs get to it before the children.

I don't think that we can smooth out the roughness of Jesus's response. I think that his dilemma was real; his bewilderment was acute; he found himself here in a new situation, in uncharted waters; perhaps, like Oskar Schindler in the film, his first reaction was one of anger. Some commentators tell us that Jesus is only "testing" the woman. To my mind, that paints Jesus in a far worse light than to allow for a natural human reaction of bewilderment, anxiety, and annoyance. No, it is not the woman who is tested; it is Jesus who is being tested here: he is in a new situation in which he must work out all over again what it means to proclaim the kingdom of God. And the woman is doing the testing, and by means of her natural and spontaneous anxiety for her daughter, gives Jesus himself a new perspective on his own main task. She seems to see the point that he is making; but desperation sharpens her wits, and she turns his parable back on himself. Feeding the children? Dogs under the table? Well, whoever heard of a family mealtime when no food was dropped on the floor? There's bound to be something spilled, something for the poor hungry dogs to snatch at. After all, they are part of the household too, aren't they, even if they're not the children of the house?

St Matthew is careful to point out that she calls him "Son of David"; that is, she recognizes him for who he is; implicitly, she acknowledges his main mission of preaching the kingdom to the people of Israel. She doesn't ask him to turn aside from that mission; but she begs some place for her and her daughter within the scope of his mission, even if it's on the floor under the table. Jesus is moved. In his mind, perhaps, the kneeling figure of the foreign woman in front of him awakens an echo of that prophecy of Isaiah, of foreigners who join themselves to the Lord; of that vision of Zechariah, of Gentiles plucking the sleeves of the Jews and saying, "Let us go with you, for we have heard that God is with you." If that is not what the woman is asking, then what is it? And Jesus responds to her with a kind of grateful, relieved, exhausted admiration: "Woman, great is your faith! Let it be done for you as you wish." And we read that her daughter found healing at that moment.

I do not think that we need be troubled by a picture of Jesus sufficiently human to show him sometimes confused, acknowledging a wrong direction, accepting from another an enlargement of his vision of God's kingdom. It is true that Christian piety down the centuries has been shy of seeing such vulnerability in Jesus; but Christian orthodoxy affirms his entire humanity, and the Gospels plainly say that his temptations, his times of testing, were real, and not over and done with in a day. In the epistle to the Hebrews, we read that "he learned obedience in the school of suffering"—which is not the picture of a supernatural know-all, effortlessly playing a pre-determined part: it suggests something much less tidy in the mental make-up of the Lord, painful, stumbling, ambiguous, struggling to find his way amid conflicting demands; and it suggests that at least sometimes it was through other people that he himself learnt.[7]

The humanity that God took to himself in Jesus was a real humanity, fragile and unfinished. We share that humanity and God accepts us in our fragile and unfinished state. And like the Canaanite woman, we, too, are nourished with the bread prepared for God's children. Every time that we celebrate this eucharist, every time that we receive the holy communion, the Lord reminds us that we, too, are part of the family:

---

[7]   Hebrews 5:8 (New English Bible).

Our hands were unclean,
our hearts were unprepared;
we were not fit
even to eat the crumbs from under your table.
But you, Lord, are the God of our salvation,
and share your bread with sinners.
So cleanse and feed us
with the precious body and blood of your Son [...]
that we, with the whole company of Christ,
may sit and eat in your kingdom.
Amen.[8]

---

8   *Common Worship: Services and Prayers for the Church of England* (London: Church House Publishing, 2000), p. 181.

5

Reading for prayer and reading for pleasure[1]

Sometimes I'm asked to lead a quiet day and sometimes I'm asked to lead a study day. I think that there is a difference between the two, but I wouldn't press the distinction too far. The difference to my mind is simply one of style. A quiet day is a day blessedly free of handouts, flip charts, PowerPoint presentations, reading lists, small groups, plenary sessions, and (I trust) evaluation sheets; a day when we can be quiet, when we can (I hope) be nourished, when we can pray. On a quiet day, a subject or a theme is there to be received, absorbed, digested, pondered. On a study day, the subject or theme is there to be questioned, probed, discussed, analysed, taken to pieces. The methods of the two days are different; but the theme or subject could well be the same. And this is the first point that I want to make in this address: the blurring of the boundaries between what we think about on a quiet day and what we think about on a study day; the smudging of the distinction between the devotional and the theological; or, to put it positively, the unity of our prayer and our thought.

Let me offer some examples. It was said of one of the greatest English theologians of the twentieth century, Austin Farrer, that "as he grew older his intellectual and devotional life and his practical activities became steadily more unified and his habitual mode of expression at once more simple and more individual [. . .] There was no discernible difference of tone between preaching and lecturing or between lecturing and everyday

---

[1]   Addresses given at Stanbrook Abbey on Tuesday, 26 February 2008, at a quiet day for clergy of the deanery of Kingswinford.

speech."[2] Here was a man who wrote huge books of philosophical theology and controversial studies of the New Testament, a notable preacher, and an effective academic administrator. That sounds like a life of compartments, but there were none. The same thoughtful and prayerful tone permeated his whole life; in him the practical, the social, the intellectual, and the devotional were all of a piece. It is hard to think that Austin Farrer would make much of the difference between a quiet day and a study day. If he were addressing you today, the subject would almost certainly be the Trinity; and by the end of it, your thoughts would have been enlarged and your prayers deepened, and both those things would have happened simultaneously. I cannot hope to achieve the same effect, but I do want to suggest to you (or to remind you) that this is both possible and desirable.

Another quotation, this time from Farrer's friend and contemporary, C. S. Lewis: writing in the foreword to a translation of St Athanasius's treatise, *De Incarnatione*, as part of a popular series of theological classics, he referred to the distinction between "devotional" and "theological" reading. He went on (and I must warn you that there is a masculine donnishness about these words, so you will need to make allowances for a significant cultural gap between his day and ours):

> Nor would I admit any sharp division between the two kinds of book [the "devotional" and the "theological"]. For my own part I tend to find the doctrinal books often more helpful in devotion than the devotional books [...] I believe that many who find that "nothing happens" when they sit down, or kneel down, to a book of devotion, would find that the heart sings unbidden while they are working their way through a tough bit of theology with a pipe in their teeth and a pencil in their hand.[3]

2   Basil G. Mitchell, "Austin Marsden Farrer", in Austin M. Farrer, *A Celebration of Faith*, ed. J. Leslie Houlden (London: Hodder & Stoughton, 1970), pp. 13–16 at 15–16.

3   C. S. Lewis, "Introduction", in *The Incarnation of the Word of God: Being the Treatise of St Athanasius* De Incarnatione Verbi Dei, tr. a Religious of CSMV (London: Geoffrey Bles and Centenary Press, 1944), pp. 5–12 at 10.

Making due allowance for a world of pipes (and indeed pencils) far remote from our own, there is still wisdom in those words.

◆

Well, I've started by pondering the difference between a quiet day and a study day, and this has given me a theme that I want to explore for the rest of the day—a day in which I hope that we may find both our thought enlarged and our prayer deepened. Let us look at how we turn our thinking into praying, and our praying into thinking.

There is, I rather think, a sort of geological fault that runs right through the Judaeo-Christian tradition, a fault that separates thought from prayer. And yet, to call it a fault, is at once to suggest that the separation ought not to have occurred. We see it, I think, in the wisdom literature of the Old Testament, where the writers take delight in all sorts of things: the nature of God, the nature of humankind, and the nature of the created world. We read of Solomon, whose "wisdom surpassed the wisdom of all the people of the east", who spoke "of trees, from the cedar that is in the Lebanon to the hyssop that grows in the wall; he would speak of animals, and birds, and reptiles, and fish".[4] The book of Proverbs sets out to give

> learning about wisdom and instruction, for understanding words of insight, for gaining instruction in wise dealing, righteousness, justice, and equity; to teach shrewdness to the simple, knowledge and prudence to the young—let the wise also hear and gain in learning, and the discerning acquire skill, to understand a proverb and a figure, the words of the wise and their riddles.[5]

Later on, the author of the Proverbs tells us that he wants to know "the way of an eagle in the sky, the way of a snake on a rock, the way of a ship on the high seas, and the way of a man with a girl".[6] Here is an intellectual

---

[4]   1 Kings 4:30,33.

[5]   Proverbs 1:2–6.

[6]   Proverbs 30:19.

tradition that is interested in *everything*; a later era might have described the author of Proverbs as "Renaissance Man".

And then, every so often, we are reminded that all this curiosity about the world can be a big distraction from knowing God. "The fear of the Lord is the beginning of wisdom," says the Psalmist; and there is a warning implicit in those words.[7] Wisdom is all very well, says the Psalmist, riddles and facts about the natural world and curiosity about what human beings get up to—but if you want *real* wisdom, well then, you must fear the Lord.

Here, I think, is the beginning of an ambivalence about human thought, about culture, about intellectual curiosity, that runs right on into the Christian tradition. We find it in Paul, where he contrasts the wisdom after which the Greeks run, with the foolishness of God (which is wiser than human wisdom).[8] We find it in early fathers such as Tertullian, who famously asked what Athens had to do with Jerusalem.[9] We find it among the mediaeval theologians who suffered from the same intellectual curiosity as the wisdom writers of the Old Testament, and struggled to justify it.

And the same geological fault runs through the Church today; and to some extent through each one of us. I was brought up in a tradition of Christianity in which there were those who feared, despised and distrusted the activity of the mind; and even more, the power of the imagination. But as a boy, I had a lively mind and a very active imagination; I loved literature and art and history, and I was puzzled to know why things that gave me such delight were apparently displeasing to God. It is no coincidence that I mentioned both C. S. Lewis and Austin Farrer at the beginning of this address; because those two writers played a significant part in bringing me to see that the mind and the imagination could both be sanctified, and that it was possible to be (or at least to aspire to be)

---

7   Psalm 111:10.

8   1 Corinthians 1:25.

9   Tertullian, *De Praescriptione Haereticorum* (7), in *Tertullian on the Testimony of the Soul and on the 'Prescription' of Heretics*, tr. T. Herbert Bindley (London: SPCK, 1914), p. 45.

both prayerful and thoughtful; both believing, and at the same time full of curiosity.

If we were to try and define this geological fault in theological terms, I suppose that we might say that it is a product of the fall. Unfallen humanity enjoyed all the fruits of creation in God's garden—revelled, we might say, in the whole rich variety of the world—without any sense of separation from God before whom man and woman stood naked and unashamed. But fallen humanity has a divided experience: shame before God and an urgent need to recover knowledge of God; and at the same time a wistful memory of that garden in which the whole natural order lay open for exploration and enjoyment. The fall introduces a tension between our delight in God's creation and our search for God; or, as I have suggested, a geological fault that runs between the activity of our minds and our aspiration for God's presence. In that vision of redeemed and glorified humanity that we are given at the end of the Apocalypse, all the kings of the earth bring their treasures into the city, by which we might understand the redemption of all civilization. The tree of life is there, with leaves to make humankind whole again. Astonishingly, there is no temple; for the presence of God fills and encompasses everything. Here, there is no separation of things human and things divine; no geological fault between the intellectual and the spiritual; no tension between thought and prayer.

Historically speaking, one of the biggest challenges to Christian thinkers has been the intellectual heritage of ancient Greece and Rome. Living as we do in the immediate aftermath of the almost complete collapse of classical learning, it is perhaps difficult for us to grasp this. But from New Testament times onwards, both the philosophy and the literature of the Greeks (absorbed, amplified and handed on by the Romans) constituted the intellectual milieu within which *all* Christian thinking took place. Some Christian thinkers feared it (as we have seen, Tertullian asked what Athens had to do with Jerusalem). Others saw classical learning as a friend and ally. Clement of Alexandria had no doubt that Greek philosophy was a sort of counterpart to Moses, "a schoolmaster to bring [us] to Christ".[10] The builders of Chartres Cathedral in the twelfth century boldly put statues of Aristotle and Cicero on the west front, alongside the prophets and the martyrs, all paying homage to Christ and his mother.

Those were the adventurous spirits. More timid souls both loved and feared classical learning at the same time, and wondered how to reconcile their love for God and their love for learning. They had two favourite allegories, drawn from the Old Testament. One was "plundering the Egyptians". That is to say, when the people of God made their exodus from Egypt, they took the wealth of pagan Egypt with them.[11] So maybe, said these Christian thinkers, it is legitimate for us to plunder the intellectual wealth of pagan Greece and Rome, and take it with us on our Christian pilgrimage. The other was "going down to the Philistines to sharpen their axes". This is an odd little story in the first book of Samuel that tells how there was no blacksmith in the land of Israel; so the Israelites had to go to the Philistines to sharpen up the tools and weapons that eventually they would use against them.[12] In just the same way, said these Christian thinkers, if we are to sharpen our intellectual tools in defence of the faith, where can we go but to the classical authors, the only people who know about such things as rhetoric, logic, and dialectic.

But these were justifications. For centuries, educated Christians (monks, nuns, theologians, bishops) adored the pagan classics, and found enormous intellectual delight in them. It is the equivalent of Solomon and the wisdom writers taking delight in all aspects of the natural world, and then getting anxious in case it distracted them from the fear of the Lord.

That classical world has become a closed book to many of us today; but we have our contemporary equivalents. We would all, I am sure, have some intellectual or scientific passion that is our version of Solomon's delight in "wisdom" or the schoolmen's delight in Aristotle or Cicero. Perhaps it is reading novels, or reading poetry. Perhaps it is looking at

---

[10]   *Stromata* (1.5), in *The Writings of Clement of Alexandria: Volume 1*, tr. William L. Wilson, Ante-Nicene Christian Library 4 (Edinburgh: T&T Clark, 1867), p. 366.

[11]   Exodus 12:36.

[12]   1 Samuel 13:19–22.

pictures in an art gallery; or films. Perhaps it is listening to music—listening, that is, with attention and appreciation. Perhaps it is travel. Perhaps it is the stern and self-effacing discipline that is involved in learning another language. Perhaps it is some hobby that requires accurate observation, such as bird watching or (who knows?) even train spotting. Perhaps it is collecting things, with all the knowledge and discrimination that collecting requires. Perhaps it is physical rather than intellectual exercise (and of course for the Greeks and Romans they went together). Whatever our personal "wisdom", we have all experienced moments which have certainly given us delight, perhaps even ecstasy; and probably we have asked ourselves how that is connected to the fear of the Lord. Is reconciliation possible between such secular delight and Christian faith? And just as the mediaeval schoolmen justified their delight in the classics by telling themselves that they were going down to the Philistines to sharpen their axes, so perhaps we have found ourselves hunting for similar justification: we have told ourselves that our secular interests "help" our ministry, give us common ground with our parishioners, keep our minds active, provide us with illustrations for our sermons—the justifications are varied; but actually, we know deep down that we love those things—those books, those films, that music, those pictures, those places, those games, those hobbies—simply because we love them; they are sources of joy and delight in our lives, and we are the better for them.

"Joy" and "delight" are words that have a certain theological seriousness about them: let me use another word, with an altogether more dangerous sound: "pleasure". Perhaps this is the root of the age-old ambivalence, suspicion or downright fear about intellectual curiosity, from the wisdom literature onwards. Is it the fear of pleasure? "Thou shalt shew me the path of life; in thy presence is the fullness of joy: and at thy right hand there is pleasure for evermore"—words which we recite in Psalm 16, but Christians have found it hard to mean them.[13] We speak of pain far more readily than we speak of pleasure. Oh, how we speak of pain—your pain, my pain, everybody's pain. We manage penitence better than we manage thanksgiving. We do Lent better than we do the Easter season. If we are beating the breast, we think that we are serious;

---

[13]   Psalm 16:12 (BCP).

if we are having pleasure, we think that we are being frivolous. Yet at the right hand of God, there is pleasure for evermore; and the meaning of the word "paradise" is a pleasure garden.

◆

I have gone as far as I want to in this first address. If you would like some particular question or exercise to guide your thoughts for the rest of the morning, may I suggest the following. Think of the things that really give you joy, delight—yes, pleasure. Think why you find them so pleasurable. Then ask yourself if you ever have qualms of conscience about them. Ask why that should be so. Try to plot those pleasures on some graph or landscape in relation to God; identify their place, so to speak, in the order of creation. And thank God for them.

And then think if there are any things that you once enjoyed, and do so no longer. Is some God-given appetite being denied; some capacity for pleasure becoming closed up? Ask why that should be so. And decide what you will do about it.

This afternoon, I will reflect in particular on the purpose of reading, and how our secular reading "for pleasure" might just be a source of strength and inspiration to our prayer.

◆   ◆   ◆

We saw this morning how, for many centuries, Christian scholars felt themselves beguiled, captivated or seduced by the pleasures of classical learning; and how they fought against it, justified it, or just surrendered to it. We saw how the wisdom writers of the Old Testament perhaps felt a similar tug of conscience: whether their delight in "wisdom" were not a distraction from the fear of the Lord. And I suggested that this geological fault that runs through the Judaeo-Christian tradition between intellectual curiosity and pleasure on the one hand, and the demands of faith on the other, is symptomatic of humanity's fallenness; and that it is right to seek to overcome it. I suggested that a positive doctrine of "pleasure" will help us here.

This afternoon, I would like to reflect on the purpose of reading. I am going to take it that we agree that there is a positive place in our lives for whatever our equivalent of "wisdom" may be: books, films, music, travel, hobbies, sport. I shall take books as my main example, because that is where I probably find the greatest pleasure, so I speak from experience. The question that I am asking, and will try to answer, is what my so-called "secular" reading can contribute to my life of prayer.

I'm not going to offer you any justifications along the lines of going down to the Philistines to sharpen my axe. I'm not going to tell you that my secular reading opens up pastoral conversations in the pub, or provides me with illustrations for my sermons, or even improves my written style. These things may or may not be so, but that's not the point of reading. I read for "pleasure". Oh, I read for knowledge; but then I acquire knowledge for pleasure. I read to enlarge my mind; but that, too, is for pleasure. I believe that literature can make me a more interesting and a more sympathetic person; that "humane" letters can make a more humane person; but the end is still pleasure. Let me be plain about that.

But I read for some kinds of pleasure and not for others. There is a pleasure in falling asleep; but I don't read (as some people do) to send myself to sleep. There is a pleasure in sexual or horrific gratification, and some people read for those pleasures; and though I've sometimes been guilty of that, I don't count that as my purpose in reading. There is a pleasure in the sheer acquisition of information, of facts and figures; and some people find their pleasure in that. That, I suppose, is the pleasure to be had from *Whitaker's Almanack* or *Wisden* or an encyclopaedia or *Debrett's*. In the days of Bradshaw's railway timetable, some people read that for pleasure. I have heard of clergy who read *Crockford's* for pleasure, but I don't believe it. I am not criticizing that sort of reading; I'm just saying that it's not what I do.

I read, I suppose, because it enables me to travel in my imagination in a world evoked by someone else; a world that I could not otherwise enter on my own. I find myself in other people's lives, whether fictional, as in the case of a novel, or factual, as in the case of biography. I enter other lands and places, as in historical writing. I see the world through someone else's eyes, as in poetry. I think another person's thoughts in their philosophy; and feel the pleasure of a difficult argument taking shape in my own mind, knowing that my own mind could never have done this on its own. So I am enriched and enlarged by what I read; but I did not set out to improve myself. My purpose was pleasure.

Pleasurable reading, or play going, or film going, or music listening, is sometimes criticized for being "escapist". That has always seemed to me an odd criticism to make of anything. In any other context, "escaping" has a positive meaning: you escape from captivity, you escape from prison; the condition from which you escape is by definition a negative one. So yes, I read to escape. I escape from the narrowness of my own mind into the breadth of others; I escape from the smallness of my world into the largeness of others. So three cheers, I say, for escapism; and if you want to give it a theological name, you could call it *exodus*.

Now, the connection of this with my prayer is twofold. One is to do with *what* I read, and the other is to do with *how* I read. First, what I read: in the course of reading, we may come across a thought or an idea, a situation or an argument that illuminates our faith; that has, as we say, "theological implications". God forbid, I say, that we should ever sit down to read a novel, just to have extracted some theology from it by the end; but theological discovery can be an illuminating by-product of the pleasure of reading. Sometimes the theological discoveries come thick and fast. You can't turn many pages of an Iris Murdoch novel without some theological or philosophical excitement. The same is true of Chesterton's stories of Father Brown. There are, of course, some novels written with deliberate Christian intent, such as the *Chronicles of Narnia*, or indeed with deliberate anti-Christian intent, such as Philip Pullman's *Dark Materials*. But the possibilities of theological discovery are not confined to the author's own polemical intentions: and you will have your own list of books where you have come across a sentence, a scene or a character that has lit up some aspect of your faith. And no doubt you have found the same to be true of plays and films.

Now there is a danger here. The danger is that we say to ourselves, "I can get my theology from novels—or plays—or films—quite as well as I can get it from books of theology", and then we stop reading books of theology, and we rely on novels, or plays, or films for what we call our theological education. I think that there are two mistakes here. One is that we are no longer reading those novels or seeing those plays or films primarily for pleasure; in other words, we have started not to enjoy them but to exploit them, to use them for their by-products and not for their principal purpose. The other mistake is that without a proper theological education, we are not actually going to make those interesting theological discoveries; or at any rate, not find as much pleasure in them as we might. The more philosophy you've read (serious philosophy out of books), the more you will delight in Iris Murdoch's novels. The more scholastic theology you've read, the more you will delight in Father Brown. Cut off the theological reading, and you close down the opportunities to make illuminating theological discoveries in your novels, your plays or your films.

Let me give an example, this time from a film. There is a scene in that awe-inspiring film *Schindler's List*, that I think may shed some light on that most difficult episode in the Gospels, the Lord's (initial) refusal to cure the Syrophoenician woman's daughter. Oskar Schindler, you remember, is a German arms manufacturer, who uses his wealth and his playboy image as a distraction from the fact that he gives employment in his factories to as many Jews as possible, giving them "essential worker" status and thus saving them from the concentration camps. But he has to measure the risk, and he cannot jeopardize the whole operation by overdoing it. There are times when he has to say no; and there is one scene where he refuses to take in the elderly parents of a friend because they are too old to pass plausibly as factory workers. He has to balance his "mission" against his limited resources; and that, perhaps, lay at the heart of the Lord's initial refusal to say no to the Syrophoenician. In the end, for whatever reason, Schindler takes the risk and says yes; as did Jesus.

Now whether or not there is any interesting parallel here between the film and the gospel is not the point. My point is that until one has wrestled with the story of the Syrophoenician woman, studied the commentaries, ruminated on the text, and tried (a few times, without success) to preach about it, then there is very little chance that a novel or a film will suddenly bring new light to bear. The theological study must come first, ploughing up the ground; only then does the germ of an idea taken from that novel or film have any chance of bearing fruit.

◆

The second way in which ordinary reading can make connections with our prayer is to do with *how* we read.

There are many ways of reading. Sometimes it is necessary to "gut" a book, or to skim it, or to use the index to find the thing that we want. But that's hardly reading at all. Then there is browsing, a much more pleasurable activity, and the reason why I hope and pray that bookshops will survive the eBay revolution. If you know the book that you want, you can order it online and you don't need a bookshop. If, blissfully, you don't know the book that you want, why, there's the value of a bookshop in which to browse.

And then there is reading proper, taking the words that the author wrote in the order in which he or she wrote them; submitting to their mind and imagination, and being taken into whatever world they have created. This requires attention; and often cannot be hurried. I have always been a slow reader; I'm not very good with complicated plots; and I know that it will be time wasted if I hurry, because it only means that I will have to go back and retrace my steps for the things that I've missed. So real reading is an attentive, almost contemplative activity. With poetry, it cannot be otherwise. It is much the same as listening attentively to music, or closely looking at a great picture. We find ourselves in the presence of that which commands our respect. A great book or a great poem requires that we not only "read" it but that we "mark, learn and inwardly digest" it—which is what we pray that we may do with the Bible.[14]

There is, then, a sort of reading which is required of us by great books, whatever their subject. It is that careful, patient, attentive, contemplative reading which any serious text demands of us. We may have learned first to read the Bible in that way, and then discovered that we gain more from other books if we approach them in the same respectful spirit; or we may have learned to read quite profane literature with care and attention, and so bring the same qualities to the sacred text of scripture.

One of the most telling images of reading is in the book of Revelation. The angel tells the seer to take the scroll and eat it, and he finds it sweet

---

[14]   *Common Worship: Services and Prayers for the Church of England* (London: Church House Publishing, 2000), p. 422.

as honey in his mouth but bitter in his stomach.[15] The same bittersweet experience comes to us in all serious reading. There is the pleasure of reading, the pleasure of a good style, of words and sentences well crafted, of an argument compellingly developed. But then there is the sharp tang as we feel a prejudice challenged, a bad argument swept away, a point of view that we have long held, now held up to ridicule. But that sharp tang can also be part of the pleasure.

In the little time left this afternoon, think about what you read. Are you reading for pleasure, with all the possibilities of enlargement of mind and imagination that that can bring? And are you doing that guiltily or not? Are you going to tell yourself once again that you have "no time" to read? And when you say that to yourself, do you believe it? What *do* you have time for, and why is that more important than your reading? And do you read in order to "mark, learn and inwardly digest" what you read? And are there moments, when you are working through some tough book, as there were for C. S. Lewis (leaving aside the pipe and the pencil), when your heart sings?

---

[15]   Revelation 10:9,10.

6

Judgement and mercy[1]

Shakespeare's tragedy *Othello* will be performed this week in the cathedral. We cherish our reputation as the only English cathedral that has an annual Shakespeare performance, which, given the fact that Shakespeare was born, baptized, married, dead and buried in what was in his day part of the diocese of Worcester, is only right. Let me reflect on what it means to perform a play such as *Othello*, not in a theatre but in a sacred place such as this.

We read Shakespeare, and perform him, and view him, and admire him, for his insight into human nature and human motive, and his gift for illuminating them in irresistible stories and transcendently beautiful words. In no play is this more true than in *Othello*. It is the tale of a heroic figure, Othello "the noble Moor", commander of the armies of Venice, who brings catastrophic downfall on himself and the woman he loves, deluded by the deliberate malice of his enemy, Iago.

Iago is a wicked man. His aim is to destroy others. In this play, Shakespeare makes us confront the reality of human wickedness. Not all people are wicked, but some are. Not all people are motivated by malice alone, but some are; and Iago is one. The grammar school that I attended in the 1960s had a proud tradition of producing Shakespeare, but *Othello* was a play which the headmaster would not allow to be performed. No impressionable teenage boy, he said, should be made to play the part of an entirely evil man. For that to be said in those far-off and far from squeamish 1960s was significant. And today, as we reflect upon the work of Her Majesty's judges, and the operation of the criminal justice system,

---

[1]   Sermon preached at evensong in Worcester Cathedral on Sunday, 15 October 2017, attended by the high sheriff and Her Majesty's judges.

we might as well start with Iago, and acknowledge the possibility in some human beings of sheer wickedness.

Those are no longer easy words to say, at any rate in church. We look for the good in people, the divine spark in every person, the image of God in every human face, however marred; we speak of forgiveness and the possibility of redemption. And we are right to do so, for that is the gospel of our Lord Jesus Christ. We support programmes of restorative justice; but sometimes, I guess, those of us who are *not* immersed day by day in the very difficult and demanding task of restoring and rehabilitating offenders make it sound easier than it is. We speak of it in ways that allow us to go on talking optimistically of the good in everyone. Last Sunday, in this cathedral, to mark Prisons Sunday, we heard from two prison chaplains (one Christian, one Muslim), and they spoke of their hope for every person in their care, but that was a hope born of many hours of patient attention to people, and they would be the first to acknowledge their many failures and frustrations along the way. Shakespeare forces us to confront the fact that some human beings are wicked; and no one watching *Othello* would come away supposing that Iago could be redeemed by putting him on a programme.

Then there is the figure of Othello himself: noble, able, a supremely accomplished soldier; but in personal relationships unsure, diffident, a prey to the delusion and deceit of others. This is accentuated by the fact that Othello is an outsider; his race sets him apart in that early modern European society; it is hard for him to thread his way through the customs and courtesies of Venetian society. And it is the fragility in his character through which Iago gets to work; and this leads to his destruction and that of the woman he loves. I dare say that the judges have often been faced with fundamentally good and decent men and women, not wicked like Iago, but brought down by their simplicity, their not knowing whom to trust.

And then there are some remarkable women in this play: Othello's wife Desdemona, whose love for her husband remains firm, but not firm enough to elicit his trust in return. And Iago's wife Emilia, at first unquestioningly loyal to her husband, but who so grows in strength of character that in the end she can see him for what he is. So Shakespeare holds up a mirror to human nature; and that alone is sufficient reason for performing him in a sacred place where human sin is confessed and divine mercy sought.

And what, in the end, of that divine mercy? In a world in which men and women bring themselves down through simplicity or folly or misplaced trust in the wrong people, we may readily speak of the divine mercy which embraces all of us, however stupid or wrong-headed we may be. But in a world in which there are also men and women, wicked to an altogether different degree, we will be slower to speak of forgiveness; slower, perhaps, to speak at all; lest our glibness or easy optimism fails to acknowledge the depths of sin. But, in the end, Christians *must* speak of mercy, because the gospel teaches us that it is mercy and not judgement which is God's last word. And we who believe in the life of the world to come, do so in part because we believe that God's mercy goes on working.

How we speak of God's mercy in the face of evil freely chosen; *how* we reconcile the irresistibility of God's love with the ultimate freedom of the individual—this is not a dilemma to be reconciled at a philosophical level. But what philosophy cannot demonstrate, poetry can intimate. And I turn here not to Shakespeare, because the subject of his play is the inevitability of Othello's downfall and not the possibility of Iago's redemption. I turn instead to words from the Irish poet James Stephens, who died in 1950. This poem is entitled "The Fullness of Time", and it canvasses the possibility of the ultimate reconciliation of God's love and the freedom of the creature, by daring to imagine even the redemption of the devil. May all of us, whose task it is to pass judgement on others, dare to believe that, in the "fullness of time", God's love reaches as far as this:

> On a rusty iron throne
> Past the furthest star of space
> I saw Satan sit alone,
> Old and haggard was his face;
> For his work was done and he
> Rested in eternity.

And to him from out the sun
Came his father and his friend
Saying, now the work is done
Enmity is at an end:
And he guided Satan to
Paradises that he knew.

Gabriel without a frown,
Uriel without a spear,
Raphael came singing down
Welcoming their ancient peer,
And they seated him beside
One who had been crucified.[2]

---

[2]   *The Oxford Book of English Mystical Verse*, ed. D. H. S. Nicholson and A. H. E. Lee (Oxford: Clarendon Press, 1917), pp. 505–6.

7

The great antagonist[1]

There he lies: John, king of England, John Lackland, "Bad King John".
This week marks the eighth centenary of his death at Newark. Eleven
days later, he was buried here, and the day after that, the young Prince
Henry was crowned at Gloucester. John's intention was to be buried in
his own foundation of Beaulieu abbey in Hampshire, but at the time of
his death, the south of England was in the hands of the French and the
rebel barons, and so on the evening of his death, he directed that his
body should be brought here, to Worcester: as he says in his last will
and testament preserved here in the cathedral library, "to the church
of Saint Mary and Saint Wulfstan"; to Worcester, whose castle he had
fortified, where he had spent his last Christmas, and where he had found
a devotion to the newly-canonized St Wulfstan. This afternoon, at the
annual judges' service, we shall remember those solemn events of eight
centuries ago. Judges, sheriffs, barons, and bishops (all the people who
resisted and opposed John) will be here, not to rehearse old conflicts or
controversies, but to pay the respect due to the office of a king of England
(however unworthy the office holder) and to pray for the repose of a
Christian soul, which is the last duty that we can give to anyone, however
good or bad.

In today's Gospel reading, Jesus paints the picture of an unjust judge,
who withheld justice from his people. We might be talking about King
John. John screwed ever higher taxes from his people to pay for his

---

[1]   Sermon preached at the eucharist in Worcester Cathedral on Sunday,
16 October 2016 (Proper 24), marking the eighth centenary of the death
and burial at Worcester, of King John. The readings were Genesis 32:22–31;
2 Timothy 3:14–4:5; Luke 18:1–8.

French wars; he seized lands, and on occasions he murdered. But the unjust judge in the parable is taken on, not by a coalition of the high and mighty, but by a solitary widow, who wins justice for herself by her sheer persistence. The Magna Carta barons might have been glad of her help.

So runs the parable, but Jesus, as usual, is talking about something different from what lies on the surface of the story. The persistence that that old woman showed in her approach to the wicked judge, says Jesus, is the same persistence which Christians need to bring to their prayers to God. As can happen so often in the parables of Jesus, we are taken through a sudden change of scene, from the wicked judge to God himself. The only thread connecting the two scenes is the need for persistence.

And if we are shocked by the comparison of the wicked judge to God himself, if we feel that here is one parable where Jesus really was laying himself out to be misunderstood and misquoted, then what do we make of the reading from the book of Genesis? This is one of the most awesome and dramatic stories in the Old Testament. Jacob the wanderer, the fugitive, encounters an unnamed adversary in the dead of night. They wrestle, and Jacob is injured. The adversary tries to escape; but Jacob persists; there is one thing that he must know—who is this person whom he is fighting? And his strange antagonist replies by giving him a new name, Israel, meaning that he has fought not only with human adversaries but with God himself. And as the grey streaks of dawn appear, Jacob exclaims, "I have seen God face to face, and yet my life is preserved."

So the picture of a human soul wrestling with God is not only there in the parables of Jesus; it is there in one of the early stories of the Old Testament. And it is there in the book of Psalms and it is there in the book of Job. There is that in religious faith, there is that in the spiritual life, which is nothing to do with serenity or peace of mind, but is akin to wrestling with God, struggling with God, even fighting God. And if we turn the pages of St Luke's Gospel to the end of the book, we read that in the garden of Gethsemane, praying to his Father, Jesus himself was in—well, the Greek word is *agōnia*.[2] We translate the word as "anguish" or "agony", which makes it an emotional thing, but the word means a

---

[2]   Luke 22:44.

struggle, or an athletic contest. Jesus, like Jacob, was wrestling with God, the great antagonist.

Jesus compared that spiritual struggle to doing battle with an unjust judge, and he shocks us into attention by the comparison. But of course, God is *not* unjust, he is justice itself, and mercy, and supremely he is love. So why the struggle? If God is love, why is our relationship to him not one of serenity and peace of mind? Well, I could get Shakespearian and say that the course of true love never did run smooth.[3] We are never more struggling, wrestling, anguished, and agonized, than in our love affairs; and if the love of God is the supreme thing in the world, then it will call forth all our effort, energy, concentration, and anxiety. Do I really love God? Does God really love me? Am I lovable? Am I forgivable? Will he speak to me? Has he even noticed me? We experience that in our loving encounters with one another; we experience the same in our encounter with God.

In 1742, Charles Wesley published a poem. We sing it as a hymn; we shall sing it this morning. By now you will recognize the Genesis story behind the poem. See how Wesley beautifully transforms that ancient tale into one of the Christian soul wrestling with God:

> Come, O thou Traveller unknown,
> whom still I hold, but cannot see;
> my company before is gone,
> and I am left alone with thee;
> with thee all night I mean to stay,
> and wrestle till the break of day.
>
> I need not tell thee who I am,
> my misery or sin declare;
> thyself hast called me by my name;
> look on thy hands, and read it there!
> But who, I ask thee, who art thou?
> Tell me thy name, and tell me now.

---

[3] William Shakespeare, *A Midsummer Night's Dream* (1.1.136), in *Complete Works*, ed. A. Jonathan Bate and Eric Rasmussen (Basingstoke: Macmillan, 2007), pp. 369–411 at 372.

In vain thou strugglest to get free;
I never will unloose my hold.
Art thou the man that died for me?
The secret of thy love unfold:
wrestling, I will not let thee go,
till I thy name, thy nature know.

Yield to me now, for I am weak,
but confident in self-despair;
speak to my heart, in blessings speak,
be conquered by my instant prayer.
Speak, or thou never hence shalt move,
and tell me if thy name is Love!

'Tis Love! 'tis Love! Thou diedst for me!
I hear thy whisper in my heart!
The morning breaks, the shadows flee;
pure universal Love thou art:
to me, to all, thy mercies move;
thy nature and thy name is Love.[4]

And King John? There is little sign that he knew the pure universal love of God; though he had a devotion to the saints, and was no doubt sincere in his hope that Wulfstan and Oswald would aid him by their prayers. But if we dare to believe in that pure universal love which is God himself, then we may dare to hope and pray that John's soul is not beyond the reach of God's mercy, any more than the souls of those whom he harmed and injured and tyrannized in this life. And we dare to hope that because it is the same mercy on which we ourselves depend.

---

[4]   *Ancient & Modern: Hymns and Songs for Refreshing Worship* (London: Hymns Ancient & Modern, 2013), no. 616.

8

Wrestling with God[1]

The Old Testament lesson today is puzzling or profound, depending on your point of view. For no reason that is ever explained, Jacob wrestled one night with a man; having wrestled all night with him and failed to find out his name, Jacob comes to understand that he has fought with God. It is puzzling; people do not have spiritual wrestling matches except on *Buffy the Vampire Slayer*; people do not fight with God, and come away with no more than a dislocated hip. At that level, we can put it down as one of the quaint and puzzling passages of the Old Testament.

People do not fight with God. Oh, but they do. As soon as we put it like that, we begin to see that here is a profound story, a myth of humanity's long struggle with God: struggling to find his name, struggling to win his blessing; a long struggle, through a long night; a wounding and bruising experience, though one that brings blessing in the end. Anyone who has ever wrestled with matters of faith and doubt knows something of Jacob's struggle.

That same struggle was part of the Lord's own ministry. From the temptations in the wilderness at the outset of Jesus's ministry to the agony in the garden of Gethsemane at the end of it, the Gospel writers show us someone who struggled, who wrestled, who at the very end was in so fierce a battle with God's will that we are told that his sweat was like great drops of blood.[2] Jesus wrestling with the Father's will in the garden of Gethsemane beside the brook Kidron through the night of Maundy

---

[1] Sermon preached at the eucharist in Chichester Cathedral on Sunday, 17 October 2004 (Proper 24). The readings were Genesis 32:22–31; 2 Timothy 3:14–4:5; Luke 18:1–8.

[2] Luke 22:44.

Thursday is Jacob all over again wrestling with God through the night beside the river Jabbok.

And the Lord not only struggled: he also gave his disciples parables about struggling with God; and doubtless those parables reflect his own experience. We heard one in the Gospel reading this morning: prayer, says Jesus, is like the struggle to extract justice from a bad judge. You have to keep at it; you mustn't let him get away with it; you have to pester him day and night until he gives his verdict. What? Is God a bad judge? The judge in the story, we are told, neither feared God nor respected people; so he's hardly a picture of what God is like. Oh yes, he is; says Jesus (the Lord's parables so often shock us into some fresh apprehension of God by seeming to totter on the brink of blasphemy). Oh yes, he is: God can seem exactly like a bad judge whom we must badger for his judgement: there is that in prayer which is just like badgering, persevering, persisting, keeping on at it. This is not to change God's mind, but it is to *find* God's mind, and let our mind and his come to a *common* mind, so that he can act through us, and we through him. And it's a *task* for us to do that. There's a *wrestling* quality to prayer that can't be explained in the terms in which we so often hear prayer talked about: such as quietness, and silence, and serenity. Those images of prayer have their place; and we find them in the scriptures; but they are not the whole story, and to correct the balance, Jesus told this morning's parable, and others.

When we turn to the New Testament reading, we seem at first to breathe a different air. Here the Christian life is ordered. "Continue", says the author of the epistle, "in what you have learned and firmly believed"—and he goes on to speak of the Christian as "trained in righteousness", "proficient", "equipped for every good work". The sense here is that the spiritual life is a discipline, something that can be taught, understood, practised, completed. And there is a truth in that picture. There *are* spiritual disciplines to be learnt and practised. There is much in prayer which is quite properly technique. Just as in the life of a musician, an artist, or a writer there are techniques to be mastered, skills to be acquired, a discipline to be followed, so in the Christian life, the life of prayer. A musician who has never mastered the techniques of music is not a musician at all: an artist who has not acquired the techniques of painting is not an artist at all. But then technique and skill do not of themselves make great music or great art: and that is where the struggle begins, the wrestling through the night of doubt and sorrow, the winning through to a great blessing but at great personal cost. In just such a way, the person who has seriously embarked on a life of prayer will work hard to master the proper techniques of praying, the age-old tried and tested skills of it; but that is not of itself prayer: then comes the great, raw, dark, lonely encounter with God, Jacob's night, Jesus's night, our Gethsemane experience when sweat turns to blood. Even the author of the second epistle to Timothy, with all its orderly images of the Christian life as "training", "instruction", "proficiency" and "equipment", starkly goes on, "endure suffering". Nothing less than that can begin to measure the depths of the soul's meeting with its maker.

Is God then the great enemy? Not the enemy but the antagonist; the one with whom we have to wrestle; the one whom we encounter in the dark, the one whose name we can never quite make out. Not the enemy: but there is a strand of imagery running right through the Bible that comes close to saying so. The Lord's parable of the widow and the unjust judge is strongly reminiscent of the book of Job, where the righteous Job is undeservedly put through every kind of torment. He experiences God as unjust, unfair; Job brushes aside the bland advice of his friends that somehow he himself is to blame for his misfortunes; his one great desire is to come before God and have it out with him. He speaks of it as a "contest" between himself and God. But God is elusive; God hides himself; Job cannot find the way to where God is. Job's anger with God rings through the book, chapter after chapter; it is one of the moral peaks of the Old Testament.

But surely (someone will say) Christ is the answer to all of this. Where people once walked in darkness, Christ comes as the light. Where people once struggled to find out the name of God, Christ has made him known. Where people wrestled with God, Christ discloses him as Love. True; but we've got there too quickly. As we've seen already, the images of struggle are not confined to the Old Testament: they fill the life of the Lord himself from start to finish, and his parables as well. So the one who brought light to others, himself struggled in darkness. The one who made God known to others still wrestled with the will of God. The one who brought healing and blessing to others was himself wounded, battered to death, in his Job-like, Jacob-like, contest with the Almighty. And what is true of his life will be true in some measure of ours: "Christ leads me through no darker rooms", wrote Richard Baxter in one of his hymns, "than he went through before"—but some of our rooms may at times be almost as dark as his.[3]

The theme that we have explored this morning is not the whole of the gospel. There are other notes struck, and that is why we read the Gospels in an orderly way, so that the note that we don't hear struck today may be the one that we hear next week or the week after. We've not heard the note of, "Come to me, all who labour and are heavy laden, and I will give you rest."[4] That's another word of the Lord, and another day it will be the word that we hear in the day's Gospel. But today the Lord's word is about perseverance, not about repose: it is the word that inspired Maria Willis to write the hymn that we've already sung:

> Father, hear the prayer we offer:
> not for ease that prayer shall be [. . .]
>
> Not for ever in green pastures
> do we ask our way to be [. . .]
>
> Not for ever by still waters
> would we idly rest and stay [. . .][5]

It's interesting, isn't it, that it is those very *biblical* images of green pastures and still waters that the hymn writer rejects. Those are the images for another day; the hymn writer recognizes that they don't contain the whole of our often turbulent relationship with God. Today's word is perseverance: "Jesus told them a parable about their need to pray always and not to lose heart."

---

3   "Lord, it belongs not to my care", *Ancient & Modern: Hymns and Songs for Refreshing Worship* (London: Hymns Ancient & Modern, 2013), no. 306.

4   Matthew 11:28 (RSV).

5   "Father, hear the prayer we offer", *Ancient & Modern*, no. 629.

One of the greatest imaginative representations of perseverance in all Christian literature is the figure of Mr Valiant-for-Truth in Bunyan's *Pilgrim's Progress*. Bunyan creates a series of symbolic characters, and in them we see different psychological and spiritual types. There is the central character, plodding, average Christian; but then there is Hopeful, whose pilgrimage passes swiftly and contentedly; there is Faithful, who goes to his reward by way of martyrdom; and there is Mr Valiant-for-Truth, who stands for the principle of perseverance. It is Mr Valiant-for-Truth who tells the other pilgrims how he fought his assailants: "I fought till my sword did cleave to my hand; and when they were joined together as if a sword grew out of my arm, and when the blood ran through my fingers, then I fought with most courage."[6] The picture of pressing on, keeping at it, and (when there is nothing more to do) still keeping at it, has never been better put. It is Mr Valiant-for-Truth who first sings that great hymn of perseverance:

> Who would true valour see,
> let them come hither;
> one here will constant be,
> come wind, come weather;
> there's no discouragement
> shall make them once relent
> their first avowed intent
> to be a pilgrim.[7]

---

[6]   John Bunyan, *The Pilgrim's Progress* (London: Frederick Warne & Co., undated), p. 324.

[7]   John Bunyan, "Who would true valour see", *Ancient & Modern*, no. 823 (inclusivized).

9

Interpreting the present time[1]

It's not difficult to guess where a sermon on this morning's readings might go. Jeremiah denounces public figures who tell public lies, and he calls on faithful people to speak God's word faithfully. The author of the letter to the Hebrews reminds readers of the great names of the past who were people of courage and integrity, who stood up for justice and were prepared to suffer for it—people, the writer says, "of whom the world was not worthy". The writer goes on to urge the people of his own time, "surrounded by so great a cloud of witnesses", to be ready to run fearlessly in the same race. And in the Gospel, Jesus paints a picture of a divided world, a divided society, families split down the middle, and he urges his hearers to "interpret the present time".

The task of a preacher this morning looks pretty straightforward. Surely it's to draw some obvious parallels between the times of Jeremiah, Hebrews, and the Gospel of Luke, and our own time. There are public figures who tell public lies. There is the moral decay of the present time. Our leaders bear but poor comparison with the moral giants of the past. Our country is in a destructive state of internal division. We have both the *word* of Jesus, bidding us to "interpret the present time", and we have the *example* of Jesus, whom we are to keep firmly in view while we do our best to lift ourselves above the moral squalor of the world and run the race that is set before us. The job of this morning's preacher is surely to draw a sharp contrast between "a world of lunacy, violence, stupidity, greed" (as

---

[1] Sermon preached at the eucharist in Worcester Cathedral on Sunday, 18 August 2019 (Proper 15). The readings were Jeremiah 23:23–9; Hebrews 11:29–12:2; Luke 12:49–56.

T. S. Eliot once put it) on the one hand; and the clear, calm, courageous witness of the Church and its faith in Jesus Christ, on the other.[2]

Except that it's not as simple as that. I don't for one moment dispute the picture of a world of lunacy, violence, stupidity, and greed, especially just at present, especially in the conduct of public affairs in both this and other countries. I am quite as much in despair as anyone else at the mountain to be climbed if we are ever to re-assert the virtues of honesty, decency, courtesy, and duty, in public life. We need to heed the words of Jeremiah, and Hebrews, and the Lord himself.

But (and this is where it gets more difficult) Jeremiah and the author of Hebrews and the Lord Jesus Christ all spoke with *authority*. Jeremiah was a prophet who spoke the truth, and suffered for it; he suffered public obloquy, regal disapproval, and imprisonment. The author to the Hebrews wrote from and to a Christian community which also was undergoing persecution on account of its faith in Jesus Christ. And Jesus Christ himself spoke out, and provoked hostility, and divided those who listened to him, and in the end, as the epistle reminds us, "endured the cross" with all its shame. Our three readings this morning all come to us marked with the authority and authenticity of those who have been prepared to suffer for what they had to say.

The challenge that this presents to the Church today, or to a preacher faced with this morning's readings, is whether the Church has that same moral authority to speak as Jeremiah, or the author of Hebrews, or Jesus himself. The Church is often urged to "speak out" on all sorts of questions, though in my experience many of those who urge the Church to "speak out" expect the Church to agree with them (if the Church doesn't agree with them, then the Church is not speaking out, but meddling). But the very idea that the Church should "speak out" implies that the Church has some authority to do so; and that is what very many other people today would question, and for good reason.

When the history of Christianity in the twenty-first century comes to be written, I fear that a significant chapter will be devoted to the crisis of sexual abuse in the Church which has emerged in recent years and

---

2   T. S. Eliot, "The Cocktail Party", in *The Complete Poems and Plays of T. S. Eliot* (London: Faber and Faber, 1969), pp. 351–440 at 418.

shows no sign of abating—at any rate, no sign of abating in terms of the *disclosure* of historic abuse. It is timely to speak about this, given the continuing disclosure of abuse all around the world, and the question of the Church's moral authority in the light of this morning's readings.

The sexual abuse of young or vulnerable people by clergy and lay church leaders is truly appalling. It is an abuse of trust, an abuse of ecclesiastical position, and a betrayal of the gospel. It has happened in all Churches, Catholic and Protestant, Anglican and Orthodox, evangelical and Pentecostal. It has happened in all parts of the world. The abusers have been clergy and lay church members, married and unmarried, straight and gay. It's not possible to push the problem on to one part of the Church, or one type of Christian, and say "that's the problem".

Of course, sexual abuse is not confined to churches: it has happened in government, in schools, in universities, in companies, in youth organizations, in towns and villages, among those of other faiths and those of no faith. But it *has* happened in church as well as in those other communities, and that is what we have to think about. Of course, the abusers have been a tiny minority, but there has been a wider culpability on the part of all the institutions in which abuse has taken place: the culpability that comes from negligence, from a lack of vigilance, and from sheer naivety about the motives and behaviour of others—which is why today, belatedly but still urgently, safeguarding the vulnerable and the young has become such a priority. And when those historians of the future reflect on this appalling chapter in the history of world Christianity, they will also try and estimate how many people left the Church during these years, disillusioned and despondent, indignant and disgusted. I suspect that the Church's complicity in sexual abuse will be seen as one of the accelerators, if not the originator, of secularization.

So when we are faced, as we are this morning, with readings that encourage us to "speak out", like Jeremiah, against wickedness in public life, then we must tread warily, and humbly, because, in the minds of many people, the Church no longer occupies the moral high ground. If houses are to be put in order, we have our own house, the household of the Church, to think about first. And how do we do that?

First, we should remember that while the Church is charged to *preach* the word of God, it must first of all *listen* to the word of God. When we come together on a Sunday as a community of Christian people, we sit *under* the word of God, to be searched by it, and judged by it, to allow ourselves to be changed by it, to be brought to repentance by it. When, in this morning's Gospel, Jesus tells us to "interpret the present time", he means us and our place (our sometimes compromised place) in the modern world. Jesus's words about removing the beam in our own eye, before we worry about the speck in other people's eyes, apply here.[3]

Second, the disclosure of widespread abuse of young and vulnerable people over recent decades, in church as well as outside it, should place upon us a new and urgent obligation to make our churches and our church communities places of welcome, security, and acceptance for all. Safeguarding is more than vigilance; it is more than policing; it is building a culture of welcome and acceptance that is reflected in all the things that we do together, and reflected even in our buildings. In this cathedral, for example, we have done much to make the building accessible for those with particular physical needs, but we have much more to do in that respect. The physical accessibility of the building should be a sacramental sign, an outward and visible sign, of a community which welcomes everyone into a safe place.

And third, the Church can claim no authority to "speak out" on any subject at all, until we are fully engaged with all people of goodwill the world over, in addressing the fundamental dangers facing the life of the planet. We think especially at present of the climate crisis, but the dangers are interlinked: climate change, pollution, population growth, disease, hunger. Even the tiniest steps, such as the use of biodegradable coffee cups for our after-service refreshments, are tiny steps in the right direction, and the fact that they are tiny is not a reason for not taking them. A church community collectively and visibly committed to the kind of simple and responsible lifestyle which alone can offer hope to the next generation: that is a community which has humbly sat under the word of God, and been changed by it, and which has heeded the Lord's warning to "interpret the present time".

---

[3] Matthew 7:3–5.

1 0

The story within a story[1]

In C. S. Lewis's story *The Lion, the Witch and the Wardrobe*, the curse that lay on the land of Narnia was that it was always winter and never Christmas. A winter without a winter celebration would certainly be bleak, and most cultures have felt the need for something to bring warmth and light to the darkest time of the year. From this point of view, Christmas is one among many winter festivals, and a spectacularly successful one.

But the story that lies at the heart of Christmas is surprising. It is not, on the face of it, a story of light and warmth, or one to gladden the dark days of winter. It tells of a birth (which, as we know, is a glad event) but the baby was born to parents who were displaced from home, and caught up in the turmoil of great political events, unable to find shelter except in the stable of an inn. The story tells of angel voices celebrating this birth, but they went unnoticed except by a few shepherds outside the town.[2] And when we turn from St Luke's familiar Christmas story to St Matthew's version, it becomes bleak indeed: for the birth of this child provokes anger and resentment, which leads to murder and to the exile of the child to a foreign land.[3] There is, on the face of it, something profoundly wrong about this birth.

So if we are to find a reason for celebrating the Christmas story, we must dig deeper. We must dig until we find within it another story. And that deeper story tells how the maker of all things—God almighty—entered

---

[1] Sermon preached at the eucharist in Worcester Cathedral on Christmas Day 2007, televised live by the BBC.

[2] Luke 2:1–20.

[3] Matthew 1:18–2:18.

his own world to live a human life and die a human death. God put himself among us to be one of us. "The Word", says St John, commenting on the birth of Jesus, "was made flesh, and dwelt among us."[4] And that homeless unregarded birth, and that murderous intrigue, and that flight into exile—those things were done to a human child, but they are also done to God himself. "He came to his own home", says St John, "and his own people received him not"[5]—which seems to make the story bleaker still.

So what is it that turns this story from sadness to happiness, from darkness to light? It is this: that when God entered this world and met with rejection and cruelty and death, he answered them with love. The child grew up to be a man, and the man proclaimed the love of God, and practised it. Even as he hung upon the cross, he asked forgiveness for those who killed him.[6] And in that deeper story, it is God himself who dies with words of reconciliation on his lips. The story of our Lord Jesus Christ is the story of God's love, put to the test by human hatred, and then set free to change our world.

And that makes this birth profoundly right, and gives us the best of reasons to celebrate it, and brings light into our dark world, and warmth into our cold world, and turns our winter into Christmas.

---

[4]   John 1:14 (AV).
[5]   John 1:11 (RSV).
[6]   Luke 23:34.

11

Brightest and best[1]

"The dean preaches the homily", says your order of service. But it's the words that come before that which interest me: "Reginald Heber (1783–1826)", the author of the beautiful Epiphany hymn that we have just sung, "Brightest and best of the sons of the morning". So by way of an Epiphanytide homily, here is a reflection on the life of one whose words have enriched our celebration of this season.

Reginald Heber was a scholar, a parish priest in Shropshire, and a writer of hymns—perhaps his best-known is the Trinity Sunday hymn, "Holy, holy, holy". He was something of a campaigner for the authorization of hymn singing in the Church of England, then regarded as an activity of dubious legality. At the age of 40, he became bishop of Calcutta, which at that time was the only Anglican bishopric for the whole of the Indian sub-continent, Australia, and New Zealand.

> Brightest and best of the sons of the morning,
> dawn on our darkness, and lend us thine aid;
> star of the east, the horizon adorning,
> guide where our infant Redeemer is laid.[2]

Heber must often have reflected on the fact that he was the only English bishop in the world whose diocese, like the magi, looked *west* to the place

---

[1] Sermon preached at the Epiphany carol service in Worcester Cathedral on Sunday, 10 January 2016.

[2] *Ancient & Modern: Hymns and Songs for Refreshing Worship* (London: Hymns Ancient & Modern, 2013), no. 96.

of Christ's birth. Though he wrote this hymn long before he went to India, perhaps he felt that he was treading in the steps of the magi.

> Cold on his cradle the dew-drops are shining;
> low lies his head with the beasts of the stall;
> angels adore him in slumber reclining,
> Maker and Monarch and Saviour of all.

Heber found himself making vast journeys, for which his life as a priest and scholar in England had scarcely prepared him. Like the magi, his travelling was arduous; and like the one whom the magi sought, he knew what it was to sleep in the cold of a stable.

> Say, shall we yield him, in costly devotion,
> odours of Edom, and offerings divine,
> gems of the mountain, and pearls of the ocean,
> myrrh from the forest, or gold from the mine?

In Heber's day, the East India Company was all-powerful, and the English clergy were expected to provide the colonial enterprise with a religious gloss. Gems, pearls, gold, the riches of mountain and forest, were all at the Company's command, and expected to open all doors. Heber, on the other hand, was keen to foster an indigenous Church in India, and was often at odds with the colonial endeavour.

> Vainly we offer each ample oblation,
> vainly with gifts would his favour secure:
> richer by far is the heart's adoration,
> dearer to God are the prayers of the poor.

In Calcutta, and throughout India, Heber encountered a depth of poverty that he had never known in England. He devoted his life to nurturing the prayers of the poor, and (in spite of his grand status in colonial India) knowing himself to be poor before God.

His life was short. He worked tirelessly for three years; he was worn down by fever; and he died when he took too cold a bath on too hot a day. His death sealed a life which had been made rich by the adoration of the heart and the prayers of the poor. The stars of the east led him at last to his Redeemer.

His life, as I have suggested, has something of the magi about it: living in the east; commanding wealth and influence and status, but seeking out the company of the poor; ready to wear himself out in labour and travel for the sake of his Lord; laying his life and his heart at the feet of Christ.

> Brightest and best of the sons of the morning,
> dawn on our darkness, and lend us thine aid;
> star of the east, the horizon adorning,
> guide where our infant Redeemer is laid.

Finally, a footnote: many years ago, my wife and I were rummaging in a second-hand shop (in York, as I recall). I unearthed a framed print of some Indian scene; there were palm trees and elephants. The title read: "The Death of Bishop Heber". I said, "I have to buy that." My wife said, "There can be no one else in the world who would want a framed picture of the death of Bishop Heber." I said, "That is why I have to buy it." And I did. And now you know why.

12

Ceremony and merriment[1]

Those of you who attended the sung eucharist on St Wulfstan's Day, the week before last, may remember that I told one of the stories of that great saint, who, as most of you know, was a monk and bishop here in the eleventh century, and began the building of the great Norman church in which you are sitting. The story concerns the first archdeacon of Worcester, Ailrec, who had seen to the building of a new parish church somewhere in the diocese, and now needed the bishop to come and dedicate it. Bishop Wulfstan told him one evening that he would dedicate the church at dawn the next day, which threw the archdeacon into a panic of last-minute preparation. By dawn, all was ready, with one exception. The hapless archdeacon had failed to lay on a stock of mead for the feast that would follow the dedication ceremony and had only been able to borrow one small bottle from a neighbour. But when the time came, all was well. The presence of the saintly bishop Wulfstan was enough to ensure that, from that one small bottle, enough mead flowed to keep the feast going for three days; and even then, the bottle was not empty. William of Malmesbury, writing the biography of St Wulfstan a generation later, gravely remarks that the "the mead held its own with the drinkers".[2]

Many of the mediaeval miracle-stories stretch our credulity, but that's not my point this morning. The stories told of the saints are not random.

---

[1] Sermon preached at the eucharist in Worcester Cathedral on the Fourth Sunday of Epiphany, 29 January 2017. The readings were 1 Kings 17:8–16; 1 Corinthians 1:18–end; John 2:1–11.

[2] William of Malmesbury, *Life of Saint Wulstan, Bishop of Worcester*, tr. James H. F. Peile (Oxford: Blackwell, 1934), pp. 83–4.

They point beyond the merely marvellous to remind us of the stories that we read in the Bible. If a mediaeval saint is said to have healed the sick, or made the lame to walk, or even to have raised the dead, the point of the story is to ask the question, "And who does that remind you of?" If a martyr died a painful death with words of pardon on his or her lips, again the story asks the question, "And who does that remind you of?" And the story that I have told you today, of a saintly bishop whose very presence caused the mead to flow without a pause for three days, puts the same question: "Who does this remind us of?" And the answer, of course, is in this morning's Gospel. In this morning's Gospel, Christ is the bringer of joy, the author of all festivity, the one whose presence makes the wine to flow in absurd abundance at a village wedding.

St John, who tells the story, calls it not a "miracle" but a "sign". His emphasis is not on the marvel but on the meaning of the marvel. Like the mediaeval chroniclers, the evangelist tells his story to put the question, "And who does this remind you of?" As St John tells the story, Jesus embodies the sheer extravagant creativity of God himself. And St John goes on throughout his Gospel to recount a succession of such signs, until, at the very end, St Thomas, the doubting disciple, speaks on behalf of all of them, and says, "My Lord and my God!"[3]

But a sign works in more than one direction. A story of Jesus causing wine to flow and festivity to happen tells us that Jesus is Godlike, and that is part of St John's purpose. But it also tells us something about God. If we have never thought of God as generous or creative or as one who longs to bring joy to the world, then we would miss the sign in this morning's Gospel. St John is not only telling us that Christ is Godlike, he is also telling us (as Archbishop Michael Ramsey memorably put it) that God is Christlike.[4] Look at Jesus at the wedding feast at Cana: look at him sensing the sadness and the anxiety as the preparations fail and the wine runs out; look at him with a heart for these people and a longing to put joy back into their faces: look at him whose sheer presence is creative

---

[3] John 20:28.

[4] A. Michael Ramsey, *God, Christ and the World: A Study in Contemporary Theology* (London: SCM Press, 1969), p. 98.

enough for the great stone water jars to run with wine. This, says St John, is not only what Jesus is like; this is what God is like.

So the fundamental question put to us by this morning's Gospel story is this: "What is your God like? What is my God like?" Is your God, or my God, the bringer of joy, the generous and creative transformer of life, the one who takes the water of your life or my life and turns it into wine? Or, to go back to that lovely and absurd story of St Wulfstan, is your God or my God remotely like a God whose priority for his people is that they have enough mead to drink at a village feast?

And if the answer that you, or I, have to give to that question is that, frankly, there isn't that much joy in the way in which we think of God, and that, even more frankly, the idea that God might give a village wedding 120 gallons of wine to drink rather diminishes our idea of God—makes God somehow *undignified*—well, maybe we need to spend more time, you and I, reflecting on this, the first of his signs, that Christ did at Cana in Galilee. And if we *do* think that the story of Cana is somehow *beneath* God, that the things that we say of God should be more *serious* than this, then I suggest that we are being children of our time. Let me explain what I mean by that.

Let's go back to the story of St Wulfstan and the miraculous flow of mead at a feast following the dedication of a church. The occasion is not accidental. It was what the people of the time would have called a "solemnity". The word "solemn", both in Latin and in Middle English, meant all at once an occasion of pomp and circumstance and ceremony, and *also* an occasion of festivity and geniality and laughter and delight. The word "solemnity" encompassed both the awesome deed of dedicating a church and the mead-drinking festivity that followed it. Public life was expected to be "solemn" in that sense: ceremony and merriment blended. We have only to see what we have done to the word "solemn" to see what we have lost. We have drained the merriment out of solemnity, and left only the gravity and the pomp.

As a matter of simple observation, I think that the Church preserves a better memory of true "solemnity", of that ancient unity of ceremony and merriment, than any other part of our society. We catch glimpses of it when liturgy is done really well in a way that allows laughter as well as tears. We catch glimpses of it at a really joyful wedding, or, indeed, a really joyful funeral. There is a good deal of that old blend of ceremony and merriment in the way in which the Church celebrates Christmas. We have lost much of it, I venture to say, at Easter. We have lost practically all of it at Pentecost.

Well, you may say, but these are serious times. We have just observed Holocaust Memorial Day with its appalling reminder of what human beings can do. We have leaders unfit for public office, who are a danger to the world. We live in a country deeply anxious and uncertain about its future. This is the world we live in, and what is the use of a sermon on merriment? But that, I believe, is absolutely the point. What gospel do we have, what good news do we preach, if we can do no more than mirror the state of the world? St John begins his Gospel by starkly saying that God in Christ entered the world and the world rejected him.[5] It is the story of God touching the most terrible parts of the world with his presence, and knowing its darkness, and sharing its pain. It is a story which reaches its climax in crucifixion. If you want gravity, go no further than St John. But St John himself goes further than gravity. This is not *just* the story of an empathetic God who feels the pain of his creatures. It is *also* the story of God who brings new joy to those creatures. It is the story of God who rises from the grave, and announces that he has come to bring life in all its fullness. It is the story of God who even as he begins his long journey to the cross has time to keep high festival at a village wedding. And it is a central part of our calling, as a Church and as individuals, to model that celestial solemnity, that divine joy, that heavenly hilarity, that Christian merry-making, to a sad and serious world.

---

[5]   John 1:10,11.

13

Lady Wisdom[1]

For reasons that are, I must confess, not entirely clear to me, the Gospel reading this morning reverts to the great prologue of St John which we read often enough and read not so long ago at Christmas. The challenge both to preacher and to hearer is to find something here that doesn't lead us unimaginatively back to a Christmas message. And perhaps that is a challenge worth accepting. Maybe those rather predictable Christmastide conclusions are not the only truth to be extracted from this passage. A more oblique approach might yield some surprises; as John Donne said:

> On a huge hill
> Cragged, and steep, Truth stands, and he that will
> Reach her, about must, and about must go.[2]

So let's tackle the Gospel reading this morning, going about, and about; and begin this roundabout approach far back in the first reading that we heard this morning, from the book of Proverbs.

What we listened to there was a hymn in praise of wisdom. Wisdom was an important concept in the culture in which the Proverbs were written. Old Testament wisdom was that practical intelligence which enabled men and women, families and tribes, cities and empires, to function effectively. The book of Proverbs is nothing if not pragmatic.

---

[1]   Sermon preached at the eucharist in Chichester Cathedral on the Second Sunday before Lent, 19 February 2006. The readings were Proverbs 8:1,22–31; Colossians 1:15–20; John 1:1–14.

[2]   "Satire III", in John Donne, *Complete Poetry and Selected Prose*, ed. John D. Hayward (London: Nonesuch Press, 1972), pp. 127–30 at 129.

But practical human wisdom was also seen as the reflection of God's wisdom: and that, too, was a practical intelligence; it was what God used to make the world and keep it going. So, said the reading we heard, before making anything at all, God needed wisdom; God needed that practical intelligence before proceeding to make anything else. Wisdom, then, was the "first of his acts". "When he established the heavens", says Wisdom, "I was there [...] when he marked out the foundations of the earth, then I was beside him, like a master worker; and I was daily his delight, rejoicing before him always, rejoicing in his inhabited world and delighting in the human race." (Oh, and one other thing, before we move on from this passage: did you notice at the beginning that wisdom is feminine—"Does not wisdom call, and does not understanding raise her voice?" This first of God's companions, before God makes anything else, is a she. We'll come back to that.)

Well, that personified figure of Wisdom continued to fascinate and tantalize the people of Israel down the centuries. Repeated conquests and exiles scattered the Jews across the known world, and the century or so before Christ was a time in which many of them were found living in the orbit of Greek culture. How could one comfortably breathe the surrounding intellectual climate, and at the same time remain true to the teaching of one's ancestors? The answer for what the historian calls the "Hellenistic Jews" lay in the concept of wisdom: it provided a natural bridge between the books of the Old Testament and the writings of the Greek philosophers. And round about the beginning of the first century of the Christian era, an unknown Hellenized Jew writing under the pseudonym of King Solomon, wrote a brilliant treatise that restated the old Hebrew notion of wisdom in language that a Greek would find respectable. The book of the Wisdom of Solomon, as it is called, is a panegyric to Lady Wisdom: "she is a reflection of eternal light", we read, "a spotless mirror of the working of God".[3] It had tremendous vogue not only among the Jews but among the first Christians as well. Paul probably knew it; and it survives among the apocryphal books of the Christian Bible.

---

[3]   Wisdom of Solomon 7:26.

Let's now turn to the epistle to the Colossians, which we heard for our second reading this morning, and to our Gospel reading, the first chapter of St John. Perhaps we can begin to see that something very remarkable is going on. Both writers pick up that figure of Lady Wisdom, she who was "with God when he established the heavens" and was "at his side, like a master worker". St Paul, in Colossians, speaks of the figure who is the image of the invisible God, who is before all things, the one who has first place in everything, and in whom all things were created: and all of this is a very clear and very precise echo of the figure of Wisdom both in the book of Proverbs, and in the later book of Wisdom. St John, in his Gospel prologue, speaks of the "Word" who is in the beginning with God, through whom all things came into being; in whom was life, and the life was the light of all people—again, a very clear echo of what has already been said of Lady Wisdom. And both writers are, in effect, saying to their readers: you've heard of Wisdom, the first of the works of God. You know that she was God's companion before anything else was made. You know that she runs through the whole fabric of the universe, and that she is the quality that you must cultivate if you wish to live wisely and well in this world—well, I'll tell who she is. She is Jesus. And she (Wisdom)—he (Jesus)—is not only enthroned at God's right hand: she (Wisdom)—he (Jesus)—has taken flesh and lived among us. She (Wisdom)—he (Jesus)—has made peace by the blood of the cross.

So there are two very remarkable things about our readings today. The first is that the figure of Wisdom, thought of for centuries as feminine, is identified with Jesus Christ. And the second is that the figure of Wisdom, thought of for centuries as eternally assisting at God's right hand, takes human flesh, and lives a human life, and makes peace by the blood of the cross. Wisdom "delights in the human race", we read in the book of Proverbs; now she has rolled up her sleeves and got involved in the human race, and become very bloody in the process. Let's think for a moment more about both those two points.

Some people are troubled by the masculine language which the Judaeo-Christian tradition uses of God. Of course, this language is conventional: we do not believe God to be of the male gender. However, we do believe God to be personal; *more* than personal, of course, personal in ways that we cannot begin to imagine within the mystery of the divine Trinity; but not *less* than personal, not *impersonal*. But, as gendered human beings, we have no personal language at our disposal to use of the more than personal God, except gendered language. If we call God "it", God becomes less than personal. On the whole, the Judaeo-Christian tradition, received and reinforced by Christ himself, has decided to use personal language of God; and of the choice between masculine and feminine language, the tradition has generally used the masculine. But it is, as I say, a convention. That same tradition, on the whole preferring masculine words for God, from time to time subverts itself, and uses feminine words, or feminine images, for God as well. The prophet Isaiah spoke of God carrying the people of Israel in the womb, and delivering them as a child.[4] And one of the most significant uses of feminine language is to cast the image of wisdom as a woman, God's first companion and agent in the task of creation.

Both St Paul and St John, as we have seen, claim Jesus as the image of God's wisdom, Lady Wisdom. So it is not surprising that in his parables, Jesus likened the kingdom of God to a housewife sweeping the house to find her lost coin; and he likened himself to a mother-hen gathering her chicks under her wings.[5]

And my second point was that both St Paul and St John depict Christ, representing the Lady-Wisdom-Companion of God, not as some eternal heavenly reality; but as one who has taken flesh, lived among us, and made peace by the blood of the cross. If there is a divine wisdom at work in Jesus, then it is a very messy, tender, bloody, compassionate, empathetic kind of wisdom; there is nothing remote or rarefied about her: she "delights in the human race" indeed, and rolls up her sleeves to get involved. We are reminded more of the picture of God in the second chapter of Genesis, moulding a world with his fingers out of mud and breath, than the picture of God in the first chapter, who makes the world just by saying so.

Those who have embraced wisdom, the "wise", are frequently commended by Christ in the gospel. We are to be wise and faithful stewards, wise men building their houses upon rock, wise maidens

---

[4]   Isaiah 46:3; cf. 66:13.

[5]   Luke 15:8–10; 13:34.

prepared for the coming of the bridegroom; we are to combine the wisdom of the serpent with the innocence of the dove.[6] Christians are called to receive and practise wisdom. But now we can see something of the long biblical pedigree of that wisdom. We have not left behind the humane practical wisdom of the book of Proverbs. But to it we have added the figure of God's Wisdom, God's lady-companion on the first day of creation now made flesh for us in the person of Jesus. And Jesus shows us the full extent of God's wisdom: a wisdom that comes in search of her lost children, a wisdom that sweeps her house until she has found what she is looking for; a wisdom that takes flesh, and makes peace by the blood of the cross; a wisdom that breaks bread to become God's body, and pours wine to become God's blood. This is the wisdom that we are called upon to practise. It is a wisdom that bids us go out and get very dirty redeeming the world and delighting in the human race.

---

[6]   Luke 12:42; Matthew 7:24–5; 25:4; 10:16.

1 4

Now is the favourable time[1]

You may be familiar with a short piece of prose called "Footprints", which tells of someone who dreamt of there being two pairs of footprints in the sand—their own and those of the Lord, set side by side. The person in the dream is distressed that the two sets of prints are reduced to one precisely at those times in their life when they most needed the Lord's presence and help. "Why did you leave me at those moments when I needed you most?" they ask; and the Lord replies that he had *not* left them: those were the moments when he *carried* the person in the dream—hence the single set of prints.

It's a familiar passage to many; too familiar, perhaps, and over-used; but even if we feel that such passages can't quite sustain the heavy use that they get, it's worth our asking why they should appeal to so many people. In the case of "Footprints", it's evidently an attempt, however sentimental, however superficial, to answer a serious question. And the question is, "Why does God seem to be absent when I need him most?" No doubt each of us has had such moments, and no doubt each of us has had to try to find the words to speak to other people going through such a moment.

The readings for Ash Wednesday, however, suggest that the question is put the wrong way round. The question "Why does God seem to be absent?" puts the onus on God to explain himself. "Where were *you* when *I* needed you most?" God, the question implies, is in the wrong place. But the readings today suggest that it is *we* who are in the wrong place. If

---

[1]   Sermon preached at an ecumenical liturgy in the Church of St Francis Xavier in Caravita, Rome, on Ash Wednesday, 17 February 2010. The readings were Joel 2:12–18; 2 Corinthians 5:20–6:2; Matthew 6:1–6,16–18 (Jerusalem Bible).

God seems to be absent, then the truth is that *we* have got ourselves out of touch with *him*, not the other way round. The first question that God put to Adam and Eve, when they had fallen from grace, was: "Where are *you*?"[2] It is *we*, fallen men and women, who are the absentees.

Now I don't mean that when someone comes to us with an agonized question about where God is, that we tell them bluntly that their question is the wrong one. Ash Wednesday, however, is an opportunity for us to face up to the sterner truths of the Christian faith; and this, surely, is one of them. And yet God's question to Adam and Eve, while there may be reproach in it, is full of yearning as well. That yearning, that longing of God for us to be with him once again, comes over powerfully in the prophecy of Joel:

> But now, now—it is the Lord who speaks—
> Come back to me with all your heart,
> Fasting, weeping, mourning [. . .]
> Turn to the Lord your God again,
> For he is all tenderness and compassion,
> Slow to anger, rich in graciousness,
> And ready to relent.

And it comes over just as powerfully in St Paul's second epistle to the Corinthians:

> It is as though God were appealing through us, and the appeal that we make in Christ's name is: be reconciled to God [. . .] we beg you once again not to neglect the grace of God that you have received. For he says, "At the favourable time, I have listened to you; on the day of salvation I came to your help." Well, now is the favourable time; this is the day of salvation.

He is the present one, *he* is the attentive one, *he* is the listening one; and if there is absence, or a lack of attention, or a failure to listen, then the fault is ours. As I say, this is probably not what we would say to

---

2   Genesis 3:9.

those who ask where God is, but they are, all the same, the words which scripture addresses to us, as we embark today on the journey of Lent. That journey, if it is to mean anything at all, is a journey back to God, a journey revisiting his compassion, re-exploring his tenderness, re-appropriating his graciousness; a journey that acknowledges with some fasting, weeping, and mourning, that once again we have been adrift; once again a year has gone past in which we have too much taken God for granted, and "neglected the grace that we have received". As with Adam and Eve in the garden, it is time to stop hiding among the trees, and come out to face the God who is calling for us.

The Lord's words in the Gospel reading invite us (changing the metaphor) to go into our inner room, and pray to our Father who is in that secret place. Now if that is where God is, and at the same time we suffer from a sense of his absence, then that must mean that at some profound level, we are absent from ourselves. We are cut off from the deepest recesses of our own hearts, the inmost chambers of our own minds, our most secret selves. We are not, after all, the lonely rugged hero of so many films and novels, bravely self-sufficient in our individuality. We have lost touch with what makes us ourselves. But if we come back to ourselves, and search those secret places of our hearts, where Jesus tells us that God is, then we shall surely find him there; and if we come back to *him*, who is present in those secret places of our hearts, then we shall find *ourselves*. The Lenten journey of return, of repentance, is a twofold journey of rediscovering both God and self.

There is a rubric at the beginning of the Ash Wednesday liturgy in the missal which says that the ashes used on Ash Wednesday come from the branches blessed the preceding year on Passion—or Palm—Sunday. Year after year, I used to collect the old palm crosses, and burn them down to ash, and bless them on Ash Wednesday, without the significance of what I was doing dawning on me. And then the penny dropped. Each year on Palm Sunday, we bless those branches of palm, and we carry them in procession, and we join in the triumphal "Hosanna" of those first pilgrims who celebrated the Lord's arrival in Jerusalem. We welcome the Lord's coming into our city, into our lives, into our hearts. We rejoice at his presence with us. Those are the moments when our faith is easy, and our courage high, and we are carried along with the enthusiasm of our fellow pilgrims. That is good, and we need such moments in our lives. But then the testing times arrive, and faith is hard, and courage is low, and our fellow pilgrims are perhaps more of a hindrance than a help; and then God seems absent from our hearts, and we stumble, and maybe we stop, or wander away from the path. And those palm branches, that we carried with such fervour and such devotion, now seem like a reproach. Are we really the same people whose song was once "Hosanna"?

And now nearly another year has come round, and we are within a few weeks of taking those palm branches once again, and joining in the Church's song of "Hosanna". So today, before we reach that moment, we take back our palm branches of a year ago, now ground down to ash by all the failures and sins and disappointments and missed opportunities of the past year, and we receive them as a sign of that "fasting, weeping, mourning" of which the prophet Joel spoke. "Lord", we say, "here are our Hosannas of a year ago. They have become the reminder of our shame. Make of them today a sign of your forgiveness, a symbol of the way in which you call us back again and again, of the way in which you are present though we are so often absent, of the way in which you live in the secret places of our hearts whether we visit you there or not, of the way in which you carry us when the path is hard whether we know it or not." Truly, now is the favourable time; today is the day of salvation.

15

Cyrus my anointed[1]

If I had to submit a list of the 50 most astonishing verses in the Bible, one of them would certainly be the first verse of the forty-fifth chapter of the book of the prophet Isaiah, words which we heard read in the first lesson this morning: "Thus says the Lord to his anointed, to Cyrus, whose right hand I have grasped." I wonder if they struck you in that way? The question is, who was Cyrus?

Cyrus the Great was emperor of Persia, the founder of a formidable dynasty which eventually ruled most of what today we call the Middle East: Egypt, Palestine, Syria, Turkey, Mesopotamia, Afghanistan, and as far as the borders of India. He ruled in the second half of the sixth century before Christ; and his empire at its height was the largest that the world had yet seen. It might be helpful if we forget the old and romantic name of "Persia", and think of Cyrus as an Iranian, an Iranian warlord who came to dominate the Middle East. Not surprisingly, he left his name on the pages of the Bible: 22 times, in fact, in Daniel, Ezra, Chronicles, and Isaiah. From both inside and outside the Bible, we know him to have been a wise and beneficent ruler, displaying an unusual tolerance to his subject peoples. It was Cyrus who gave permission to the people of Jerusalem to rebuild the temple, which had lain in ruins since the Babylonians had destroyed it a generation before. As we might imagine, the writers of the Old Testament speak of Cyrus with some appreciation. Appreciation, yes; but Isaiah goes well beyond mere appreciation in this morning's first reading: "Thus says the Lord to his anointed, to Cyrus,

---

[1] Sermon preached at the eucharist in St Mary's, Wimbledon, on Sunday, 19 October 2008 (Proper 24). The readings were Isaiah 45:1–7; 1 Thessalonians 1:1–10; Matthew 22:15–22.

whose right hand I have grasped", and again, "who says of Cyrus, 'He is my shepherd, and he shall carry out all my purpose.'"[2] The prophet calls this Iranian ruler the "anointed" and the "shepherd". In other words, he calls him by two of the titles reserved for the sacred kings of God's own people: the titles of King David and his successors. He calls him by the title that one day would be taken for the coming great king who would once and for all establish God's kingdom on earth: the "anointed", the "messiah", the "Christ". Thus says the Lord to Cyrus, his anointed. Thus says the Lord to Cyrus, his messiah. Thus says the Lord to Cyrus, his christ. The prophet Isaiah pulls out all the available vocabulary for saying that this foreign ruler was directly and intimately instrumental in God's purposes for his people.

And that is why these words are so remarkable. Up until that time, the people of Israel had worked with a fairly simple set of ideas: that there is a God, and he is (without question) on our side, and he legitimizes what we want to do. Sometimes he may be angry with us, but not for long; in the end, he is always there for us, and he guarantees our long-term survival, indeed our eventual victory over our enemies. It's a simple but vigorous theology, and it's far from dead today: it's fuelling a great deal of energy, for example, in the American presidential election. It's alive and well and kicking all over the Middle East. It's occasionally seen lurking in the corridors of the Palace of Westminster.

It was the prophets of the Old Testament who began to question this theology. The prophet Amos listed all the nations that would fall under the judgement of God (that was conventional stuff for the prophets of the time) but then added Israel to the list. And he recounted how God had brought Israel out of Egypt and gave them a promised land (again, conventional stuff) but went on to say that God had equally positive purposes for other nations as well. That made Amos unpopular, and he was thrown out of the royal shrine.

And the prophet Isaiah (or rather, the unknown author of the second part of the book of Isaiah from which we read this morning) went even further than Amos, and painted a picture of God whose writ ran to the ends of the earth. No tribal God here; no domestic God who is by

---

2   Isaiah 44:28.

definition on our side; but a God whose concern embraces the whole of humanity—whether they know it or not.

The Emperor Cyrus was not a believer in the God of Israel. The prophet says in this morning's passage:

> I call you by your name,
> I surname you, though you do not know me.
> I am the Lord, and there is no other;
> besides me there is no god.
> I arm you, though you do not know me,
> so that they may know, from the rising of the sun
> and from the west, that there is no one besides me;
> I am the Lord, and there is no other.

Cyrus, unbeliever, ignorant of God's true nature, yet the means by which people from east and west might come back to God: what the prophet here is celebrating is Cyrus's benign policy of allowing the Jewish exiles to return to their homeland and rebuild their temple. He was the unwitting instrument of the reunification and restoration of the people of God.

Never before had an Old Testament prophet spoken of a foreign ruler in such a way. Never before had the titles of "servant", "shepherd", or "anointed one" been used in this fashion. Here is a whole new reading of history, a fresh insight into the ways of God. So universal was the scope of God's concerns that even the pagan ruler of the Middle East could unknowingly become the servant of the Lord.

So there is no "other side" for God. There is no favouritism with him. He has no tribal loyalties. His benign purposes are achieved in hidden and surprising ways; and anyone, however unlikely, may appear (with prophetic hindsight) to have been the anointed servant of those purposes, the shepherd of God's people.

We live in times in which there is a strong temptation to see the human race in tribal terms, in terms of "us and them", to see right and wrong geographically defined by continents, to make an easy identification of good and evil across the globe. It is a small step then to press religion into the same tribal mould: to press God into the same set of local loyalties. There is a terrible temptation for western Christians to think of Christianity as the religion of the west; and other religions as belonging somewhere "east". That of course is a misreading of Christianity: for Christianity is in origin eastern, and other religions (notably Judaism and Islam) have made their contributions to the culture of western Europe.

But that is not just a misreading of Christianity: it is misreading of Christ. "In Christ there is no east or west" runs a hymn, echoing the words of Christ himself that "many will come from east and west" and "sit down in the kingdom of God".[3] Christ did not demarcate the world into his side and the other side. He commended the faith of a Roman centurion and a Syrophoenician mother, and he told surprising and subversive stories of Samaritans who were good, and collaborators with the foreign government who found their way to God's kingdom.

Each time we celebrate the eucharist, we celebrate a breaking and a remaking. Christ gives his body to be broken; but when his body was broken on the cross, a whole world was broken too: a world of preconceptions about what God must be like, a world in which different sections of the human race were divided up from one another. Christ's body was broken on the cross, precisely because he suffered the effects of human sin and division; but in stretching out his arms upon the cross, he embraced that divided humanity and made it one.[4] There was a curtain in the temple that signified separation and division; and the Gospel writers tell us that at the moment of Christ's death, it too was torn apart, signifying reconciliation.[5]

When we receive the eucharist, we receive not only Christ's living body, but God's world remade. He gives it back to us to live in without division, without tribal loyalties, without God made in our own image. And in the eucharist, he says to us—as he said to Cyrus—as he says to all the unlikely and surprising instruments of his love:

---

[3]   John Oxenham (William Arthur Dunkerley), "In Christ there is no east or west", *Ancient & Modern: Hymns and Songs for Refreshing Worship* (London: Hymns Ancient & Modern, 2013), no. 679; Matthew 8:11 and (AV) Luke 13:29.

[4]   Cf. Ephesians 2:14–16.

[5]   Mark 15:38.

I call you by your name [. . .] though you do not know me,
so that they may know, from the rising of the sun
and from the west, that there is no one besides me;
I am the Lord, and there is no other.

1 6

Who do you say that I am?[1]

It is always disconcerting when people change their names. I know a young woman, baptized as Elizabeth, who in her teenage years decided to be Libby. This news reached everyone except her father, who would take phone calls from young men asking for Libby and always firmly replied that there was no one there of that name. It took Libby's father some years to discover his mistake.

Place names also change. The world in which I grew up had cities with famous names such as Peking and Bombay. Again, I was probably slower than most people in noticing when they became Beijing and Mumbai, names which more accurately reflect the proper pronunciation. In other cases, a city has changed its name for political purposes. St Petersburg became Leningrad, and now it is St Petersburg again. Byzantium became Constantinople, and Constantinople became Istanbul; and each change of name signified one more chapter in the story of that extraordinary place.

Caesarea Philippi, where this morning's Gospel reading is set, is another place of many names and multiple significances. It was a town on the edge of Galilee, a borderland where people of different races and cultures mixed. It was one of the sources of the Jordan, and springs and river-sources were always significant and mysterious places. Its ancient name was Panion, a shrine of Pan, the wild nature god of the Greeks. The Romans built a temple there for the divine cult of the emperor. At about the time of the birth of Christ, the emperor Augustus Caesar gave

---

[1]   Sermon preached at the eucharist in Worcester Cathedral on Sunday, 16 September 2018 (Proper 19). The readings were Isaiah 50:4–9a; James 3:1–12; Mark 8:27–38.

the town to King Herod, and Herod's son Philip changed its name to
Caesarea Philippi, named after Augustus and himself.

The place was important in Old Testament history as well. Not far
from here was Dan, one of the two most ancient sanctuaries of the
Israelites, marking the extremities of the promised land. "From Dan to
Beersheba" is a phrase that we often find in the Old Testament, and it
simply means from end to end, Land's End to John O'Groats.

So today's Gospel reading is set in a place of significance for the
different races and cultures and religions which were mingled there. And
it was there, in this place of many significances, of many possible ways
of understanding the world, of many alternative answers to the meaning
of life, that Jesus posed his question to his disciples, "Who do you say
that I am?"

We read that there were already theories circulating about Jesus. There
were those who said that he was John the Baptist, come back from the
dead. Others said that he was Elijah, of whom it was said that he would
return to earth to usher in the end of the world. Others said that Jesus
was a prophet, in the line of the prophets of the Old Testament. Peter
gives a different answer, a seemingly decisive one: "You are the Messiah";
"you are the Christ".

At one level, Peter was right, and in St Matthew's Gospel, Jesus says
to Peter that his answer had been given him by God.[2] Of all possible
answers to the question "Who is Jesus?", "the Messiah" was the best, the
most accurate, the completest. Peter gave the right answer.

And yet, as we also heard in the Gospel reading, it's not as simple
as that. In the tiresome phrase beloved of philosophers, "it all depends
on what you mean" by the word "messiah". Jesus took the opportunity
to begin to tell his disciples what it meant: that he would be rejected by
the religious authorities, that he would be executed, but that he would
rise to new life. Peter, fresh from the triumph of acclaiming Jesus as the
messiah, cannot believe that this is what being the messiah means. He
takes Jesus on one side to rebuke him. The moment is almost comic.
Can you imagine taking Jesus on one side? But the rebuker becomes
the rebuked. From being told that he spoke with God's voice when he

---

2   Matthew 16:17.

confessed Jesus to be the messiah, Peter is now told that if he thinks that he knows better than Jesus what it means to be the messiah, then he is speaking with the devil's voice. And Jesus continues the lesson: to be the messiah is to face rejection and suffering and death before the moment of final victory; and to be the disciples of the messiah will also mean self-denial, and shouldering the messiah's cross, and walking in his footsteps, and being prepared to lay down one's life, and not being ashamed of being a follower of Jesus, however hard at times that may be.

We live in a world of multiple meanings, alternative stories clamouring for our allegiance, and familiar landmarks constantly changing before we are aware of it. The political landscape, the moral landscape, the cultural landscape, certainly the religious landscape, the way in which we receive information and assimilate it and evaluate it and share it: the kaleidoscopic world which we inhabit gives us a glimpse of that cross-border fluctuating world that was first-century Caesarea Philippi. And for those of us, like the people of Caesarea Philippi, who had caught a glimpse of Jesus and were trying to work out in their own minds who he was, he poses that same question, "Who do you say that I am?"

In a few moments' time, when we stand to recite the creed, we will give, like Simon Peter, an answer. It will be a slightly expanded version of the answer that Peter gives in this morning's Gospel. He said simply, "You are the Messiah"; "you are the Christ". We will go a little further, and with the benefit of the whole Gospel story (which Peter did not yet have), we will say (among other things) that Jesus is the Son of God, that for our salvation he came down from heaven, that he was crucified under Pontius Pilate and rose from the dead, and that his kingdom will have no end.

These are words that we have inherited from the tradition of faith in which we stand. We should not accept them uncritically, or unquestioningly, or blindly; but on the other hand, we haven't just made them up for ourselves. In saying these words of the creed, we place ourselves in a certain inheritance of Christian belief and practice which we make our own. That's rather like Peter's initial spontaneous answer to Jesus: "you are the Messiah". Peter hadn't invented the term; it was there in the inheritance of faith that he had received, and when he needed a word with which to respond to Jesus's challenging question, it was the word which sprang to his mind.

Yet Peter, as we have seen, only partially understood it. There was much to learn about the messiah, many misconceptions to be discarded; much to learn and much to explore, and not merely intellectually. The meaning of the word "messiah", and the meaning of being a disciple of the messiah, were to be for Peter a lifetime of exploration and experiment; a lifetime of mistakes, and setbacks, and starting again. And it's just the same when we recite the words of the creed, when we give those words to Jesus's question, "Who do you say that I am?" Learning to be a disciple of the messiah, learning to be a Christian, learning the deep meaning of the creed, is the agenda for the rest of our lives. And we will certainly die in the attempt. As in the case of Peter, so for us there will be no moment of arrival, no moment of final and complete understanding, this side of death. The New Testament rules out that kind of certitude. "Now we see through a glass, darkly."[3]

St John, in his Gospel, tells of another moment in Peter's life. Again, Jesus had been teaching his disciples, and again, his words were hard and challenging. They were too much for many people, and they were going elsewhere for answers. "Will you too go away?" Jesus asks his closest circle. Again, it is Peter who replies. "Lord", he says, "to whom can we go? You have the words of eternal life. We have come to believe and know that you are the Holy One of God."[4] Peter knew that he did not know all that Jesus's words meant. He knew that he was on a lifetime of discovery, some of it painful. But at the same time, he had seen enough to know that here was someone to whom he needed to hold on; whose words, however hard, were life-giving; and that, in the end, he did not need to look elsewhere.

---

[3]   1 Corinthians 13:12 (AV).

[4]   John 6:68,69.

17

Jesus prayed[1]

"In the morning, while it was still very dark, he got up and went out to a deserted place, and there he prayed." *Jesus prayed*. Well, of course, Jesus prayed. It is part of the Gospel story, these night-time visits to the hills or to the wilderness; or to the garden of Gethsemane, where, we are told, he often went, when he was in Jerusalem. What else should we expect of the messiah, than that he should pray to the God who sent him? So Jesus prayed.

But the more we think about those two words, the more they open up a depth of meaning that we shall never exhaust. They are like a tiny crack in the ground that suddenly opens up a cavern of treasures. Let's start to fetch a few of them out, and see what's there.

Jesus prayed. In his regular daily prayer (the prayer of any Jew), this particular Jew sustained his regular daily communion with the God of his ancestors. He wasn't simply sent from God; he remained in communion with God throughout his earthly life. A hymn of St Thomas Aquinas puts it like this: "The Word of God, proceeding forth / Yet leaving not his Father's side".[2] That regular daily remaining close to God was sustained in prayer.

Jesus prayed. And his disciples wanted to pray as he did. "He was praying in a certain place", says St Luke, "and after he had finished, one

---

1   Sermon preached at the eucharist at Holy Trinity, Sloane Street, London, on the Fourth Sunday before Lent, 5 February 2006 (Proper 1). The Gospel reading was Mark 1:29–39.

2   Thomas Aquinas, "Verbum supernum prodiens", tr. John M. Neale, Edward Caswall, et al., in *The English Hymnal*, 2nd edn (London: Oxford University Press, 1933), no. 330.

of his disciples said to him, 'Lord, teach us to pray.'"[3] And his response to them was to teach them the words that we all call "the Lord's Prayer". So the prayer of Jesus is not just a part of his story; it becomes an example to his followers—to his first followers within the Gospel narrative; and then, by extension, to us. We are to notice how Jesus prayed; and we are to draw the same conclusion as did those first disciples: we are to say to him, "Lord, teach us to pray." And because his teaching about prayer arises from his example of prayer, we can reasonably conclude that what he taught his disciples to pray, he was in the practice of praying himself. If he taught his disciples to pray "Father", using that lovely Aramaic word "Abba", that is because he spoke to God in that way himself. It's not surprising that in Gethsemane he began his prayer, "Abba, Father".[4] And if in the Lord's Prayer, he taught his disciples to pray "thy will be done", we can be sure that that was what he prayed daily himself. Again, in the garden of Gethsemane, as we know, he made those words his prayer all the more urgently, more agonizingly, than ever before: "Let this cup pass from me"; "nevertheless not my will, but thine, be done."[5] So reading back from his instruction on prayer to his own example of prayer, we can begin to see of what his prayer consisted: the Lord's Prayer was not just the prayer he taught his disciples, but the prayer that he had first learned himself; and learned, we may be sure, not without cost. The author of the letter to the Hebrews tells us, in a daring phrase, that Jesus "learned obedience in the school of suffering".[6] His life of obedience was not ready-made; certainly not without effort; he learned a costly obedience, and he learned it in the school of suffering. The words of his Prayer—words which we repeat so easily—were first fashioned in that secret school to which he went under cover of darkness, in the hills, in the garden, in the desert places.

There is a unity of the life of Jesus and the prayer of Jesus: each shapes and informs the other. But his life is more than one of exemplary holiness. As Christians, we believe God to be uniquely present in the life of Jesus:

---

[3]   Luke 11:1.

[4]   Mark 14:36.

[5]   Matthew 26:39; Luke 22:42 (RSV).

[6]   Hebrews 5:8 (New English Bible).

so much so that we say that here, God took into himself a human life, and a human experience, and a human identity, and made them his own. God took human nature upon himself. And therefore the prayer of Jesus to his Father, of which we get such a brief and tantalizing glimpse in the Gospel story, is in fact a dialogue that takes place in the heart of God. I don't mean God talking idiosyncratically to himself. I mean that in that deep mystery of the nature of God that we call the Holy Trinity, God the Son in his human nature prays to God the Father; and the cost of that encounter (the "school of suffering" in which that prayer was fashioned) is borne by God himself. Everything we read about Jesus in the Gospels finds an echo in the heart of God. Even that most bewildering moment of all, when from the cross Jesus asks his God why he has forsaken him, even that terrible dereliction is something carried, and felt, and contained by God himself.[7]

And all of this means that when we pray, we are treading on some very holy, and very loving, and very terrifying ground. In giving us his prayer, Jesus has given us more than a set of words, more than a personal example: he has opened the door on his own costly relationship with God, and given us a glimpse of the potential cost of our own discipleship.

No Christian writer has more held up to us the cost of discipleship than the German theologian Dietrich Bonhoeffer, born 100 years ago yesterday, and widely commemorated today in both England and Germany. One of the most radical theologians of his time, Bonhoeffer went on to become a prophet of the German resistance to Hitler, and was executed in the closing days of the war. He reminded us that there is no easy grace of God; or, as he put it, no *cheap* grace.

But that is not quite the same thing as saying that the life of discipleship is simply difficult; just something with which we have to struggle on our own. "We do not know how to pray as we ought," says St Paul in his letter to the Romans; and there are few words in the whole of the New Testament more reassuringly down-to-earth than those. "We do not know how to pray as we ought, but [the] Spirit intercedes for us with sighs too deep for words." "When we cry, 'Abba! Father!' it is that very

---

7   Mark 15:34.

Spirit bearing witness with our spirit that we are children of God."[8] Do you see where St Paul is taking us here? We need only a few, stumbling words—just the first word of the Lord's Prayer in fact: "Abba! Father!", and at once the Spirit of the Lord is taking that word, and is investing it with all the Lord's meaning; the Spirit of the Lord packs it with all the depth and experience and pain with which Jesus himself prays that word. The Spirit of the Lord prays in us "with sighs too deep for words". Another translation gives us "groans too deep for words".[9] Where have we heard something like that before? Surely in the garden of Gethsemane, where his prayer and anguish turned to blood and sweat? There the sighs, the groans, of Jesus were too deep for words. And Paul tells us that we have only to echo the Lord's word "Abba", and at once the Lord is praying his Gethsemane prayer in us. Our hearts, our minds, become the secret place where Jesus re-enacts his loving and costly dialogue with the Father.

And all that means that our praying—or our trying to pray—is very much less a matter of our finding some suitable words and phrases of our own; and very much more a matter of opening our minds and hearts and wills to the everlasting prayer of Jesus within us. "He ever liveth", says the letter to the Hebrews, "to make intercession for [us]."[10] If we line up those words with what St Paul says in Romans, then we have a picture of the eternal prayer of Jesus, the eternal response of the Son to the Father within the mystery of the Godhead, being re-enacted within us. That is what our prayer is. However stumbling our words, that is what *God* makes of them. Probably the fewer words of our own, the better. In any case, Jesus has told us that we will not be heard for our much speaking. "We do not know how to pray"—and that is not a rebuke; that is almost the necessary condition for the Spirit of God to intercede within us with the sighs of Jesus that are too deep for any words of ours.

And what is the effect of this Jesus-prayer within us? Well, it is simply one way of describing how we become Christlike. The prayer of Jesus becomes our prayer. Our minds become the place where Jesus prays, "Father, hallowed be thy name." Our hearts become the place where

---

[8]   Romans 8:26,15b–16.

[9]   New International Reader's Version.

[10]   Hebrews 7:25 (AV).

Jesus prays, "Thy kingdom come." Our wills become the place where Jesus prays, "Thy will be done." We cannot pray increasingly like Jesus without becoming increasingly like Jesus; and becoming increasingly like Jesus is the whole life of grace, the whole path of discipleship, our whole purpose and destiny as human beings.

One final thought: I have spoken of the life of prayer as costly, as entering into Christ's struggle, even his agony. And there is no escape from that truth. But there is another truth about prayer as well; and that is, that in the prayer of Jesus we enter into rest. At the very beginning of his Gospel, St John gives us another glimpse of the life of the Holy Trinity; and there the Son reposes eternally in the "bosom"—in the heart—of his Father.[11] So there is repose as well as struggle in that divine conversation. There is reward as well as cost. And the more that the prayer of Jesus becomes a reality of our lives, the more that we too "repose" in God. St John uses just the same words to describe how the unnamed "disciple whom Jesus loved" reposed upon the breast of Jesus at the last supper.[12] As the Lord rests in the heart of his Father, so his disciples rest in the heart of the Lord, and know themselves to be beloved.

Just how prayer can be all at once both a wrestling and a reposing, is hard to put into words; but it is what each person who prays begins to find. And the note of repose in prayer must have the last word, because prayer is also a foretaste of heaven. "There we shall rest and we shall see; we shall see and we shall love; we shall love and we shall praise."[13] Those words of St Augustine, from the very end of his great work, *The City of God*, mark out the final destination for those who begin the journey of entering into the prayer of Jesus.

---

[11] John 1:18.

[12] John 13:23.

[13] Augustine, *The City of God* (22.30), tr. John Healey, ed. Randolph V. G. Tasker, vol. 2 (London: J. M. Dent, 1945), p. 408.

18

The worst has already happened[1]

I would like to take you first of all deep into the Paris sewers—not, I hasten to add, for a one-man rendition of *Les Misérables*, but to tell you about a plague of both snakes and dormice that afflicted Paris 1400 years ago. The snakes and the dormice came out of the sewers, and to deal with the infestation, the city authorities made a bronze serpent and a bronze dormouse and buried them deep under the city. When someone inadvertently dug up these replicas, the real snakes and the real dormice returned, so they quickly put them back again. So we are told by Gregory of Tours, the great historian of early France.[2]

And if that seems to us an odd way to deal with a plague of anything, there were many ancient cultures in which it wouldn't have seemed at all odd. In the first book of Samuel, we read of another plague of mice, among the Philistines, and they put an end to the plague by making little gold models of them. And the Philistines, we are told, were also stricken with tumours; so they made, unpleasant as it sounds, five golden tumours and sent them off to God on the back of an ox cart.[3] Make a replica of your plague, say these ancient cultures, and that will keep it at bay.

And so to this morning's first reading, from the book of Numbers, and another plague of serpents. As the people of Israel travelled through the desert on their weary way to the promised land, they were attacked by

---

[1]   Sermon preached at the eucharist in Chichester Cathedral on the Fourth Sunday of Lent, 26 March 2006. The readings were Numbers 21:4–9; Ephesians 2:1–10; John 3:14–21.

[2]   Gregory of Tours, *The History of the Franks* (8.33), tr. Lewis G. M. Thorpe (Harmondsworth: Penguin, 1974), p. 467.

[3]   1 Samuel 6:1–12.

poisonous snakes. And when they cried to the Lord, Moses was given the remedy: make a serpent of bronze and set it on a pole, so that everyone who has been bitten by a real snake may see it and live. The poisonous serpent, the sign of death, was changed into the means of healing and became the symbol of health and life. And that sign of death changed into life has remained to this day the symbol of the medical profession. Moses's bronze serpent, together with the crozier of St Richard of Chichester, forms the badge of the Royal West Sussex Hospital Trust.

The ancient Israelites were not alone in making this curious identification of life, death and the serpent. The Greeks worshipped Asklepios as their god of healing, and his symbol, too, was the serpent. Pilgrims came from all across Greece to the temple of Asklepios at Epidauros, where live snakes were kept; they spent the night in the temple in the hope of being licked by one of the sacred serpents, and so being healed. Make a model of what plagues you, say these ancient cultures; externalize your fear and construct a replica of it; contemplate the source of your affliction, or even embrace it; and you will find ways of overcoming it. You will find health and healing. You will live.

Well, I don't know what you make of all that; to my mind, there is rather more sound psychology implied in that admittedly rather quaint range of remedies than might at first sight appear. But the Gospel reading takes us a step further. In St John's Gospel, the Lord picks up the story of the bronze serpent in the book of Numbers and puts it to work in a new way: "as Moses lifted up the serpent in the wilderness, so must the Son of Man be lifted up, that whoever believes in him may have eternal life."

All through St John's Gospel, parallels are drawn between what Jesus is doing in his own time, and what God did for the people of Israel in the time of the exodus. Parallels, and contrasts: for what Jesus does in his time is also far greater than what God did in the days of the exodus. For instance, God gave the Israelites miraculous bread in the wilderness to feed their physical hunger: but Jesus offers the "bread of life" that "whoever eats of this bread will live forever".[4] God gave the Israelites water from the rock: Jesus offers a "spring of water gushing up to eternal

---

4   John 6:51.

life".[5] God gave the Israelites the bronze serpent lifted up on a wooden beam so that anyone bitten by a serpent might look at it and live: Jesus— well, what does Jesus offer? "So must the Son of Man be lifted up, that whoever believes in him may have eternal life." And that phrase "lifted up" is heartbreakingly ambiguous. It means exalted, raised up in glory. It means the ascension. "I, when I am lifted up from the earth, will draw all people to myself."[6] It equally means lifted up on that wooden beam which was the instrument of his death. It means the crucifixion. "I, when I am lifted up from the earth, will draw all people to myself." As the evangelist comments: "He said this to indicate the kind of death he was to die."[7]

Over the next weeks, Christians retrace the story of that death. Once again, we look upon the Son of Man, lifted up that we might live. We "survey the wondrous cross on which the Prince of glory died".[8] Like the Israelites and brazen serpent, we make in our minds an image of the crucified, we contemplate him, we embrace him, and we look to him for healing. Look again at the great window in the south transept where the stories of the Old Testament are mirrored by the stories of the New; and see the bronze serpent of Moses matching the figure of the Son of Man, lifted up that he might draw all people to himself.

Now Christians have not been unanimous in their attitude to the crucifix. In the earliest Christian centuries, when real crucifixion was still a possible outcome of Christian discipleship, there was little appetite for depicting it in art. The earliest artistic Christ-figure is the warm and reassuring one of the good shepherd. But as Christianity became first lawful, then popular, and finally fashionable, a growing need was felt for visible reminders of the austere truths at the heart of the Christian faith, for symbols of the awful death and passion of the messiah. And so the figure of Christ upon the cross became widespread; though at first it

---

[5]   John 4:14.

[6]   John 12:32.

[7]   John 12:33.

[8]   Isaac Watts, "When I survey the wondrous cross", *Ancient & Modern: Hymns and Songs for Refreshing Worship* (London: Hymns Ancient & Modern, 2013), no. 157.

was the living Christ, the risen Christ, Christ reigning from the tree. The truth proclaimed by the crucifix was that of Christ's victory.

Later, much later, a new mood gripped Christians, especially in the west, and that was one of sympathetic identification with Jesus in his suffering. We see this mood stealing over western Christianity in the tremendous pathos of the Lazarus carvings in this cathedral. But it reached its most extreme point, perhaps, in a remarkable altarpiece painted by the German artist Matthias Grünewald in about the year 1515. He was commissioned to paint a crucifixion scene for the altar of a hospital chapel at Isenheim. Many of those who first looked at it were victims of the plague. And the Christ-figure which Grünewald created for those plague victims to gaze upon is one of the most dreadful figures in the whole history of art. The Christ of the Isenheim altarpiece is not only crucified. His body is twisted, distorted, desecrated by something else. This Christ is a victim of the plague. Plague sufferers would look upon him and in his agony see their own. And yet the effect of the Isenheim altarpiece is not restricted by that; on the contrary, it makes its appeal all the more universal. It is as if Grünewald says to us: if a plague-victim can find his or her anguish mirrored in the anguish of Jesus, can you not find your anguish there as well?

This is an anecdote that I have told before, I know; but some years ago, at a time when I was feeling pretty bruised by failure and disappointment and generally at the end of my tether, I booked myself in for a couple of days at a monastery that I know. When I rang the bell, and the guest master answered it, I do not know what he read in my face or in his own heart, but he took me, without a word, straight to the monastery church, and sat me down. "I shall leave you here for a few minutes", he said, "and then I will come and take you to your room. In the meantime, look at the crucifix, and remember: *the worst has already happened*."

The worst has already happened. Plague victims looked at the Isenheim crucifixion and said to themselves, "the worst has already happened". Christians all down the centuries have looked at the Son of Man lifted up on the cross (whether in their mind's eye or in the representational form of the crucifix) and said to themselves, "the worst has already happened". The message of the death of Christ of course is more than that: the resurrection itself cannot be contained within quite so negative a statement. Nonetheless, this is where the death of Christ begins to connect with our fears, our failures, our sins, our profound spiritual sickness. Whatever those fears may be; whatever the particular plague that afflicts us; whatever our peculiar dread or secret terror or deeply buried guilt or long-borne grief: they are all focused, pin-pointed, concentrated in the figure of the crucified, upon whom the worst has already fallen. And recognizing that God has borne them for us, known them, endured them, suffered them, and outlived them, is the first step on our road back to life.

The praetorium[1]

The praetor was a high-ranking Roman magistrate. His residence and office was called the praetorium, and the name was applied to government offices up and down the empire. Though the governor (or prefect) of Judaea had his permanent residence, his praetorium, in Caesarea, he would come up to Jerusalem at the time of the Jewish festivals, more to remind the people who was in charge than from any desire to take part in their celebrations; and then the main army barracks in Jerusalem would serve as his praetorium. What is known as the Antonia Fortress, of which fragments survive, was probably the praetorium of Pontius Pilate. Intriguingly, there is a pavement outside marked out for Roman soldiers to gamble with dice. Also outside would have stood the raised seat, the judge's bench, where the prefect publicly dispensed justice and passed sentence.

In some translations of the Bible, you will find the praetorium called the "palace", in others, the "headquarters"; but praetorium is the word that Pontius Pilate would have used, and St John, even though writing in Greek, broke into Latin at that point and used the same word. No doubt it was the name by which Jesus knew the place.

We must imagine a building that embodied the power of Rome. We must imagine a place of terror and menace; a place where the justice dispensed was harsh, and the sentences severe; where prisoners were tortured, and where many came out only to go to their execution. In Pilate's time, there were many such prisoners. The Jewish historian

---

[1]   Address given at compline in Worcester Cathedral on the Wednesday of Holy Week 2021, in a series of addresses on "Places of the Passion". The reading was John 18:28–38a.

Josephus tells us that Pilate was eventually removed from office and returned to Rome in disgrace for the unusually savage measures that he took against the Jews.[2] It is to this place that Jesus is dragged after his trial before the chief priests. We must assume that he had never set foot in it before; and we cannot imagine the sense of dread as he passed from the jurisdiction of the chief priests, however hostile they were, to the alien jurisdiction of Tiberius Caesar.

At first, Pilate is not interested in the case: if the prisoner has come from the priests, it is presumably to do with their religion, and Jewish theology is not his concern—unless, of course, it is the tiresome business of the promised messiah, the future "king of the Jews". When the chief priests mention the death penalty, which the Roman government (in theory at any rate) reserved to itself, Pilate's attention is caught. He decides to see the prisoner. What follows is not so much a trial as an interview; an interview that briefly becomes a debate, until it descends into a shouting match between Pilate and the crowds outside.

So Pilate impatiently puts the question to Jesus: "Are you the King of the Jews?" Is that what this is all about? Jesus takes this as an invitation to debate, and enquires whether Pilate is asking the question on his own account, or whether others had laid the accusation. Pilate, not accustomed to being interrogated by a prisoner in imminent danger of the sentence of death, roughly cuts in. "So what have you done?" Jesus refuses to take the hint that he is wasting the governor's time, and answers, as he does so often, obliquely. "My kingdom is not from this world. If my kingdom were from this world, my followers would be fighting to keep me from being handed over to the Jews. But as it is, my kingdom is not from here."

Later in this strange interview—this trial that is not a trial, this debate between the prisoner and the judge—Pilate asks that, if his kingdom is "not from here", where is he from? Jesus refuses to answer, and Pilate asks him whether he does not understand that he (Pilate) has power of life and death over him—to which Jesus says: "You would have no power over me unless it had been given you from above."[3]

---

[2]   Josephus, *Antiquities of the Jews* (18.4), tr. Louis H. Feldman, Loeb Classical Library 433 (Cambridge, MA: Harvard University Press, 1981), pp. 63,65.

[3]   John 19:11.

Let us allow this scene to sink into our imagination. Jesus, awake all night, arrested, deserted by his friends, dragged before the chief priests, and now marched into the praetorium, confronts the calm majesty of the Roman empire. Pilate, flanked by guards, with an army at his command, looks down on this dishevelled Jew. And Jesus says to Pilate, "You would have no power over me unless it had been given you from above"; in other words, "Whatever power you have comes from the God I serve, the Father whose Son I am." When he speaks of the kingdom that is not from this world, and the power that is from above, he means the same thing. Authority is on his side, not on Pilate's; it is the authority of God above. What is Pilate? A provincial governor in a transient earthly kingdom. What is Jesus? The Son of the God from whom all authority and power derive.

That's the truth of the matter, says Jesus. Strip away the robes on the one hand and the rags on the other; look at us two—you, Pilate, and me, Jesus—and you see the true relationship of the world and God. "You say that I am a king," says Jesus. "You started this debate about kingship. All I say is that the reason that I am here, the reason that I was born, the reason that I came into the world, is to bear witness to the truth." I came to tell the truth, says Jesus. I came to show the world the truth about itself. I came to show the truth of the matter between the world and God. "Everyone who belongs to the truth listens to my voice." And the truth of the matter between the world and God is that the power and the authority and the kingdom belong to God, and not to Tiberius Caesar or Pontius Pilate or any other temporary regime or passing empire. That's the truth of the matter. "What is truth?" says Pilate.

This passage has been much quoted to prove that Jesus preached a purely spiritual kingdom, uninvolved in the messy politics of this world. I remember the late Enoch Powell, right-wing politician, classical scholar and amateur theologian, arguing from this verse that Jesus was no threat to the Romans at all, and that the crucifixion was a misunderstanding. The conclusion, of course, which Powell and others drew from this was that the Church, like Jesus, should not engage in politics.

But this is to misread the passage. Indeed, it is to import into this passage our modern English idea of what it means to be "unworldly". If something is not "of this world", we call it "unworldly", meaning vague, remote, abstract, ineffective, powerless. But the Gospel does not say 'unworldly', and if it did, it would carry none of those English connotations. The kingdom that Jesus represents is precisely what he says it is, it is not "of this world"; it is "from above", it is the rule, the authority, the sovereignty of God, to which all other authorities are subordinate. Jesus is claiming the ultimate divine authority for passing judgement on all the kingdoms, regimes, authorities, and politics, of this world. The most astounding aspect of this passage is the freedom with which Jesus, the prisoner at the bar, interrogates Pilate, the Roman governor. "Do you ask this on your own, or did others tell you about me?" "You say that I am a king." "Everyone who belongs to the truth listens to my voice." "You would have no power over me unless it had been given you from above." His words, his attitude, his demeanour, all say that here is one who recognizes no authority but that of the Father who sent him.

At the end of the inconclusive exchanges between Jesus and Pilate, the governor brings him outside to the open-air judge's bench, where justice is publicly pronounced, intending to bring this extraordinary trial to an end. Now there is a curious ambiguity in what the evangelist writes next. Pilate "sat on the judge's bench", we read in all our translations.[4] But the Greek could also mean "Pilate sat him—Jesus—on the judge's bench." You will probably find that as a variant reading in the margin of your Bible. In such cases of ambiguity, the meaning is usually established from the context. So the straightforward reading is that Pilate himself sat on the judge's bench with Jesus standing in front of him. But we also read that Pilate's guards have just dressed Jesus as a pantomime king with a robe and a sceptre and a crown made of thorns. And Pilate presents him to the people with the ironic words, "Behold your king."[5] So was this all part of the joke, part of the public humiliation of Jesus, that Pilate did indeed sit this pathetic figure on the seat of judgement? And if he did, then he acted more truly than he knew, for Jesus is the true judge in this drama, the one who all along has embodied the authority and majesty of God's kingdom, the one against whom Pilate can wield no power at all.

---

[4]   John 19:13.

[5]   John 19:14 (RSV).

The soldiers take Jesus to the place of execution, and the priests and the crowds go with them. Pilate returns to the praetorium alone. We may imagine his footsteps echoing through the deserted building. Did Pilate notice a difference in the atmosphere? A moment before, the praetorium had throbbed with the authority and majesty of a great king. An hour before that, Pilate would have believed it to be the authority and majesty of his master, Tiberius Caesar. But something has gone from the praetorium, the power and authority evaporated, and Pilate is left a diminished figure—while outside the city, the universal king, still wearing his crown of thorns, stretches out his arms to embrace the world, from the throne which is the cross of Calvary.

2 0

As our Saviour has taught us[1]

I want to begin well away from Jerusalem, and a good while before the
events of Passover Week. We don't know where it happened: St Luke
tells us only that Jesus "was praying in a certain place", and he puts it
somewhere on the long last journey of Jesus and his disciples from Galilee
to Jerusalem.[2] St Matthew gives us another account of it, but he fits it
into the Sermon on the Mount, given by Jesus in the hills of Galilee at
the outset of his ministry.[3] What I am talking about is the moment when
Jesus gave his disciples the Lord's Prayer. Later Christian tradition placed
it on the Mount of Olives and built a church there to commemorate the
scene. At any rate, Jesus "was praying in a certain place, and when he
ceased, one of his disciples said to him, 'Lord, teach us to pray, as John
taught his disciples.' And he said to them, 'When you pray, say: "Father"."
And so he gives them the words which have become so familiar to us,
and which most of us, probably, use every day. Most familiar, of course,
is the fuller form of words that we find in St Matthew's Gospel; and there
are no Christian words more familiar than these.

The Lord's Prayer is both a form of words for us to say, and a pattern
for the words of our own prayers. Jesus surely meant us to say the Lord's
Prayer, as we do privately and together; and he surely meant us to use it
as a model for our own further praying. With the Lord's Prayer in mind,
we learn that our prayers should begin with praise for God the Father,
and not be just a matter of our rushing in with a shopping list of our

---

[1]   Addresses given at the three hours' devotions at Worcester Cathedral on
Good Friday, 21 March 2008.

[2]   Luke 11:1–4 at v. 1 (RSV).

[3]   Matthew 6:9–13 (quoted in the following in the RSV).

own requirements. We learn that we should be penitent for our own shortcomings, but also forgiving of the shortcomings of other people: we can never separate our need of forgiveness from our need to forgive. We learn to pray for the coming of God's kingdom, but also for our daily bread here and now. We learn to pray that God will protect us, and guard us from harm.

But we can learn more from the Lord's Prayer than simply *what* to pray, and *how* to pray. The Lord's Prayer, which is so aptly named, also teaches us how *Jesus* prayed. If these were the words that he gave his disciples, they were surely words which had first been tested and tempered in his own experience. It is no accident that St Luke tells us that it was the experience of *watching Jesus pray* that prompted the disciples to ask him for instruction in prayer. "We want to pray like you."

And with this clue in mind, we can turn to the Gospels with fresh eyes, and begin to see the whole ministry of Jesus as an acting out of the Lord's Prayer; or, to put it better, to see his whole life as an offering up in deed as well as in word of his own constant, inward prayer; his secret day-by-day communion with his heavenly Father. His prayer was all of a piece with his teaching; and his teaching was all of a piece with his life; and his life was a sacrifice offered up to God the Father, completed when his life was consummated in death on Calvary.

Yes, you see, in case you're thinking that I've forgotten that it's Good Friday, there is a very close connection between the Lord's Prayer and the Lord's passion. In his prayer—his constant daily, nightly prayer to God the Father—he offers up his whole life. His whole life becomes an act of prayer, an act of oblation, to the Father. And on the cross, he completes that oblation, that prayer. Death, life, prayer, and the words of the Lord's Prayer, are all of a piece, an integrity, a unity. Through the words of the Lord's Prayer we can explore the meaning of the cross; and through the story of the cross we can deepen our understanding of the Lord's Prayer; and in both ways, we can learn to pray better ourselves.

Let's think first of the word that Jesus uses to address God. In St Matthew's version of the Lord's Prayer, it is "Our Father who art in heaven". In St Luke's version, it is simply "Father". The word that Jesus used in his own, Aramaic, tongue is *Abba*. It is an affectionate mode of address. It speaks of his own intimate communion with God, and it is the same communion with God into which Jesus invites his disciples. In teaching them to call God their *Abba*, he is teaching them to pray as he prays; he is teaching them to address God with the same deep intimacy that he enjoyed.

The whole of the earthly life of Jesus is an outworking, an outliving, of this deep communion with God. Nourished by those times of prayer in the wilderness, in the hills, in the garden of Gethsemane (to which, the evangelists tell us, he liked to go when he was in Jerusalem), he lived constantly in the presence of God.[4] And even as he approached the crisis of his life, he lived still in the communion of his Father. The whole of his life was dedicated to the glory of God. And that is why the first words that he taught his disciples to say, after they had addressed God as their Father, are the words, "Hallowed be thy name."

The whole of Christ's life was hallowing the Father's name, glorifying God in his words and in his deeds, in his life and in his death. St John is the evangelist who brings this out the most clearly. St John's Gospel is the book of the gradual unveiling of God's glory in the life of his Son. St John calls the miracles of Jesus his "signs". He places the emphasis, not on the fact that they are *marvellous*, but that they are *significant*. And what the miracles, the signs, of Jesus *signify* is the *glory of God*. When Jesus gives water for wine at a village wedding, when Jesus multiplies loaves in the desert to feed the hungry, when Jesus calls Lazarus from the tomb, it is the glory of *God* which people are invited to see, breaking out in the words and actions of Jesus. It is as if, in everything that Jesus did, he says, "This is to hallow the Father's name, not mine. This is to glorify God, not me."

And what, according to St John, is the climax of this step-by-step unveiling of the glory of God? It is the suffering and death of Jesus on the cross. "Now is my soul troubled," says Jesus in St John's Gospel, as he approaches the final crisis of his life. "And what shall I say? 'Father, save me from this hour'? No, for this purpose I have come to this hour. Father, glorify thy name."[5] "Father, glorify thy name." "Father, hallowed be thy name." For this purpose he came to this hour, to hallow the Father's name.

---

[4]   Luke 22:39; John 18:2.

[5]   John 12:27,28a (RSV).

And if his life was dedicated to the hallowing of God's name, so it was dedicated to the coming of God's kingdom. "Thy kingdom come." The coming of the kingdom of God, or the kingdom of heaven, is a main theme of the other three evangelists, Matthew, Mark, and Luke. Matthew calls it the "kingdom of heaven", but he uses the word "heaven" here simply as a reverential way of referring to God. By "kingdom of heaven" he means precisely what Mark and Luke mean by the "kingdom of God", and none of them mean something that we arrive at only after death. They do not mean "heaven" in that sense at all. They mean the "reign of God", God's rule, coming in this world, here and now. That, says St Mark, was the heart of the preaching of Jesus: "the kingdom of God is at hand"; "God's reign is about to begin."[6]

The ministry of Jesus was a summoning of men and women into the life of God's kingdom. To one he would say, "You are not far from the kingdom of God."[7] To others, the scribes and the Pharisees, he might have to say, "You will never enter the kingdom of God."[8] His own life was a colony, a microcosm, of God's kingdom, a life ruled perfectly by God.

And he taught his disciples to say, "Thy kingdom come." God, may you reign in our world; may you reign in our society; may you reign in our neighbourhood; may you reign in my home; may you reign in my heart. But just as Jesus longed to share the life of the kingdom with all whom he met, so if we are to pray this part of the Lord's Prayer, then we must long to share the life of the kingdom with those around us. Even on the cross, Jesus was sharing the life of the kingdom, welcoming others into it. It is St Luke who tells us of the penitent thief on the next cross. "Jesus, remember me when you come into your kingdom." "Truly, I say to you, today you will be with me in Paradise."[9]

Perhaps, then, we can begin to see how the words of the Lord's Prayer illuminate both the Lord's life and the Lord's death. We are very close to Jesus, in his life and in his death, when we begin to pray, "Our Father who art in heaven, Hallowed be thy name. Thy kingdom come." "Jesus,

---

6   Mark 1:15 (RSV).

7   Mark 12:34.

8   Cf. Matthew 5:20.

9   Luke 23:42,43.

remember [us] when you come into your kingdom." "Truly, I say to you, today you will be with me in Paradise."

◆　　◆　　◆

As we continue to explore the Lord's Prayer, step-by-step with the Lord's passion, let's think about three more lines: "Thy will be done"; "lead us not into temptation"; "deliver us from evil."

"Thy will be done." It is evident that the Lord's life was consecrated to the doing of the Father's will. "I have come down from heaven, not to do my own will, but the will of him who sent me," says Jesus in St John's Gospel.[10] It sounds easy; St John's Gospel is written in such a way that we can easily fall into the trap of thinking that Jesus found it easy. But the other evangelists help us here; and they tell of that fearful crisis in the garden of Gethsemane, on the night before he died, when Jesus struggled, wrestled, fought over the will of God and whether he could do it. "Being in an agony", says St Luke, "he prayed more earnestly; and his sweat became like great drops of blood falling down upon the ground." And what was he praying? "Father, if thou art willing, remove this cup from me."[11]

A terrible cup of suffering was held out to him; he knew that his betrayer was at hand; he could see, only too well, what lay ahead of him. And he longed to be free of it; he longed to live; all his natural human instincts for life and survival and self-preservation came welling up— how could they not? There was nothing easy for Jesus here; and yet he found the strength to say, "nevertheless not my will, but thine, be done."

This he had taught his disciples to say when he gave them the Lord's Prayer. This he had already said in his own secret communion with God. Now he had to learn, all over again, what it meant to say these words. Learn? Yes, Jesus had to learn. The epistle to the Hebrews is quite clear about this: "he learned obedience through what he suffered".[12] This doing of the Father's will was something that Jesus had to learn, again and again;

---

[10] John 6:38.

[11] Luke 22:44,42 (RSV).

[12] Hebrews 5:8.

he had to make real for himself the words that he had already taught others to say; "Father, not my will, but thine, be done."

"Lead us not into temptation." Those, too, were words that he had taught his disciples to pray; and we must take it that they were words which formed part of his own prayer. Let's think about this word "temptation". It's a word that we use with a rather restricted meaning. We've taken to using it to mean those occasions when we would quite like to do something that we know we shouldn't really—it conjures up a world of just another cake, just another chocolate, just another drink. "Ooh, you're tempting me!" We've made it almost *genteel*.

Well, the word "temptation" as Jesus used it has nothing genteel about it. It means any kind of testing, any kind of trial. Being put to the test—that's temptation. Being tried to the limits—that's temptation. "Do not bring us to the point where we can take no more." That's the effect that Jesus is driving at in this prayer. And does God do that? No, says the New Testament, God doesn't drive us beyond the limits. "No testing [no temptation] has overtaken you", says St Paul to the Corinthians, "that is not common to everyone. God is faithful, and he will not let you be tested beyond your strength, but with the testing [with the temptation] he will also provide the way out so that you may be able to endure it."[13] God does not drive us to the limits; but life may drive us to the limits, other people may drive us to the limits, we may drive ourselves to the limits; and when we are at the limits, then we are likely to blame God for it. So what's the point of praying that God will never bring us to the limit? The point is that we place ourselves in the words of the Lord's own prayer, and like him, we pray for the strength, the courage, the endurance to suffer and to do what must be suffered and what must be done. And in the spirit of the Lord's own prayer, we pray with confidence that God is indeed faithful, and we will not be left to endure what cannot be endured. We pray, in fact, that God will "deliver us from evil".

Here, again, we have words that Jesus had taught his disciples to say; words which he himself had said; words which he had to prove all over again in the final crisis of his life. On the face of it, Jesus was not delivered from evil at all. He was delivered up to the great evil of betrayal, and

---

[13]   1 Corinthians 10:13.

malicious arrest, and false imprisonment, and beating and humiliation; the evil of unjust condemnation, and agonizing death. So what did it mean for him to pray to be delivered from evil? Well, there are two ways of reading this word, as we find it in St Matthew's Gospel. It can be read as "deliver us from evil", or it can be read as "deliver us from the evil one". This is "evil" with a capital E—the power of evil which in the time of Jesus people pictured readily enough as a personal force, the devil. Even if we find the picture of a personal devil a difficult one, we can still, perhaps, see that what Jesus means here by "evil" is not just any hardship or calamity that comes our way—not even death itself—but that absolute evil that separates us finally from God. It would be a bold paraphrase, but you could almost give his words as "Don't leave us in hell."

So when Jesus prays to be delivered from the power of evil, he's not saying, "Don't let me be beaten. Don't let me be killed." He's saying, "Don't let me be cut off from God." "Don't let evil have the last word." "Whatever happens to me, let me still be with God."

But it was a dark road for Jesus, all the same. It was the valley of the shadow of death, and Jesus walked the whole length of it. St Matthew and St Mark offer very little to alleviate the darkness of the Lord's passion. They say only that on the cross, he cried out in the words of the twenty-second Psalm, "My God, my God, why hast thou forsaken me?"[14] The words of that psalm, it is true, move from despair to hope, and perhaps the evangelists mean us to understand that Jesus moved from despair to hope; but the Christian imagination has always been disturbed and troubled by these words, and challenged to think that Jesus, even Jesus, passed through a moment of believing that his Father had in fact forsaken him. God had not forsaken him; but part of the valley of the shadow of death through which Jesus passed was the *sense* that God had forsaken him. It is one more way in which Jesus endures all that it is to be human.

St Luke, in his account, offers more of a glimmer of light. As he tells the story, Jesus finds the words of another Psalm, the thirty-first, and makes of them his dying prayer, "Father, into thy hands I commend

---

14   Psalm 22:1 (RSV); Mark 15:34; Matthew 27:46.

my spirit."[15] And St John says that in the end he said, "It is finished."[16] "It is accomplished." "All that I came to do, I have done." Resignation, acceptance, a quiet release of confidence in the God who has not, after all, forsaken him: in this sense, Jesus was delivered from the power of evil; and in this sense, he teaches us to pray as well: "Thy will be done"; "lead us not into temptation"; "deliver us from evil."

◆   ◆   ◆

"Give us this day our daily bread. And forgive us our trespasses, as we forgive those who trespass against us." The remaining words of the Lord's Prayer; and where do we find in them some glimpse of the Lord's passion? Give . . . forgive. This part of the Lord's Prayer is about giving. We ask our Father to give us our daily bread, and we ask him for all for which bread stands. "The staff of life"—that's what our ancestors called bread; bread signifies all that sustains life; bread is life itself. So in begging God for our daily bread, we beg to receive at his hands our life itself; we gratefully acknowledge him as our maker and our sustainer; in prayer to him we stand at the source of life, and praise him as the Lord, the giver of life.

Jesus, the Son of Man who had nowhere to lay his head, lived his life in a very direct sense of dependence on God his heavenly Father; he had no means of knowing where his daily bread would come from. We (most of us, at any rate) live a different sort of life; we reckon we know how our life will be sustained, for we have incomes, and pensions, and benefits, and insurance; we have a structure of financial security which much of our time and energy go into arranging. And yet we know that we are the lucky ones. We know how many human lives, the world over, are lived far more simply, far more vulnerably, far more precariously, than ours. We know, too, in our more realistic moments, how much there is from which our web of financial protection will *not* keep us: disease, and infirmity, and grief, and loneliness, and death. There is far more to our "daily bread" than we can secure financially: we too, quite as much as our

---

[15]   Luke 23:46 (AV); Psalm 31:5.

[16]   John 19:30.

brothers and sisters in the poorer world, stand with empty hands before God and can only say, "Give us this day our daily bread."

But there is a deeper layer of meaning in these words. The word "daily", in the biblical languages, is an odd one. You could almost translate the Lord's words as something like this: "give us today our bread for tomorrow." And what is that supposed to mean? When Jesus first taught these words to his disciples, he was thinking of more than bread; more than all that bread stands for, the sustenance of our lives. He was thinking of the coming of God's kingdom: that long-promised dream of God's people which Jesus suddenly announced had arrived. "The bread for tomorrow" was the bread of God's kingdom. To have tomorrow's bread *today* was to welcome God's kingdom *now*. All that God had promised his people had arrived in the person of Jesus: he was the embodiment of the kingdom, he was tomorrow's bread, given today.

It is St John who builds this into a main theme of his Gospel. "I am the bread of life," says Jesus. "Whoever comes to me will never be hungry, and whoever believes in me will never be thirsty."[17] So in praying for God's gift of daily bread, we pray for all that sustains our life, in terms of our bodily survival, yes; but we pray, too, for the coming of the bread of life into every part of the world: we pray for the coming of the kingdom embodied in the bread of life, Jesus Christ; and we pray that we may feed upon him who gives his flesh for the life of the world.[18]

The other three evangelists do not give us the same words of Jesus, as we find them in St John, but they do tell us how Jesus, when he came to supper with his friends on the night before he died, took bread, and said to them, "This is my body."[19] Jesus gives them his flesh, he who is the bread of life. So the Lord's Prayer has a *eucharistic* aspect as well. In praying for our daily bread, we pray to be caught up into the great feast of God's kingdom of which each eucharist that we celebrate is the foretaste and sign: this is how we feed on Christ the living bread; this is *how* he gives his flesh for the life of the world.

---

[17]   John 6:35.

[18]   John 6:51.

[19]   Matthew 26:26; Mark 14:22; Luke 22:19.

But there is still more that God gives us. He *forgives* us. "Forgive us our trespasses." Our lives deny life; our lives disown the God who gave them; our lives betray the Christ whom we claim to follow; there is so much that needs forgiving; and *Jesus knows that*—he knew that when he told his disciples to pray for God's forgiveness.

Mercifully, he had taught them to say these words before they came to need them. When he first heard these words, Peter was still confident that he could serve Jesus beyond reproach. James and John still thought that they deserved the best thrones next to Christ in glory. The others could not imagine that the day would come when they would run away, leaving their Lord in the hands of his enemies. And as for Judas—who knows what Judas thought when he first received the Lord's Prayer, and tried out for the first time those words, "Forgive us our trespasses"?

But there is more to God's forgiveness than simply asking for it. Oh, I don't mean that we have to earn it, or pay for it; we can never do that. But God does place one condition on our receiving of his forgiveness. "Forgive us our trespasses, as we forgive those who trespass against us." "If you forgive others their trespasses", says Jesus in the Sermon on the Mount, "your heavenly Father will also forgive you; but if you do not forgive others, neither will your Father forgive your trespasses."[20] It's not that God *withholds* his forgiveness; it's rather that unless we are forgiving towards others, we cannot *receive* God's forgiveness for ourselves. Forgiveness is indivisible; we cannot claim it for one sin but withhold it for another; we cannot claim it for ourselves and withhold it from others.

Jesus, sinless Son of God, needed no forgiveness from his heavenly Father. But he had much to forgive; and the story of his suffering and death is the story of his infinite forgiveness. To the dying thief on the next cross, as we have seen, he promises a place that day in paradise. To Simon Peter, denying him three times, he gives opportunity three times to say that he loves him, and three times recommissions him as a pastor to his people.[21] Even to Judas, as we read St John's Gospel, there is a moment of proffered reconciliation: their hands meet in the same dish at the last supper; bread is broken between them, the sign of sacred fellowship; but

---

[20]   Matthew 6:14,15.

[21]   John 21:15–17.

Judas rejects the moment, and goes into the night.[22] All these are moving episodes in the Gospel story; but there is none so moving as the words given us by St Luke. As the soldiers hammered home the nails, Jesus said, "Father, forgive them; for they know not what they do."[23]

These words bring us very close to the heart of the Lord's passion. The story of the passion has an outside and an inside. The outside story is the story of Jesus and his preaching of God's kingdom, opening up God's friendship to Gentile as well as Jew, woman as well as man, prostitute as well as pharisee, tax-collector as well as scribe. And that brought hostility, and eventual betrayal, imprisonment, condemnation, and death. He preached the love of God, and suffered death for it.

But the inside story is the story of what God was doing in all of this. "God was in Christ", says St Paul, "reconciling the world to himself."[24] In other words, in the life of Jesus, God himself was present, submitting himself to human hostility, taking into himself the hatred of the world, and meeting it all with his own love and forgiveness. On the cross, God himself endures the worst that the world can do to him; and he meets it with love. As the soldiers nail Jesus to the cross, the inside and the outside stories are indivisibly united. Jesus meets the soldiers' violence with a prayer to his Father that they may be forgiven. His Father is not somewhere else; his Father is there with him; God is nailed to the cross, and God offers the world his forgiveness.

"Forgive us our trespasses, as we forgive those who trespass against us." In saying these words, as we do so easily, so readily, day by day, it is easy to think only of our own shortcomings, and how much we don't want them to stand against us. But we are taking on our lips words which belong to the very heart of God; we echo the dying words of Jesus on the cross, and words which in their turn express the essence of the love of God. These words should burn our lips every time that we say them.

Christ gives us life: all that we mean by our daily bread. He gives us new life, the life of his kingdom, the forgiveness of our sins. We cannot celebrate Good Friday without thinking of the resurrection; just as we

---

22   John 13:21–30.

23   Luke 23:34 (RSV).

24   2 Corinthians 5:19.

cannot celebrate Easter Day without thinking of the cross. We are only here in church today because of the resurrection, because Christ who gives us life and forgiveness is the living Christ and not a dead one. And while it is true, as I hope that I have shown just a little, that the Lord's Prayer illuminates the Lord's passion; it is also true that we only *say* the Lord's Prayer because of the living Christ who has called us into fellowship with himself. Indeed, if we were to plumb the New Testament further, we should begin to see that whenever we pray, whatever the words we use, it is the living Christ who is actually at prayer within us; our prayers are only ever the echo of his own, our efforts at prayer the stirrings of his Spirit.

2 1

Endings and beginnings[1]

Stories are judged by their endings. However enthralled we have been by the *The Night Manager*, it is the final episode tonight that counts.[2] What we long for in a good story is for knots to be unravelled and mysteries cleared up, for evil to be defeated and good come out on top. As Aristotle argued many centuries ago, even a tragic story, well told, can have a purifying effect on our minds.[3]

The story of the resurrection of Jesus, however, defies any tidy description. At first appearance, it is a classic happy ending. An innocent person dies, but God raises them to life, and the grief of their friends turns to joy. That is the way that we would like the world to be. We wish that the violence in Syria, Paris, or Brussels would stop. We wish that the refugee crisis were resolved. When disaster or tragedy strikes, we would like the clock turned back. We would like the world to be other than it is.

The resurrection is not that kind of story. It's not an improbable tale of injustice which God miraculously puts right, the clock put back to the time before Jesus died. For one thing, Jesus's experience of death is

---

[1]   Sermon preached at the eucharist in Worcester Cathedral on Easter Day, 27 March 2016, broadcast live by BBC Radio 4. The readings were Acts 10:34–43; Luke 24:1–12.

[2]   A British television spy thriller directed by Susanne Bier, based on the 1993 novel of the same name by John le Carré and adapted by David Farr. The six-part series began broadcasting on BBC One on 21 February 2016. The final episode was shown on Easter Sunday evening. In the United States, it began on 19 April 2016 on American Multi-Cinema.

[3]   *The Poetics of Aristotle* (6), ed. Samuel H. Butcher, 4th edn (London: Macmillan & Co., 1922), p. 23.

a vital part of the story. It is not a pretence of death with one eye on the resurrection; it's a real death. In the Gospel narratives, the risen Jesus still bears the marks of the crucifixion: he is the one who has come to know what death is like.

Nor is it a story in which his followers live happily ever after. As we heard in the Gospel reading, the disciples heard the news with bewilderment and disbelief. Mark puts it more strongly: they ran away in terror. And when the risen Jesus did bring them together, it was not to round off the story, but to charge them with the good news, to bring others to know him and follow him. Far from being the end of the story, the resurrection is the start of a new one, the story of the lives of his disciples lived in this world. We glimpsed that in the reading from the Acts of the Apostles. We might say that when the credits come up on the final episode of the Gospel story, the next series is already scheduled.

Nor is the resurrection a simple story about the world being put right. The violence on the streets of Jerusalem when Jesus died did not stop, as his followers found out; and that violence has continued in the Holy Land, and across the world in countless conflicts, as we know well. It is into that world that the followers of Jesus went, many of them to suffer as he suffered. There are still places in the world where Christians die for their faith.

The resurrection is not a story about the instant transformation of Jesus's followers. Christians fail, and sin, and sometimes betray their faith. As we know only too well today, Christian pastors (people like me) can be unworthy of their calling. We can damage the lives of those whom we are called to help, betray the Church that we are called to represent, and dishonour the God whom we are called to serve. There is no excuse for this, and every ground for shame, but from the beginning, Jesus entrusted his message to fallible people, and he made no promise of instantly transforming sinners into saints. Every Christian is a pilgrim, still on a journey, still exploring, still making mistakes and taking wrong turnings. A Christian is not someone who has arrived at the journey's end.

The story of the resurrection, then, is not a simple happy ending. It is the start of a new experiment in human living, fraught with difficulty and danger, entrusted by God to fallible men and women. So from the Acts of the Apostles onwards, the followers of Jesus formed cells and colonies of

Christian living, breaking bread together as we do this morning, and (as St Luke puts it) knowing him in the breaking of that bread.[4]

The good news is that when we Christians get it partly right, and are faithful to God and recognize his presence in our lives, then those cells or colonies of Christian living that we call the Church can be a power for good. The Church does good, less perhaps on the public stage, than in the unsung lives of Christian women and men serving God in the ordinary circumstances of daily life. At the end of *Middlemarch*, George Eliot suggests that "the growing good of the world is partly dependent on unhistoric acts [. . .] half owing to the number who lived faithfully a hidden life, and rest in unvisited tombs".[5] Such "unhistoric acts" belong to all people of goodwill, whatever their religious faith or lack of it, who today must stand united in the face of violence and terror. There is no Christian monopoly of courage or virtue. But Christians are those who have specifically recognized the call of God to live such lives, and have found the presence of Jesus the source of strength to do so.

In a world in which disaster and tragedy still strike, in which wars go on, and the power of virtue is hard to measure, in which human lives are forgotten and tombs unvisited, Christians believe that the human journey does not end there. To the followers of the risen Jesus, life here is the opportunity to contribute to the "good of the world", and death is the doorway to a life which has *no* ending.

---

[4]   Luke 24:35.

[5]   George Eliot, *Middlemarch: A Study of Provincial Life* (London: Folio Society, 1999), p. 759.

22

The one not chosen[1]

Ours is a culture which prizes success and holds failure in contempt. It is, moreover, a culture which draws the definition of success very narrowly, and the definition of failure very widely. Take, for example, the recent election. From a dispassionate point of view, one might think that in a rational society which valued democracy, an election might consist of a range of proposals being put forward by various parties as constructive ideas for how the country might be governed; from which the electorate must, if it is to be governed at all, choose one; but that no special blame would attach to those parties whose point of view the electorate had politely passed over. But, as we know, that is not the way of the world. No sooner has the electorate chosen one party, by the slimmest of margins, than the disappointed parties plunge themselves into a frenzy of recrimination and self-justification. Not only are the policies, which a week before were laid before the electorate for its serious consideration, now held up for self-mockery in the bitter wisdom of hindsight; it is the way in which each campaign was conducted which elicits the most savage reprisals; for apparently, the true test of a party's fitness to govern consists not in having the right policies to put before a sovereign electorate, but in knowing how to kick a slavish electorate successfully into submission.

All this is characteristic of a culture in which success is overrated and failure undervalued; in which making a mark is everything, and failing to make a mark is unforgivable. In our personal lives, we do fail from time to time: we do not always come first, we do not always make a mark. A

---

[1]   Sermon preached at evensong in Lincoln College, Oxford, on the Sunday after Ascension Day, 17 May 2015. The readings were Acts 1:15–17,21–end; John 17:6–19.

rational approach to life would be to take into account the probability of failure, and the likelihood of not making much of a name, and to work out some strategies for dealing with it. But that is not easy in a world in which the person who does not win the prize is judged to be both knave and fool.

The reading from the Acts of the Apostles tells of a rather odd election; and of the one who was chosen and the one who was not chosen. It is a story which invites us to reflect on success and failure, fame and obscurity. The story is set between the ascension of Jesus and the outpouring of the Holy Spirit; which is why the passage is read today, with Ascension Day behind us, and Pentecost next Sunday. The election was caused by Judas Iscariot's act of betrayal and subsequent suicide, leaving a space in the sacred number of the twelve apostles. So the company of disciples, under the presidency of St Peter (a sort of apostolic returning officer), looked for someone to make up the twelve. They put forward the names of two people, both eminently qualified for the position, both of whom had been disciples of Christ from the earliest days, both of whom had witnessed the resurrection: one called Joseph Barsabbas Justus, and one called Matthias. At that point, the democratic process was superseded by a method that perhaps reduced the likelihood of post-electoral recrimination: the electorate prayed, and cast lots, and Matthias was chosen.

Of Matthias, we know nothing more; though legend has stepped in to fill the gaps in our knowledge, and tells of heroic missionary work among the Anthropophagi. Of Joseph Barsabbas Justus, even legend is silent. The one whom Jesus might have chosen to be one of the original twelve—but didn't; the one whom the Church might have chosen to succeed Iscariot—but didn't; the one who might have had churches dedicated to him, and his face in icons and stained glass windows the length of Christendom—including the windows of this chapel—but didn't: Joseph Barsabbas Justus, the one who wasn't elected, and who, after his brief appearance in the Acts of the Apostles, disappeared from the pages of history.

But because this is a Christian story, it is not one of failure, and the obscurity into which Joseph disappeared is not a shameful one. The Christian tradition rates this sort of obscurity very highly. Jesus spoke of the importance of obscurity when it comes both to our prayers and to our acts of generosity.[2] Prayer is something for the private inner chamber, he said, not the street corners. Acts of generosity should be so unobtrusive that even the left hand does not know what the right hand is doing. He himself looked for dark and secret places to pray—the mountainside, the garden, the desert, under the veil of night—and his ultimate act of self-dedication to God was in the valley of the shadow of death. St Paul used the image of that final isolation as a way of describing our own Christian discipleship: "you have died," he wrote, "and your life is hid with Christ in God."[3] "Hid with Christ in God": that is what it is to be a Christian. That is the hiddenness of Joseph Barsabbas Justus. That is the hiddenness of the Christian way, which does not need to make a name, or court publicity, or go down in history.

There is a curious passage in the book of Ecclesiastes, and it reads as follows: "There was a little city with few people in it. A great king came against it and besieged it, building great siegeworks against it. Now there was found in it a poor wise man, and he by his wisdom delivered the city. Yet no one remembered that poor man."[4] Nothing else: who the poor man was, and how he used his wisdom to save the city, we are not told. But those haunting words are a kind of Unknown Warrior's memorial to those who do good without their right hand knowing what their left is doing; and they are a salutary caution to politicians and others who see themselves as the saviour of the city by more glittering methods.

George Eliot strikes the same note in the closing lines of *Middlemarch*. Speaking of her main character, Dorothea, she says, "The effect of her being on those around her was incalculably diffusive: for the growing good of the world is partly dependent on unhistoric acts; and that things are not so ill with you and me as they might have been, is half owing to the number who lived faithfully a hidden life, and rest in unvisited tombs."[5] So, too, Wordsworth wrote that "the best portion" of a good person's life

---

2   Matthew 6:1–6.

3   Colossian 3:3 (RSV).

4   Ecclesiastes 9:14,15.

5   George Eliot, *Middlemarch: A Study of Provincial Life* (London: Folio Society, 1999), p. 759.

are their "little, nameless unremembered acts of kindness and love".[6]
And the great bishop of Lincoln (and visitor of this college) a century
ago, Edward King, also wrote of holiness as "the exercise of unselfish,
untiring love; quiet lives lived away in holes and corners and not known
to the public while alive".[7] Here again is the life that is hid with Christ in
God; the unremembered wisdom of the poor man who saved a city; the
honourable obscurity of Joseph Barsabbas Justus, the one not chosen.

We should no more court failure than we should be obsessed by
success; there is no virtue in doing less than that of which we are capable.
This is not a doctrine of mediocrity, or half-heartedness, or failing to
bother: far from it. But it is a gentle reminder from the wisdom of the
Christian tradition that the good of the world is largely done by unhistoric
acts, and that God alone sees the life that is hid with Christ in him.

---

6   "Lines Written a Few Miles Above Tintern Abbey", in William Wordsworth,
     Selected Poems (London: Everyman's Library, 1975), pp. 120–4 at 121.
7   Quoted in George W. E. Russell, *Edward King, Sixtieth Bishop of Lincoln: A
     Memoir* (London: Smith, Elder & Co., 1912), p. 48.

The exhausting mystery of God[1]

In the name of God: Father, Son, and Holy Spirit. Amen.

It is that name of God, Father, Son, and Holy Spirit, which is the theme of today's festival, Trinity Sunday; three Persons in one God, the mystery of the Holy Trinity.

There are people who say that the mystery of the Trinity is not to be found in the New Testament. There are people who say that the mystery of the Trinity was invented hundreds of years after the time of Christ. There are people who draw a contrast between the primitive simplicity of Jesus's teaching in the Gospels, and the later complexities which St Paul or the Church fathers then foisted upon it. In David Hare's 1990 play *Racing Demon*, about a group of clerics in the diocese of Southwark, one of the priests asks miserably, "Why can't it all be more simple?"—a line which, I recall, got a round of applause when the play was revived at the Chichester Festival Theatre a few years ago.

But the picture, however attractive, of a simple gospel preached by Jesus then made complicated and difficult by the Church, won't do. When the curtain rises on what we call the New Testament, the earliest books of which were written scarcely 20 years after the time of Jesus, we can tell that the earliest Christians were already struggling with ideas of incredible complexity. The earliest New Testament books, of course, are not the Gospels, which came later, but the letters of St Paul. And the picture that those letters give us is not of someone taking a simple religion and trying to make it complicated, but of someone wrestling with dazzling, overwhelming, mind-blowing ideas, and trying to make sense

---

[1]   Sermon preached at the eucharist in Worcester Cathedral on Trinity Sunday, 7 June 2009. The readings were Isaiah 6:1–8; Romans 8:12–17; John 3:1–17.

of them. There is no doubt that for the very earliest followers of Jesus, the experience of seeing the messiah first crucified (which was shocking beyond words) and then resurrected (which was literally unthinkable) put all their inherited beliefs into meltdown, from which emerged some very new and very powerful ideas—ideas which they couldn't put neatly into words. Take those lines from Paul's letter to the Romans that we heard read a moment ago:

> all who are led by the Spirit of God are children of God. For you did not receive a spirit of slavery to fall back into fear, but you have received a spirit of adoption. When we cry "Abba! Father!" it is that very Spirit bearing witness with our spirit that we are children of God, and if children, then heirs, heirs of God and joint heirs with Christ—if, in fact, we suffer with him so that we may also be glorified with him.

It's contorted stuff—Paul is falling over himself in the attempt to put into words some huge experience of God which both he and his readers have in common. And there's no "simple gospel" in the background. Here we are, about 25 years after the crucifixion, with a very large Christian community in Rome well established; but no Gospel has been written down, and it is very far from clear to us how much of the familiar teaching of Jesus—which we know so well from those Gospels—has yet filtered through to those Christians in Rome.

So what was it that they and the apostle Paul (whom they had never met; Paul wrote his letter to the Romans as a letter of self-introduction, paving the way for his first visit there)—what was it that they and he had in common? Let us unpick those words that I have just quoted. First of all, Paul takes it for granted that both he and his readers are "led by the Spirit of God". He and they have a shared experience of being caught up in some great spiritual movement. God is moving among them, and they are being stirred and moved and *led* by him. This experience has given them a sense of liberation, and a sense of confidence. "You did not receive a spirit of slavery to fall back into fear," he says, knowing that his words will resonate with them. On the contrary, he says, "you have received a spirit of adoption". Now this is Paul's first attempt in this particular passage to interpret this mighty experience of God which he and his readers share. He gives it an image, a metaphor—it is, he says, as if we have been "adopted" by God. On the face of it, that's a surprising thing to say about God, and it's not immediately clear what Paul is driving at.

Let's leave that for a moment, and look at what comes next: "When we cry 'Abba! Father!' it is that very Spirit bearing witness with our spirit that we are children of God." "When we cry 'Abba!'" Fascinatingly, Paul takes it for granted that those mostly Gentile Christians in Rome have already learnt to pray to God, using the Aramaic word for "Father". Only much later on, when we get to read the Gospels, do we find that this was how Jesus taught his disciples to pray. Yet here we are, with some shared Christian practice which Paul has learnt in Antioch, and the Roman Christians are using in Rome, of using Jesus's own word for God when they pray. So when you use the word "Abba" in your prayers, Paul says, you are being caught up in that huge spiritual movement, which we call the Spirit of God: we are being caught up to him whom we call "Abba! Father!"; and the Spirit of God, as it were, endorses who we are, the children of God.

Now, says Paul, if we are children of God, then we are heirs of God: we are the recipients of all the blessings that God can give us. And if we are heirs, why then, he goes on, that makes us "joint heirs with Christ". Why is that? Because (and this is a point that Paul does not spell out here, though he has done so earlier in the letter) Jesus is the first, the pre-eminent "child of God". He is, as it were, God's natural child; and we—well, it is as if we are "adopted" into God's natural family: no less beloved of God than God's natural child; but that which Jesus shares by nature with God, we share by way of extension, by way of God's choice, by way of adoption.

And then, just to give his mixture of ideas one more vigorous stir, Paul adds that we only become the "heirs of God" and "joint heirs with Christ" if "we suffer with him so that we may also be glorified with him". We must, says Paul, identify with Jesus in his suffering, if we are to enjoy the blessings and the glories of being God's children.

Now on any showing, that's a pretty tortuous cluster of ideas. We might well have expected Paul, in writing to introduce himself to the Christian community in Rome, to have stuck to something safe and straightforward.

The trouble was, there wasn't anything safe or straightforward to stick to: up and down the Mediterranean basin, groups of Christians were pondering their great new experience of God, and trying to find words to express it. Paul's best chance of being accepted by the church in Rome was to offer some fresh ways of putting that experience of God into words.

What we call the doctrine of the Trinity is not a complicated set of ideas foisted onto an original simple gospel. Almost the reverse: it is the attempt, refined over the early centuries of the Church, to read some order and intelligibility into that first bewildering explosion of ideas that caught up the first followers of Jesus in the aftermath of his death and resurrection. Paul's letter to the Romans is one of the earliest surviving written efforts to do just that.

The doctrine of the Trinity helps us to see the action of God, first, in the one to whom we pray, the one whom we call "Abba! Father!", the one who adopts us into his family with a fatherly love, the one who calls us his children: the Father. The doctrine of the Trinity helps us to see the action of God, second, in the one who has suffered alongside us, who has taught us to pray with the words "Abba! Father!", the natural child of God into whose extended family we are called: the Son. The doctrine of the Trinity helps us to see the action of God, third, in the mighty spiritual experience of confidence and freedom which was so marked for those first Christians, and which they called the "Spirit of God": the Holy Spirit. And the doctrine of the Trinity helps us to see that these are not three separate actions of God, or the action of three separate Gods, but the one action of the one God, all at once summoning us, and suffering with us, and inspiring us: Father, Son, and Holy Spirit.

I have no illusion that this thumbnail sketch of what we celebrate on Trinity Sunday will have done much to dispel the mystery. If it has, then I've certainly got it wrong. Augustine said a long time ago that the only thing that we can understand about God is that he cannot be understood: "if you can grasp it, it isn't God".[2] But I do want to leave you with the idea

---

[2]   Augustine, *Sermons on the New Testament* (117.5), *The Works of Saint Augustine: A Translation for the 21st Century*, part 3, vol. 4, tr. Edmund Hill, ed. John E. Rotelle (New York: New City Press, 1992), p. 211. The editor is grateful to Robert Beattie for assistance with this reference.

that nothing started off simple, which the Church, for devious reasons of its own, then made difficult; but rather that Jesus Christ stirred up such a revolution of religious ideas, and unleashed so powerful a spiritual movement, that his followers have been trying to make sense of it ever since. Not that we shall ever succeed in making sense of *him*: but he has given us enquiring minds, and our minds will not forgive us until we have exhausted them upon the mystery of God.

Given for the life of the world[1]

This time last week, I was in the congregation at mass in the ancient abbey church of La Lucerne on the Cotentin peninsula in Lower Normandy. The abbey was founded in memory of those who perished when the *White Ship* sank in the waters of the Channel, taking with it the only son and heir of Henry I of England, whose death left both England and Normandy open to that terrible war of succession between Count Stephen and the Empress Matilda, known as the Anarchy. It was a time, it was said, when Christ and his saints slept. Every year, to this day, on the anniversary of the sinking of the *White Ship*, the abbey bell is tolled throughout the night.

But if La Lucerne Abbey is a memorial to a far-off tragedy and disaster, it is also a monument of present beauty, set in a wooded valley, with sunlight flooding the clear glass of the east windows, filtered through the foliage of the trees outside, which form a rich green reredos to the altar. Last Sunday, four swallows twisted and turned in the clerestory throughout the mass, outsinging the congregation:

> O how amiable are thy dwellings : thou Lord of hosts!
> My soul hath a desire and longing to enter into the courts of the Lord :
> > my heart and my flesh rejoice in the living God.
> Yea, the sparrow hath found her an house,
> > and the swallow a nest where she may lay her young :
> > even thy altars, O Lord of hosts, my King and my God.

---

[1]   Sermon preached at the eucharist in Worcester Cathedral on Sunday, 16 August 2015 (Proper 15). The readings were Proverbs 9:1–6; Ephesians 5:15–20; John 6:51–8.

> Blessed are they that dwell in thy house :
> they will be alway praising thee.[2]

Now the readings at the eucharist in the Church of England are usually the same as those in use throughout the Catholic world, so the same readings were read at La Lucerne last Sunday as were read in this cathedral: the story of the journey of Elijah through the wilderness, an extract from St Paul's letter to the Ephesians, and part of the Lord's discourse on the bread of life, from the sixth chapter of St John, a further instalment of which we have heard this morning.

Hearing those readings in French was a particular pleasure. "Bread" and "wine" occur rather often in the Bible, and it is easy to hear them simply as liturgical words, with smooth theological associations. But when "bread" becomes *pain*, it sets off quite a different set of associations. I thought of the *baguette* that I had that morning for breakfast, warm from the baker's shop in the village. And when "wine" becomes *vin*, well, where do you start? With the Burgundy that I bought for a few euros in the supermarket the day before, or the jug of *vin de pays* with which I meant to while away the afternoon in the garden? And as for the story of Elijah in the wilderness, did you know that the "cake", which the angel baked for him on hot stones, was not a cake at all, but a *galette*, that delicious savoury pancake which is one of Normandy's gifts to the world?[3]

By now you are thinking that this is not a very spiritual sermon. The dean, you fear, is concerned more for his stomach than for his soul. But that is actually the point of this sermon. God was not being very "spiritual" when he decided that he would convey to us the great mystery of our religion, not directly to our mind (intellectually) nor by way of our cultural sensibility (aesthetically) nor even immediately to our heart (emotionally) but rather to our digestive system in the gifts of bread and wine. It used to be said to young women that the way to a man's heart was through his stomach; and whatever truth or untruth there is in that gender-stereotyping remark, it is profoundly true that the divinely chosen

---

2   Psalm 84:1–4 (BCP).

3   1 Kings 19:6.

path to the human soul is through the stomach. "Take, eat." "Take, drink." Not "Take, think", or "Take, enjoy", or "Take, feel"—though thinking, enjoying, feeling all have their place as well—but first and foremost, "eat" and "drink".

And this means that the eucharist is something in which all can participate, in equal measure, and on equal terms. Our intellectual gifts may differ, as do our aesthetic sensibilities; and as for our feelings, they are wayward and unpredictable; but the Lord's command to eat and drink levels us all. C. S. Lewis wrote that before his conversion to Christianity, he thought that religion ought to be a matter of praying alone, and meeting by twos and threes to talk of spiritual matters; and I suspect that many people (Christians and otherwise) do indeed suppose that that is what properly "religious" or "spiritual" people are like.[4] But solitary prayer and spiritual discussion are things for which some people are temperamentally better suited than others. Solitary prayer and spiritual discussion have their place, but not the central place that Christ gives to the eucharist, when he tells us to "eat" and "drink".

Of course, the gift of the eucharist, which we come to share again this morning, *is* a spiritual gift. When Christ took bread and wine, he freighted them with supernatural meaning far beyond their ordinary day-to-day significance: "the bread that I will give for the life of the world", he says in this morning's Gospel, "is my flesh [...] Those who eat my flesh and drink my blood have eternal life [...] for my flesh is true food and my blood is true drink." We must often reflect on that miracle of transformation which God works in bread and wine, so that they become for us the body and blood of our Lord Jesus Christ, his very life implanted to our lives. But we must not so reflect on that transformation as to forget that which is transformed. We must begin where God begins, with the bread and the wine themselves, and reflect on how it is in the very ordinariness, the mundaneness, the earthiness, the humbleness, of bread and wine, that God works the miracle that gives life to our souls.

Just as the eucharist levels us all, so it connects us all. What we call the "catholicity" of the Church—its universality—is rooted in the eucharist.

---

[4]   C. S. Lewis, *Surprised by Joy: The Shape of My Early Life* (London: Geoffrey Bles, 1955), p. 220.

That which we do this morning is that which Christ did on the night before he died. It is what the Church has done Sunday by Sunday and day by day ever since; as we say in the Eucharistic Prayer: "at all times and in all places". What I take part in here today is what I took part in last Sunday in another place, another country; and what I took part in there was what had taken place there all the way back to the tragedy of the *White Ship* in the twelfth century; and it is the same thing that has taken place here for almost twice that length of time. The story of humankind has known no other action, rite or gesture which has connected so many hundreds of millions of people—"doing this", because Christ told us to.

"The bread that I will give for the life of the world is my flesh," says the Lord. He gives that bread, which is his flesh, for our lives, to nourish our souls, to strengthen us in grace, to sustain us day by day as we seek to serve him. But the "life of the world", for which Christ gives his flesh, is more than my life and your life; more even than the lives of the hundreds of millions of Christian people who have fed on the bread and wine of the eucharist. The "life of the world" is greater still: it is the story of all people, Christian or otherwise; it is the story of the world, and not just of human beings; it is the story of the earth.

I began with a vision of loveliness: the eucharist celebrated on a summer morning in an ancient abbey church in a forest with swallows overhead. But that loveliness was born of an ancient tragedy and disaster. The eucharist which we continue to celebrate equally calls to mind the tragedy and disaster: a world in which people still drown—not mediaeval princes off the coast of Normandy, but refugees from Africa off the coasts of Italy and Greece. This is the world, for the life of which Christ gives his own flesh and blood. This is the world in which we celebrate the eucharist this morning. And having celebrated, it is the world into which we go, giving of ourselves for its life and in its service.

2 5

Abiding friendship[1]

We begin with the passage which, in one way or another, we have touched on every day of this retreat. Jesus said,

> As the Father has loved me, so I have loved you; abide in my love. If you keep my commandments, you will abide in my love, just as I have kept my Father's commandments and abide in his love. I have said these things to you so that my joy may be in you, and that your joy may be complete.
>
> This is my commandment, that you love one another as I have loved you. No one has greater love than this, to lay down one's life for one's friends. You are my friends if you do what I command you. I do not call you servants any longer, because the servant does not know what the master is doing; but I have called you friends, because I have made known to you everything that I have heard from my Father. You did not choose me but I chose you. And I appointed you to go and bear fruit, fruit that will last, so that the Father will give you whatever you ask him in my name. I am giving you these commands so that you may love one another.[2]

In this passage, we see at once two of the architectural motifs of the fourth Gospel, motifs which are present in so many other passages. I call them architectural, because they help to give shape and structure to the Gospel

---

[1] Address given to clergy on retreat at the Shrine of Our Lady of Walsingham on Thursday, 4 February 2016.

[2] John 15:9–17.

as a whole. There is the motif of "My Father . . . I . . . you". And there is
the motif of "not yet . . . now".

The motif of "My Father . . . I . . . you" comes out in the first line of
our passage: "As the Father has loved me, so I have loved you; abide in
my love." There is a relationship between the Father and the Son, and
as we know from the prologue of the Gospel, this relationship is from
all eternity.[3] But there is that about the eternal relationship between the
Father and the Son which is communicable and inclusive: the Father
loves the Son and the Son extends that love to his disciples: "If you keep
my commandments, you will abide in my love, just as I have kept my
Father's commandments and abide in his love." Again, the Father "makes
known" to the Son what he is doing, and the Son, in turn, "makes known"
to his disciples what *he* is doing: "I have made known to you everything
that I have heard from my Father." So that is one motif, one idea that
gives shape and structure to the whole Gospel; and we shall meet it again.

The second architectural motif is the "not yet . . . now", and this
brings us straight to the heart of what Jesus says about friendship. We
are all familiar with the way in which the drama of the fourth Gospel
is constructed on a period of "not yet", followed by a climactic moment
of "now". In the earlier chapters, there is an insistent pointing forwards:
Jesus says to Nathanael, "you will see heaven opened";[4] Jesus says to his
mother, "My hour has not yet come."[5] Sometimes he says, as he does to
the woman of Samaria, "the hour is coming, *and is now here*, when the
true worshippers will worship the Father in spirit and truth";[6] or again,
to his disciples, "the hour is coming, *and is now here*, when the dead
will hear the voice of the Son of God".[7] The "not yet" and the "now" are
poised on a knife-edge; the hour that is coming is so imminent that the
stroke of the bell is already sounding. Nonetheless, there is still a "not yet"
and a "now", and we know that in the mind of the evangelist, the "now"
only arrives when the final terrible cluster of events which constitute the

---

[3]   John 1:2.
[4]   John 1:51.
[5]   John 2:4.
[6]   John 4:23.
[7]   John 5:25.

climax and the crisis of the Gospel are set irreversibly in train: when all have assembled for the Passover, and Jesus proclaims, almost intones, the words: "Now is the judgement of this world; now the ruler of this world will be driven out. And I, when I am lifted up from the earth, will draw all people to myself."[8]

It is in this dramatic context of "now . . . " that Jesus addresses his disciples at the last supper, and says to them, "I do not call you servants *any longer,* because the servant does not know what the master is doing; but I have called you friends, because I have made known to you everything that I have heard from my Father." There has been the period in which the disciples of Jesus have been servants, not knowing what their master was doing; but now that the final crisis has come, now that the judgement of the world has begun, now that the Son of Man is on his final short journey to crucifixion and to glory, everything changes. The disciples are at last finding out what this entire story is about. The Son is at last making known to them everything that he has heard from his Father. And so they are servants no longer, for servants do not know what their master is doing; what Jesus is doing for them now is to make them his friends. He gives them his love; the same love that he has received from his Father. He gives them his commandment, to love one another; the same commandment that he has received from his Father. He tells them that he is laying down his life for them, for there is no greater love than to do that for friends; and they are those friends. He gives them his joy, so that (even in the midst of these heart-breaking events) their joy may be complete. He tells them that they are his choice, and not the other way round. And these are all the constituent elements of this pivotal moment when Jesus calls his disciples out of servanthood and into friendship.

It is not too much to say, then, that for the fourth evangelist, *being called by Jesus into friendship* is one way of stating the whole mystery of salvation. His friends are the ones for whom he dies, the ones with whom he shares his joy, the ones whom he commands to live in love and to bear lasting fruit. Of course, there is more to be said about salvation than that; otherwise our thin and timid notions of friendship would drain

---

8   John 12:31,32.

all the strength and vigour out of our understanding of salvation. It's the other way round: we need all the strength and vigour of the mystery of salvation to make us realize how astonishing a claim Jesus is making for his notion of friendship. But the whole of salvation is at any rate implied in these words of Jesus about being friends: his redeeming death, the joy of his resurrection, the power of the Spirit, the communion-in-love which is the Church, the bearing of fruit which is the living of lives of holiness in the world.

◆

Let's now look at some of the characters of the Gospel, and see how far the theme of "being called into friendship" is worked out in individual cases. I must be careful not to overstate the argument. The fourth evangelist is not very interested in the psychology of his characters, but I think nonetheless that there are some vividly sketched scenes which reflect what I have been saying.

The most fully worked-out character is that of Simon Peter. At their first meeting, Jesus addresses him with a hint of the "not yet ... now" motif that we have already noticed. "You *are* Simon son of John. You are *to be* called Cephas [...] Peter."[9] So there is a *being Peter* into which Simon son of John must grow. He next comes to the front of the stage after the feeding of the five thousand, and the discourse on the bread of life which turns so many disciples away. Jesus asks the twelve, "Do you also wish to go away?" Simon Peter replies, "Lord, to whom *can* we go? You have the words of eternal life. We have come to believe and know that you are the Holy One of God."[10] It is a confession of faith, certainly; the fourth evangelist's equivalent of the synoptic scene at Caesarea Philippi. But I can't help feeling that there is something a shade equivocal about Peter's words. "To whom *can* we go?" "Who else is there?" There is surely more than a hint here of servants who do not know what their master is doing. They are certain that he is their master, and they will not abandon him;

---

9   John 1:42.

10   John 6:67-9.

but they are not yet in his confidence, they do not have the confidence of friends.

So we come to the last supper, and the washing of the disciples' feet. Simon Peter said, "Lord, are you going to wash my feet?" Jesus answered, "You do not know *now* what I am doing, but *later* you will understand."[11] Even now, even at this late hour, even as the paschal mystery is beginning to unfold, Simon Peter is still caught in a "not yet" moment. He, and the others whose feet Jesus is washing, are still in the role of servants. That is the significant thing about the foot-washing; they are servants, and yet Jesus serves them. And he underlines it: "You do not know now what I am doing." And yet, just a few moments later, he will say to them, "I do not call you servants any longer." So what has changed? Well, what happens between these two moments is the departure of Judas; but more of that later. Staying with Peter for now, we don't need reminding of his role in the passion narrative: his promise to follow Jesus to death, his threefold denial during the trial, his uncomprehending visit to the empty tomb, and the poignant reconciliation scene at the lakeside. Here is friendship confidently promised, cowardly denied, movingly restored. The frailty of the friendship that Peter gives to Jesus points up the gracious invincibility of the friendship that Jesus gives to Peter. Peter's story gives colour to the words of Jesus: "You did not choose me but I chose you."

And then, at the very end of Chapter 21, after the reconciliation scene, Peter asks Jesus one last question, "Lord, what about him?" He is speaking of the "disciple whom Jesus loved", and we shall think about this disciple later; but this moment is part of Peter's story too. Jesus replies, "If it is my will that he remain until I come, what is that to you? Follow me!"[12] One could say that Jesus is here declining to make known to Peter all that the Father has told him; that Peter is after all not to know what his master is doing; that this is the final rebuff, Peter reduced to the role of a servant once more. But it is of course impossible to read the Gospel in that way. Rather, I suppose, Jesus is reminding Peter that while the friends of Jesus are invited into a saving knowledge of God ("all that the Father has told him"), there is a difference between that and mere curiosity; that there

---

[11]   John 13:6,7.

[12]   John 21:21,22.

is nothing in the mystery of salvation that Peter needs to know about the destiny of another disciple; and that that, too, is part of what it means to be a friend of Jesus.

There are other characters, not so fully fleshed out, but whose stories contribute all the same to the idea of entering into friendship with Jesus. There is Nicodemus, who comes to Jesus under cover of darkness, and is baffled by talk of a spiritual birth. "Are you a teacher of Israel", says Jesus, "and yet you do not understand these things?"[13] Here is a servant who does not yet know what the master is doing. But Nicodemus perseveres, like a faithful servant; and at the end of the story, Nicodemus joins Joseph of Arimathea in the risky business of begging Pilate for the dead body of Jesus and giving it burial; the action of a faithful friend.[14]

There are Lazarus, Martha, and Mary, latecomers to the story, but identified at once as people whom Jesus "loved"; Jesus uniquely refers to Lazarus as "our friend". The raising of Lazarus is the scene that stands at the very cusp of the Gospel drama, it concludes the period of "not yet" and heralds the period of "now". So we see no progression in the story of Lazarus and his sisters. Instead, it captures, in a single episode, what Jesus will later spell out as the constituent elements of friendship: Martha's lack of comprehension turning to understanding; Mary's sorrow turning to joy; Lazarus passing from death to life in a foreshadowing of the resurrection. And in the joy of that raising, six days before the Passover, Jesus is the guest at their supper table. They are abiding in love; and the supper prefigures the communion of the Lord's table.[15]

There is Philip, who asks to see the Father, to whom Jesus replies, "Have I been with you all this time, Philip, and you still do not know me?"[16] So Philip speaks in the role of one who "does not know what his master is doing"; but Jesus enlightens him, and that is a part of Philip's being called into friendship. And there is Thomas, who makes a brief intervention in the Lazarus story to say "Let us also go, that we may die with him."[17]

---

13 John 3:10.
14 John 19:38–42.
15 John 11:1–12.8.
16 John 14:9.
17 John 11:16.

Here, too, is the language of the loyal servant, uncomprehending, unable to see any joyful outcome, but still faithful. And we see him again, of course, still uncomprehending, still unwilling to see any joyful outcome, even after the others have met the risen Lord. And so Thomas receives his own particularized invitation to friendship: "see my hands. Reach out your hand and put it in my side. Do not doubt but believe." And it falls to Thomas to make the final, comprehensive and comprehending confession, "My Lord and my God!"[18]

There are two more figures who move from servanthood to friendship. Mary Magdalene does not appear in the fourth Gospel before the crucifixion, but we may take it from her appearance at the foot of the cross with the mother of Jesus and Mary the wife of Clopas, that she is intended to be a figure of faithful waiting.[19] After that brief glimpse, we next see her in her pivotal role on Easter morning as the first person to see the Lord. Faithfully waiting, the uncomprehending servant stands at the foot of the cross; faithfully waiting, the uncomprehending servant stands outside the tomb. She is still the servant who does not know what her master is doing, or, indeed, what has become of him. With one word—her own name—Jesus beckons her into understanding, into joy, into friendship. True, she must learn the nature of that friendship: it's not to be the yearning that has led her to the foot of the cross, or to the tomb, or which now makes her want to cling to him. Being called into friendship with Jesus includes the command to "go and bear fruit"; and Mary Magdalene is told not to linger, not to cling, but to go at once. The fruit that she bears is the joy of the resurrection and the calling of the apostles into that joy.[20]

And our last figure who moves from servanthood to friendship is the mother of the Lord. We know that the fourth evangelist places her in scenes of pivotal importance at both the beginning and the end of his Gospel. She is instrumental in the first miracle that Jesus wrought at Cana in Galilee; the first of his signs; the first revealing of his glory; the beginning of the road to crucifixion and resurrection. There is

---

[18] John 20:27–8.

[19] John 19:25.

[20] John 20:1–18.

no denying, and this is very important, that in the story of Cana, the mother of Jesus appears in the role of a servant. The words of Jesus to her, "Woman, what concern is that to you and to me?" are the words of a master to a servant, a servant who does not know all that the master is doing. Her words to the other servants underline this: "Do whatever he tells you."[21] This is the equivalent of Simon Peter's "To whom shall we go?" or Thomas's "Let us go and die with him." Here is obedience, but without complete understanding; just as it was for Peter and for Thomas. To say that is not to deny all that the Church goes on to say of Mary. After all, if the author to the Hebrews has the temerity to say that the Son of God learned obedience through what he suffered, there is surely reason to think that for his mother, too, there were lessons to be learned, progress to be made towards understanding, which in the thought of the evangelist is what "being called into friendship" means.[22]

In the drama of the fourth Gospel, that friendship with his own mother is sealed at the cross. She is there, faithful, sorrowing, with her companions. As we know, Jesus provides her with a home with the disciple whom he loved. The particular aspect of the friendship which Jesus promised his disciples at the last supper, which he here offers his mother and his beloved disciple, is that of "abiding in his love" so that their "joy might be complete". The promise of hearth and home, domestic security and the fellowship of the supper table reminds us of the wedding scene where the mother of Jesus first appeared. There, disaster was threatening the household at Cana, the promise of joy was imperilled; but now, there is a promise of abiding in love and joy for these two friends of Jesus in the home that he gives them. And we see the profound importance which the fourth evangelist attaches to this moment, when we remember that he immediately goes on, "After this, when Jesus knew that all was now finished".[23] Once he had given his mother and his beloved disciple a home, he had completed everything that he had set out to do.

---

[21] John 2:4,5.

[22] Hebrews 5:8.

[23] John 19:25–8.

◆

So far, we have seen a range of characters reflecting the theme of servants called into friendship. Their backgrounds are varied: some fishermen, a member of the Sanhedrin, a brother and two sisters, one half of a twin, a single woman, a grieving mother. Their brief encounters with Jesus before and after his death and resurrection are not described in depth, but the effect is cumulative: the evangelist is building up a compelling impression of lives changed as understanding dawns, joy breaks out, fellowship is restored and celebrated. Perhaps more than anything else, these brief encounters emphasize one aspect of what Jesus says of friendship in Chapter 15: "I have *called* you." We have seen this in several of the episodes. "You are Simon [...] You are to be called [...] Peter." "The Teacher is here and is calling for you." "Jesus said to her, 'Mary!'" "Simon son of John, do you love me more than these?"[24] Jesus does not just *make* them his friends; he calls them by name.

And so we come to that enigmatic figure, called simply "the disciple whom Jesus loved". The identity of the beloved disciple, and the interrelated questions of John son of Zebedee and the author or authors of the Gospel, are an academic industry, and it is neither my purpose nor within my competence to discuss them in depth. For what it's worth, it seems clear to me that the evangelist (the one who wrote the Gospel) has unobtrusively placed himself in his own narrative, picturing himself as a close disciple of Jesus, but refraining from giving himself a name. Whether that placing of himself in the story is a literary device, or whether it is a literary device constructed on a historical identity, is one of the questions which scholars have not stopped discussing. And whether the evangelist means us to guess the name of the beloved disciple, and whether he means us to guess that that name is John son of Zebedee, and whether that identification is a literary device, or again a literary device constructed on a historical identity, are also questions which scholars will go on discussing. I suspect that they are questions which, as was rumoured of the beloved disciple himself, will remain until the Parousia;

---

[24]   John 1:42; 11:28; 20:16; 21:15.

in which case, the Lord's deflating comment "What is that to you?" may apply.[25]

At any rate, I do not have to answer those questions in order to make a few comments about the figure of the "disciple whom Jesus loved". Whoever he is in the text and in history, a figure described as "the disciple whom Jesus loved" *must be intended to be* a representative figure of *all* the disciples whom Jesus loves. "As the Father has loved me, so have I loved *you.*" Jesus addresses those words to those gathered at the last supper; and by extension, he addresses them to all those who, through them, come to believe in him, including ourselves. The way in which the evangelist reaches out from the pages of the Gospel to his future readers is one of his marked characteristics. "I ask not only on behalf of these", says Jesus in his high priestly prayer, "but also on behalf of those who will believe in me through their word".[26] "Blessed are those", he says to Thomas, "who have not seen and yet have come to believe."[27] And even more directly: "these are written so that *you* may come to believe that Jesus is the Messiah, the Son of God, and that through believing *you* may have life in his name."[28] The figure of the "disciple whom Jesus loved" is, as it were, that reaching out in reverse: in the figure of the beloved disciple, *every* beloved disciple, *every* disciple whom Jesus loves, is gathered *into* the Gospel narrative. What else is the point of the anonymity of this disciple? When the evangelist has emphasized that Jesus called his friends by name, why is there one at the heart of the story who has no name? Why else but that we are invited to write our own names in the space provided?

And the beloved disciple *is* at the heart of the story. He is not an observer, watching from the margins; he is not there making notes or recording events, even though at the very end of Chapter 21, he does turn to us and say, "This is the disciple who is testifying to these things."[29] He is in the heart of the action. He lies closest to Jesus at the last supper. He stands at the foot of the cross. He receives the mother of Jesus into his

---

[25] John 21:22.

[26] John 17:20.

[27] John 20:29.

[28] John 20:31.

[29] John 21:24.

care, as, in turn, he is commended to her care. He goes into the depths of
the sepulchre and is the first to believe the resurrection. He follows the
risen Lord along the lakeside in that final morning scene that never ends.
I think that it is clear that the evangelist is saying to us, "And this is what
it means to be the disciple whom Jesus loves. I have been that disciple,
and I am writing this so that you can be that disciple too."

All the "beloved disciple" scenes are profoundly significant; but none
more so than the first of them, at the last supper. "One of his disciples—
the one whom Jesus loved—was reclining next to him."[30] As I am sure you
know, behind that rather bald translation a Greek phrase is concealed:
en tō kolpō. The Authorized Version says: "leaning on Jesus' bosom". The
Jerusalem Bible speaks of Jesus's breast. And I am sure that you know
equally well that the evangelist uses practically the same expression, *eis
ton kolpon*, in the prologue.[31] The Authorized Version again: "the only
begotten Son, which is in the bosom of the Father, he hath declared him".
And the New Revised Standard Version: "It is God the only Son, who is
close to the Father's heart, who has made him known." So the beloved
disciple lies in the bosom of the Son of God, close to his heart; just as
the Son of God lies in the bosom of the Father, close to his heart. This is
what it means for the Son to *abide* in the Father's love, and for the one
whom Jesus loves to abide in his love. It is because the Son lies close to the
heart of the Father that he knows what the Father is doing, and can make
it known; by the same token, it is because the disciple lies close to the
heart of the Son, that the disciple knows what the Son is doing; in other
words, as we have seen, the disciple enters into friendship with Jesus. *En
tō kolpō* is the evangelist's most intimate and definitive statement of what
friendship with Jesus means.

◆

The fourth Gospel is a dramatic interplay of light and darkness. The
evangelist begins, as the book of Genesis begins, with a light that
penetrates the shadows. The theme is repeated in a hundred allusions,

---

[30]   John 13:23.

[31]   John 1:18.

scores of sayings of Jesus, and dozens of episodes that take place in daytime or at night. None is more tragic than the moment after Jesus has washed the disciples' feet, and acted as their servant in order to demonstrate that he loves them to the end, when he then gives a piece of bread to Judas. "After he received the piece of bread", says the evangelist, "Satan entered into him." Jesus said to him, "Do quickly what you are going to do." "So, after receiving the piece of bread, [Judas] immediately went out." *Ēn de nux.* "And it was night."[32]

Judas is the figure of friendship refused. Jesus offers bread, the unmistakable sacred sign of hospitality. Judas, terribly, takes the bread with a false hand and a false heart, and goes into the night. "Even my bosom friend in whom I trusted," runs the lament of the psalmist, "who ate of my bread, has lifted the heel against me."[33] The friendship of Jesus is offered to all his disciples: it is strong enough to reconcile Peter, to convince Thomas, to give joy to Mary Magdalene, but it is not enforced.

◆

We must not end on a dark note. As I have said, the Gospel begins like Genesis with light piercing the darkness, and the battle goes on between light and darkness until night settles over Golgotha and the Son of God is lying in his tomb: and then, once more, light begins to penetrate that Easter night. The glorious epilogue takes place at breakfast-time, with sunlight drenching the Sea of Galilee. In Chapter 21, so many of the themes of friendship that we have already considered are drawn together. Simon Peter, the most fully drawn of the disciples, is restored to friendship in moving terms. The third of Jesus's questions switches from *agapaō* to *phileō,* and while there is no very discernible difference in the way in which the evangelist uses the two words, there is a dramatic intensity about that third question, "Are you my *friend*?"[34] We may take it that this is another of the moments when the words of the Gospel are meant to reach out to us readers and address us directly. And, as we

---

[32] John 13:27,30.

[33] Psalm 41:9.

[34] John 21:17.

have seen, the "disciple whom Jesus loved" is there, following, silently following; and yet more than that; remaining, abiding, still close to the heart of Jesus where Jesus invites his friends to be.

Signs work in two directions. When the author of the first Johannine epistle says that God is love, that tells us something about God, but it tells us much more about love.[35] And when St Aelred tentatively considered whether the fourth evangelist might have said, "God is friendship", again that tells us something about God, but it tells us much more about friendship.[36] If friendship stands in the fourth Gospel as a sign of all that the evangelist means by salvation, then we bring all that we understand of friendship in our own experience to help us understand more of the saving mystery. Just as our experience of water and bread and wine enable us to know something of the mysteries of baptism and the eucharist, so, too, there is in the fourth Gospel a variety of ordinary scenes and experiences in which ordinary people are then transformed by friendship with Jesus. A fisherman at work all night, a rabbi troubled by a religious conundrum, two sisters grieving over the death of a brother, a wedding that needs to be rescued from disaster, a group of women gathered in grief, a man lying in the arms of his friend, a woman clinging to the body of the man she loves, a mother weeping over her dead child, a sceptic refusing to accept good news: these are the characters whom Jesus calls to be his friends. So, too, we start from our own experience of friendship: our memories of acceptance, of rejection, of grief, of loyalty, of suspicion, of companionship, of betrayal, of bliss. These experiences enable us to enter imaginatively into the stories of Simon Peter, or Thomas, or Mary Magdalene, or Nicodemus, or Judas Iscariot, or the mother of the Lord, and help to see what the transforming friendship of Jesus is like.

In a sacramental mystery, however, the sign is even more powerful in the other direction. The mystery of baptism is reflected back on common water, and tells us something of the sanctity of that common water. The mystery of the body and blood of Christ gives us a new reverence even for ordinary bread and ordinary wine. The communion of the altar

---

[35]   1 John 4:8.

[36]   Aelred of Rievaulx, *Spiritual Friendship*, tr. Mary E. Laker (Kalamazoo, MI: Cistercian Publications, 1977), pp. 65–6.

illuminates the fellowship of the common table. So, too, the Gospel stories of the friends of Jesus prompt us to rediscover spiritual depths in our ordinary experience. There is more to our experience of acceptance when we see it in the light of Christ's gracious acceptance of Simon Peter. There is more to our experience of rejection or betrayal when we set it alongside the hand and the bread which Jesus offers, even at the last minute, to his friend Judas. Our grief or our experience of bereavement is not taken away, but maybe it can be enlightened, when placed under the mystery of Jesus weeping for his friend Lazarus, or the mystery of Mary at the cross. Our moments of physical touch or intimacy take on new depth when we see the beloved disciple resting in the bosom of Jesus, or Mary Magdalene unwilling to let him go. The image of the messianic feast casts its light back upon our times of convivial fellowship with bread on the table and wine in the glass. And if God is friendship, as St Aelred thought that perhaps he is, then it is God who transfigures our own friendships, and makes them the sacraments of his presence and the vehicles of his grace.

The virtue of friendship[1]

In thanking the dean for his invitation to preach at this commemoration, and while bringing you the greetings of the dean and chapter of Chichester, I am mindful of the fact that Samuel Johnson did not have unmixed admiration for deans and chapters. In his dictionary, he quoted Sir Francis Bacon's remark that "in their first institution, [they] were of great use in the church"—which is hardly a ringing endorsement.[2] But there was one dean whom Dr Johnson did appreciate: the one who contributed a hogshead of claret to his club. Johnson was put up by the other club members to write the letter of thanks to the dean, which was to convey the heavy hint that while one hogshead of claret was good, two would be better. But I must not be lightsome. Johnson was once in the company of some clergymen who (so his biographer James Boswell tells us) "assumed the lax jollity of men of the world", upon which Johnson remarked ("by no means in a whisper", says Boswell) that "the merriment of parsons is mighty offensive".[3] So I must be serious.

My text, as it were, is a conversation that took place during Holy Week 1778 between Samuel Johnson, James Boswell, and a Quaker called Mrs Knowles. Mrs Knowles was a friend of Johnson's; indeed, on an earlier occasion, Boswell tells us that Johnson "showed visible signs of a

---

[1] The Samuel Johnson Commemoration Sermon preached at the eucharist in Lichfield Cathedral on Sunday, 24 September 2006.

[2] Samuel Johnson, *A Dictionary of the English Language* (London: W. Strahan, 1755), under "Dean".

[3] *Boswell's Life of Johnson*, ed. Robert W. Chapman (London: Oxford University Press, 1953), p. 1125.

fervent admiration of her charms".[4] Be that as it may, the subject under discussion on this occasion was the nature of friendship. A book had been published, in which it was argued that friendship was not a Christian virtue. Mrs Knowles disagreed. Johnson, despite being both a Christian and a man with many friends, took the opposite line from Mrs Knowles and sided with the book. "Christianity", he said, "recommends universal benevolence, to consider all men as our brethren, which is contrary to the virtue of friendship, as described by the ancient philosophers."[5]

Why did Johnson say this?—because he valued friendship, and in his dictionary defined it as the "highest degree of intimacy";[6] because he took trouble over his friendships, and told Sir Joshua Reynolds that "a man should keep his friendship in constant repair";[7] and because he was steeped in the classics, and the nature of friendship was a lively subject for classical authors. Plato and Aristotle both wrote about it; and Cicero's book on friendship was one of the most widely read books in the centuries between Cicero's time and Johnson's. One of the commonplaces of this classical reflection on the nature of friendship was that a person should not have too many friends. It was a gift not to be spread too thinly. Depth of commitment was the thing. "Warm friendship can be felt only for a few," said Aristotle.[8]

Now this is a point of view evidently in some tension with Christian belief. Friendship, from this perspective, is essentially exclusive: we choose some people to be our friends and not others. We know, and can probably remember, how painful it is for a child who "wants to be friends" to be told by another child, "You're not my friend." Nor are adults beyond such attitudes of preference and rejection. "They're quite nice people," we say, "but they're not people with whom I'd want to go on holiday." "He's a good colleague, but I wouldn't spend my spare time with him." Sometimes we can be harsher. "They're not our type; not our

---

4   *Boswell's Life of Johnson*, p. 776.

5   *Boswell's Life of Johnson*, pp. 945–6.

6   Johnson, *Dictionary of the English Language*, under "Friendship".

7   *Boswell's Life of Johnson*, p. 214.

8   *The Ethics of Aristotle: The Nicomachean Ethics* (9.10), tr. J. A. K. Thomson (Harmondsworth: Penguin Books, 1955), p. 282.

sort." It is easy for the hint of criticism to slip in. Difference becomes disapproval.

How, as Christians, can we justify our close (and to that extent exclusive) friendships? That was Johnson's dilemma. "Love your neighbour as yourself," said Jesus; and he defined the neighbour as anyone who crossed our path.[9] To put the matter more plainly still, he even said, "Love your enemies."[10] We all know that there's a standard cop-out to this dilemma, whereby we say "I *love* my neighbour, but that doesn't mean that I have to *like* them"; and we all know that that's just a bit too easy to be convincing.

Let's go back to the discussion between Dr Johnson and Mrs Knowles. Johnson took the classical line, and felt that there was a tension between the classical view of friendship and Christianity. Mrs Knowles disagreed, and she reminded Johnson that although the Lord had many disciples, there was still one of whom it was said that he was the disciple whom Jesus loved. There are, in other words, elements of both universality and particularity in the personal relationships of the Lord himself. The tension between "universal benevolence" on the one hand and "particular friendships" on the other is not a tension between the classical tradition and Christian faith, as Johnson supposed; it is there in the very heart of Christian faith, at the very centre of the Lord's own life. Dr Johnson liked Mrs Knowles's reference to the beloved disciple. He said ("with eyes sparkling benignantly"), "Very well indeed, Madam. You have said very well." "Had you ever thought of that?" Boswell asked him. "I had not, Sir," Johnson replied.[11]

Let's try and get inside Mrs Knowles's argument. Jesus taught us, as I have said, to love our neighbour, and to interpret the idea of neighbour very broadly; indeed, to go further, and love our enemies. In other words, the love at which we must aim as Christians is nothing less than the love of God our heavenly Father, who makes the sun rise on the evil and on the good, and sends rain on the just and the unjust.[12] His love is

---

9   Mark 12:31.

10 Matthew 5:44.

11 *Boswell's Life of Johnson*, p. 946.

12 Matthew 5:45.

universal, undiscriminating, generous, forgiving, gathering all people into his embrace. Such was the love of Jesus, calling people to follow him, and saying to them, "I call you friends."[13]

All the same, Jesus had close and particular relationships. He loved Lazarus, and Mary, and Martha; and evidently he loved to stay in their home. He loved that disciple who is mentioned again and again in St John's Gospel, never named, but traditionally taken to be St John himself. Was there something exclusive about those friendships? Were there other disciples in Jerusalem who wished that it was their house where Jesus loved to relax and feel at home? Was Peter sometimes jealous of John—John, who lay so close to Jesus at the last supper—Peter, who at the very end of the Gospel story wanted to know what would become of John?[14] How do we reconcile the Lord's general call to his disciples to be his friends, with those evident deep and particular relationships with a few of them?

The clue, I think, is the figure of John, if John it was who called himself "the disciple whom Jesus loved". This is the disciple, as I have said, who lay close to the heart of Jesus at the last supper on Maundy Thursday, who stood at the foot of the cross on Good Friday, and who was one of the first to arrive at the empty tomb on Easter Day. He is the figure of the perfectly loyal disciple, returning the Lord's love with a loving response. So he is, in fact, *every* disciple, as the Lord would have his disciples to be. John Bunyan would have called him "Christian". And the fact that the fourth evangelist does not ever give him a name, but calls him just "the disciple whom Jesus loved" is significant: it is, as it were, a row of dots on which we can aspire to sign our own name. All Christians are the disciples whom Jesus has called his friends. All Christians are the disciples whom Jesus loves. The figure of the beloved disciple is a type of all of us.

But rather than paint a picture of the Lord giving his friendship to every disciple indiscriminately, the fourth evangelist shows us *one* disciple who knew himself to be loved, who knew himself to be the Lord's friend, who lay close to his heart at the eucharist and wept at the cross and ran eagerly to greet the resurrection. Think of yourself as *that* disciple,

---

[13]   John 15:15.

[14]   John 13:23; 21:21.

says the evangelist. Don't think of yourself as a Christian in general, think of yourself as *the* disciple whom Jesus loves.

And now let's go back to the debate between Dr Johnson and Mrs Knowles. Johnson, following the classical authors, was right to insist that true friendship is something intimate and deep, not just a vague goodwill towards anyone and everyone. We learn the meaning and the cost of love in such close encounters; general goodwill does not demand so much.

Yet Mrs Knowles was right to insist that this evaluation of friendship lies at the heart of the gospel, which insists on something deeper than mere benevolence. Even the Lord himself, so the fourth evangelist suggests, experienced the depth and demands of love in close encounters with his disciples in ones and twos and threes, as much as with the crowds in general. The intimate friendship of Jesus with "the disciple whom he loved" is the type of relationship for every disciple with the Lord. So, too, our deep friendships, necessarily select and few, give us an experience of love, which we can, and must, extend to others. Every person who crosses our path is our neighbour, and so potentially our friend. Even our enemy is our neighbour, and so potentially our friend. Christianity goes beyond the wisdom of the classics, by daring us to see the gift of friendship as something through which we can take enmity and reconcile it.

Mrs Knowles, who made Samuel Johnson think through his idea of friendship all over again, was a Quaker, a member of that Christian body that calls itself by the honourable name of the "Society of Friends". That would be a good name for every church to adopt. It would at least teach us to value a gift that we sometimes take for granted. Even Johnson nearly let a valued friendship slip. "To let friendship die away by negligence and silence", he once wrote to a friend whose friendship he had nearly lost, "is certainly not wise. It is voluntarily to throw away one of the greatest comforts of this weary pilgrimage, of which when it is, as it must be, taken finally away, he that travels on alone, will wonder how his esteem could be so little."[15] That is Samuel Johnson's eloquent testimony to the virtue of friendship; one of the best gifts that we can share with a lonely world.

---

[15] Letter to Bennet Langton, 20 March 1782 (*Boswell's Life of Johnson*, p. 1179).

27

Our Lady of Worcester[1]

We are in the Lady Chapel, the Chapel of Our Lady, the Blessed Virgin Mary. We often think of St Oswald and St Wulfstan, whose shrines once stood either side of the high altar, as the two saints of Worcester. Perhaps we forget that in the Middle Ages, Worcester was as well, or even better, known as a shrine of Our Lady. The cathedral is itself dedicated to St Mary: as we say when we are being precise, "the Cathedral Church of Christ and the Blessed Mary the Virgin of Worcester". In addition to the high altar, there were two other altars dedicated in her honour: one here, and one near the north door in the nave. Pilgrims came to the shrine of Our Lady of Worcester as they went, and still go, to the shrine of Our Lady of Walsingham. Benefactors endowed Our Lady's altar with lamps and candles, vestments and plate. And when it was all taken away at the Reformation, the people of Worcester felt that they had lost a friend, their guardian and their mother. Eamon Duffy, in his great and sad book *The Stripping of the Altars,* tells how a serving-man from the parish of All Saints, called Thomas Emans, came here on the Feast of the Assumption 1537, when the great image of Mary had been stripped of its jewels and vestments, but still said his Our Father and the Hail Mary. "Lady, art thou stripped now?" he asked aloud; and the sense of loss in his voice is palpable.[2]

This Lady Chapel is part of the great rebuilding of St Wulfstan's Norman cathedral, which began in the second quarter of the thirteenth

---

[1]   Address given at a parish pilgrimage in the Lady Chapel of Worcester Cathedral on Saturday, 19 April 2008.

[2]   Eamon Duffy, *The Stripping of the Altars: Traditional Religion in England c.1400–c.1580*, 2nd edn (New Haven and London: Yale University Press, 2005), p. 403.

century. In 1216, King John was buried in the cathedral at his own request; and his son King Henry III, a deeply pious man, made frequent benefactions to the cathedral. On the strength of this, the rebuilding, beginning here at the east end, went on apace throughout his long reign; and Henry often came in person, sometimes several times a year, on one occasion celebrating Christmas in Worcester.

That was the material impulse to build; but there was a spiritual impulse as well. The English people had had a deep love of Mary since early Saxon times. Several of the great festivals of St Mary—especially that of her conception—took off in Saxon England, and from here their popularity spread to the continent. Now when the Normans came, there was something of an effort at first to stamp out anything that was characteristically Saxon about the liturgy; but Wulfstan, who uniquely served as bishop under two Saxon kings and two Norman kings, did much to salvage the native English traditions; in consequence of which, Worcester was at the forefront of a great welling-up of new devotion to Our Lady in the twelfth century. A daily mass in honour of Our Lady became common; and then a daily office to go with it—a whole parallel liturgy—and a special place in which to celebrate it; so "Lady Chapels" became the thing; and in England they were usually built as an extension to the east end of the church; so here we are in one of the earliest of them.

There are not many reminders of Mary here now, more's the pity. The east wall is a careful Victorian reconstruction of what the mediaeval building might have looked like; but we do still have some precious mediaeval fragments. Above our heads is a boss carved to represent the crowned Christchild seated in the lap of his crowned mother. In one of the spandrels in the triforium, we have the pair of them again. Amazingly, on the wall of what we now call St Andrew's Chapel, you can see sculptures of the annunciation, visitation, and nativity. I say "amazingly" since any mediaeval figures of the saints within reach were usually hacked to bits by the Reformers or the Roundheads.

But once there was a statue here, and it stood by the pillar on the north side of the chapel, the image of Our Lady of Worcester; and William of Blois, the bishop who began the building of the chapel, lay buried at her feet, and here the people of Worcester and pilgrims from further afield, came with their prayers and their thanksgivings, their joys, their sorrows, their sicknesses and sins; and here they sought help and healing; and frequently, no doubt, they found it.

◆

Let us remind ourselves of what it means (as we sing each Christmas) to "love and watch the lowly maiden";[3] at any rate, what it means to do so in the tradition of the Church of England. Despite the destruction of the shrines and images and altars of Our Lady, no fewer than five feasts of Mary are included in the calendar of the *Book of Common Prayer*: her conception, her nativity, her annunciation, her visitation, and her purification (two of them with collects, epistles and Gospels). In two other early calendars, the primer of Queen Elizabeth and the calendar of the University of Oxford, the feast of her assumption was also mentioned; and the dedication of many churches across England in honour of the assumption was preserved.[4] The name of Mary survived in common speech, from oaths to wildflowers. But these, perhaps, are only reminders of a lost devotion.

But in the seventeenth century, something of that devotion was revived. The Anglican divines preached about Mary and wrote about Mary; and the finest fruit of that period is Thomas Ken's great hymn in praise of Mary which we still sing, beginning "Her Virgin eyes saw God incarnate born", and ending with the verse:

> Heaven with transcendent joys her entrance graced,
> near to his throne her Son his Mother placed;
> and here below, now she's of heaven possest,
> all generations are to call her blest.[5]

—the doctrine of the assumption of Our Lady, alive and well in

---

[3] To use a line from C. F. Alexander, "Once in royal David's city" (*Ancient & Modern: Hymns and Songs for Refreshing Worship* [London: Hymns Ancient & Modern, 2013], no. 81).

[4] Kenneth E. Kirk, *Church Dedications of the Oxford Diocese* (Oxford: Clarendon Press, 1946), pp. 67–87.

[5] *Ancient & Modern*, no. 314.

seventeenth-century England.

The nineteenth century brought more Marian hymns into our hymnbooks, such as those of John Keble and Stuckey Coles; but even before we reach the Catholic revival, we have the remarkable hymn of Bishop Reginald Heber, himself so close to the evangelical Clapham Sect:

> Blessèd was the breast that fed thee;
> blessèd was the hand that led thee;
> blessèd was the parent's eye
> that watched thy slumbering infancy.
>
> Blessèd she by all creation,
> who brought forth the world's Salvation;
> blessèd they, for ever blest,
> who love thee most and serve thee best.[6]

A steady stream of Anglican devotion has kept alive a love of Mary; not with that popular force that brought the people of mediaeval Worcester flocking here to her shrine; but significant all the same.

◆

Authentic Anglican devotion is rooted in scripture; and of all the scriptural pictures of Our Lady, the one that I love the best is that of Mary and the beloved disciple standing at the foot of the cross. And there, of course, is the scene in the window above the altar: the Lord on the cross, and at the foot of it the blessed mother and the beloved disciple.

To make sense of this episode, we have to think about that other figure in the scene: "the disciple whom Jesus loved". He is mentioned first of all at the last supper, where he lies, as the evangelist literally and startlingly puts it, "on Jesus' breast".[7] Then he reappears at the foot of the cross, with Mary.[8] Then, on Easter Sunday morning, he comes with Peter to the

---

6   "Virgin-born, we bow before thee" (*Ancient & Modern*, no. 317).

7   John 13:25 (Jerusalem Bible).

8   John 19:26–7.

tomb.[9] And finally, in that so very moving scene beside the Sea of Galilee, he walks a little way behind the risen Lord and Peter; and the closing words of the Gospel are, as it were, from him: "This is the disciple who is testifying to these things."[10]

Now from the second century, this figure has been traditionally identified with John, the brother of James, one of the twelve apostles. He has been thought to be both "the disciple whom Jesus loved" and the author of the Gospel. And that is why, since the second century, the Gospel has been called that of St John.

Now we cannot be certain of this; and there is no time this afternoon to enter into the scholarly debate about it. Suffice it to say that nowhere in the text of the fourth Gospel is either the author or the "beloved disciple" given a name. And there is food for thought in that—whoever he was. The evangelist wrote himself into the Gospel story, and he chose not to give himself a name, but he called himself "the disciple whom Jesus loved". Was that humility, or was it arrogance? Or was it something else?

I think that it was something else. I think that the evangelist is saying to us: "I was there. I lay close to him at the last supper. I stood at the foot of the cross. I ran to the tomb and found it empty. I walked beside him on the lakeside after his resurrection. But it's not important that *I* did those things. So I'm not even going to distract you by giving you my name. The point is that any disciple beloved of the Lord can be there as well. Read my Gospel with the eyes and mind of love, and you too will lie close to him at the supper. You too will stand at the foot of the cross. You too will discover the Lord risen from the tomb, and will walk with him in his risen life. Because you too are the disciple whom Jesus loves."

Now if this is the way in which to read the mystery of the beloved disciple, what do we make of this episode at the foot of the cross? If the beloved disciple is every disciple—every Christian—then the Lord gives his mother to each one of us, and he gives each one of us to his mother. And that means that it was a true evangelical instinct which led the people of Worcester in the thirteenth century to come here to the shrine of the

---

[9] John 20:1–10.

[10] John 21:20–4.

Blessed Virgin Mary and call her "Our Lady of Worcester". She was part of their family; and they were part of hers.

So what does it mean to have the Lord's mother for our mother? Well, it means that we can learn from her. There is plenty in the four Gospels upon which to meditate: her faith; her obedience—those are the two great standbys. But it wasn't unquestioning faith. "How shall this be, seeing I know not a man?"[11] That, we might think, is a rather bold way to speak to an archangel. She wanted to understand; and that, perhaps, is how we are meant to read those repeated statements in St Luke's Gospel that she "kept all these things, and pondered them in her heart".[12] She questioned them; she puzzled over them; she wrestled with them.

Hers, evidently, was not a quiet faith. The picture which St Luke gives us of Mary singing the Magnificat puts her in the Old Testament tradition of tough and challenging women. "He has shown strength with his arm, he has scattered the proud in the imagination of their hearts, he has put down the mighty from their thrones, and exalted those of low degree; he has filled the hungry with good things, and the rich he has sent empty away."[13] There is an agenda here of social reform, not to say revolution. Mary has the character of a Deborah or a Judith.

But Mary is not only of the same character as the heroines of the Old Testament; she sums up the Old Testament and brings it to its climax. The phrase "daughter of Jerusalem" is used in the Old Testament to mean the whole people of Israel. Mary is the "daughter of Jerusalem" from whom is born the messiah. This is particularly true of the way in which St Luke tells the story of the nativity at the beginning of his Gospel. He goes out of his way to evoke a sense of the Old Testament reaching its fulfilment. Here is Zechariah, serving as a priest in the temple. Here is Simeon, righteous and devout, looking for the consolation of Israel. Here is Anna, worshipping with fasting and prayer night and day, who speaks of the Christchild to all who were looking for the redemption of Jerusalem. And this helps us to understand the figure of the woman clothed with the sun in the book of Revelation, who gives birth to the

---

[11]   Luke 1:34 (AV).

[12]   Luke 2:19 (AV).

[13]   Luke 1:51–3 (RSV).

messiah amid great tribulation.[14] She is not precisely Mary; rather she is the "daughter of Jerusalem", the whole people of Israel from whom the messiah is born amid pain and suffering; but that story comes to its fulfilment in the story of Mary.

◆

I have pointed out the boss of Mary and the Christchild above our heads. I wish that I could show you one of my favourite mediaeval representations of them, which is also a boss; but it is in the lovely gothic Church of Our Lady in Nuremberg in Bavaria. In it the boy Jesus carries something that looks like a satchel or even a lunchbox. Mary has him not by the hand, but by the wrist. They are evidently on their way to school, and just as evidently Jesus is not sure that he wants to go. Mary is not standing any nonsense. Our more modern artistic representations of the Virgin have not always had that quality of realism. They do not always suggest the toughness of the Magnificat.

There are also those surprising moments in the Gospels when Jesus seems to speak to Mary quite bluntly. Mary and her other sons try to see him during one of his preaching missions. "Here are my mother and my brothers," replies Jesus, pointing to his disciples. "Whoever does the will of my Father in heaven is my brother and sister and mother."[15] Well, it doesn't sound very gracious to his family. Jesus is teaching the important truth that obedience to the gospel is the important thing; there wasn't a privileged place in the kingdom of heaven for those who could claim blood relationship to the messiah. Does that mean that Mary isn't special after all? No, but it means that Mary is special not only because she gave birth to the messiah, but also because she then became the messiah's first disciple. "Behold the handmaid of the Lord; be it unto me according to thy word."[16] Those are the words of the true disciple; and when Jesus said that anyone who did the will of God was his brother and his sister and his mother, the first of those who did the will of God was Mary.

---

14 Revelation 12:1–6.
15 Matthew 12:49–50.
16 Luke 1:38 (AV).

And Mary is the one who points others to Jesus. That is the message of so many of the eastern icons of the mother of God: she is always shown with Jesus, and she usually points to him. That is the message, as far as Mary is concerned, of the wedding at Cana. "Do whatever he tells you," is her advice to the servants.[17] This makes Mary not only the first of the disciples, but the first of the apostles and the first of the evangelists. She shows Jesus to others, and invites them to come to him. She doesn't say, "Come to me" or "Look at me." It is always "Come to him", "Look at him", "Do whatever he tells you."

It intrigues me to read at the beginning of the Acts of the Apostles that Mary was there with the rest of the disciples awaiting the gift of the Holy Spirit. This too conveys an important truth about her: though she was filled with the Holy Spirit at her annunciation, and overshadowed by the Holy Spirit to conceive the Christchild, she is still one of the company of the Lord's disciples; she still waits with them for the outpouring of the Spirit at Pentecost; she is still, we may accurately say, a member of the Church.

So there is Mary, the Lord's mother, but also the first of the Lord's disciples, learning to do the Father's will, waiting with the rest of the disciples for the gift of the Lord's Spirit. She is one of the disciples, but also given by the Lord to be the mother of his beloved disciple, and so the mother of all disciples.

◆

The Anglo-Saxons called her "Our Lady". That of course is a title of honour; but it is also a title of great intimacy and affection. For the word "lady", in Old English, meant the "loaf-kneader"; the lady of the house in the most basic and practical and nourishing of ways. So that characteristically English title tells us how our Saxon forebears thought of her; they made the connection between their homes and the holy house of Nazareth; between their homes and the home to which the beloved disciple took her from the foot of the cross; they took her for their loaf-kneader, the one who held out to them the bread of life; and they knew that in keeping close to her, they were close to the Saviour of the world.

---

[17]   John 2:5.

2 8

Caught in a storm[1]

I am grateful for the opportunity to be with you this evening, and to preach for the first time in one of the parishes of the diocese of Worcester. And this is of course a very special parish, with a very special link with Worcester Cathedral, going back over many centuries. This priory church was a dependency or daughter house of the cathedral monastery of Worcester; two communities of monks united by their common allegiance to the Benedictine life. I wonder if you know the story of the monks of Worcester caught in the thunderstorm? Forgive me if you do, but I only learnt of it in preparing this sermon, and it seemed to me to have something to say to us today.

In the year 1303, a party of monks from the cathedral were returning to Worcester after some errand or mission of some kind; we don't know what. They got as far as Malvern where they were caught by a storm, and they took shelter here, in Little Malvern Priory. In fact, they stayed the night; and that was a serious breach of the Rule of St Benedict. To be allowed outside the monastery at all was a privilege, and under strict orders from the abbot. Any monk who had been sent out on an errand was forbidden to talk about anything that he had seen or heard while he was on the outside; so to stay out overnight without the abbot's permission was a very serious matter. And so the prior of Little Malvern wrote a letter to my predecessor, the cathedral prior of Worcester, explaining the situation. "We had pleasure in entertaining our dear brothers your fellow-monks", he wrote, "who turned aside yesterday on account of the stormy weather. As we should wish our brethren to be entertained by any

1   Sermon preached at evensong in Little Malvern Priory on Sunday, 17 June 2007.

Catholic, most of all by those who hold the faith of our house [that is to say, the Benedictine Rule], we pray your Reverence that of your gracious piety you will pardon their not returning at the hour appointed."[2] What a delightful letter to have survived more than seven centuries. I hope that the cathedral prior of Worcester was equally gracious in return.

The monks of Worcester had inadvertently broken the Rule of St Benedict by not getting home on time; but the monks of Little Malvern kept it, by welcoming the travellers in with unqualified hospitality—because, of course, St Benedict is famous for saying in his Rule that every guest in the monastery should be received as if they were Christ himself. "By a bow of the head or by a complete prostration of the body, Christ is to be adored because he is indeed welcomed in them": so Benedict writes, and he goes on to say that the entire community should assemble to wash the feet of their guests.[3]

There are very strong gospel themes running through the Rule of St Benedict. In the parable of the sheep and the goats, the Lord tells us to welcome the stranger and feed the hungry because in serving them we do him service.[4] The Lord rebuked the Pharisee who failed in his duty of gracious hospitality, and commended the prostitute who carried out his duties instead, and washed the Lord's feet.[5] The Lord himself washed the feet of his disciples and told them to serve each other in the same way.[6] And the epistle to the Hebrews speaks of the duty of hospitality, because "thereby some have entertained angels unawares".[7]

So there's much for us to think about in that. Each guest, each visitor, each person in need of shelter or hospitality or food is Christ himself. Each is to be treated as though we treated Christ himself; as indeed we

---

[2]   James M. Wilson, *The Worcester Liber Albus: Glimpses of Life in a Great Benedictine Monastery in the Fourteenth Century* (London: SPCK, 1920), p. 41.

[3]   Chapter 53: *The Rule of St Benedict in Latin and English with Notes*, ed. Timothy Fry (Collegeville, MN: Liturgical Press, 1981), pp. 254–9 at 256–9.

[4]   Matthew 25:40.

[5]   Luke 7:44–7.

[6]   John 13:12–15.

[7]   Hebrews 13:2 (RSV).

do. And that really does mean all those people who have turned up on my doorstep over the years, each with a hard-luck story more far-fetched than the one before. It doesn't mean that we buy the hard-luck story, for Christ himself taught us to be not only innocent as doves but wise as serpents as well;[8] but it does mean that deep within that scruffy, unattractive, unwanted, untimely person dwells the same Christ as I receive in holy communion. "Next to the Blessed Sacrament itself", wrote C. S. Lewis in one of his best sermons, "your neighbour is the holiest object presented to your senses." "There are", he said, "no *ordinary* people."[9]

And this applies not only to people in obvious material need: it is not just the poor, the homeless and the hungry within whom we shall find the living Christ. Christ also lives in people with different demands: those tiresome people who crave our company, who impose upon our time, who desperately want us to like them, though try as we might we don't. Christ reaches out to us through them as well; as he does through the loud and aggressive, whose loudness and aggression is perhaps only a disguise for insecurity and fear. What a lot of really rather difficult people turn out to be the brothers and sisters for whom Christ died; and in whose unhappy lives the living Christ still lives and asks us for our help.

And then—and maybe this is the hardest lesson that some of us have to learn—needy people are not only other people. Tiresome and untimely people are not only other people. We too are the people whom others find hard to like, or difficult to please, or crying out for help. Some good people love us, not because (as we like to think) we are lovable; but rather, they love us sacrificially, for Christ's sake; they love us because Christ loves us. And that reflection should make us both humble and exalted: humble, because Christ loves us not for our merits but out of his own self-giving love; and exalted for the same reason—we are the objects of his self-giving love.

I have come rather a long way from those fourteenth-century monks of Little Malvern taking in their brothers from Worcester out of the rain for Christ's sake. Yet they were only obeying the rule of the gospel; and in

---

8   Matthew 10:16.

9   C. S. Lewis, *They Asked for a Paper: Papers and Addresses* (London: Geoffrey Bles, 1962), pp. 210–11 (original emphasis).

that gospel all that I have gone on to say is implied. All are to be loved on account of the Christ that is in them, and for the sake of the Christ who loves them. And we too are loved on account of the Christ who is in us, and for the sake of the Christ who loves us. And so "to him who loves us and freed us from our sins by his blood, and made us to be a kingdom, priests serving his God and Father, to him be glory and dominion for ever and ever".[10]

---

[10]   Revelation 1:5b–6.

Richard of Chichester[1]

So he embraced the image of the Crucified which he had asked
to be brought to him [...] He devoutly kissed and tenderly
caressed the wounds as if he had just seen them newly inflicted
on his Saviour's dying body and cried out, "I thank thee, Lord
Jesus Christ, for all the benefits which thou hast granted me, for
all the pains and insults which thou hast suffered for me" [...]
He said to his attendants, "Place this wretched body down on the
ground" [...] Thus between the sighs of his pious devotions and
the words of his holy prayers [...] the blessed Richard rendered
up his soul [...] to his Creator.[2]

Richard lived at a time of deep devotion to the vulnerable humanity
of Christ. We see an early glimpse of this in the Lazarus reliefs in this
cathedral—which Richard must have known—where the figure of Christ
expresses not only majesty but pathos too. St Francis, who died when

---

[1] Sermon preached at the eucharist in Chichester Cathedral on the Fifth
   Sunday of Lent, 6 April 2003, marking the 750th anniversary of the death
   of St Richard of Chichester on 3 April 1253. The readings were Jeremiah
   31:31–4; Hebrews 5:5–10; John 12:20–33.

[2] The death of St Richard of Chichester, as described by his contemporary
   biographer Ralph Bocking: *Saint Richard of Chichester: The Sources for His
   Life*, ed. David Jones (Lewes: Sussex Record Society, 1995), p. 213. His death
   was commemorated in a ceremony on 3 April 2003 in the very building where
   he died, the Maison Dieu of Dover. Earlier that same day, Richard's successor
   in the see of Chichester, Bishop John Hind, celebrated the eucharist in the
   chapel of St Edmund across the road, dedicated by the saint a few days before
   his death.

Richard was a child, and whose followers he admired and encouraged, did much to spread a devotion both to Christ in his nativity (and so to his mother as well), dwelling on the poverty of his birth, and to Christ in his passion, dwelling on the pains of his suffering and death. Think of the delicate roundel of the mother and child in the bishop's chapel—again which Richard knew; think of Ralph Bocking's vivid picture of the dying saint clasping the crucifix and asking—like St Francis—to be laid on the ground to die. In death, Richard longed to be like Jesus, the Son of Man who had nowhere to lay his head.

There are some aspects of this mediaeval identification with the suffering Christ which we would find it hard to make our own. Philip Jackson's statue of St Richard outside the west doors shows him with a whip: literally unhistorical, since there is no record of Richard having used one, but not inappropriate, since beneath his clothes he did wear a hair-shirt, a breastplate, and a knotted belt. Richard was a child of his time, and there were expressions of Christian piety then which we can only regard as dangerously wrong-headed.

More dangerous and more wrong-headed still was yet another way in which Richard's generation interpreted the Lord's word that we should "take up the cross".[3] They applied those words to the taking up of arms in defence of the holy places of Palestine; and Richard, a famous orator, died in the course of a preaching tour in support of the Crusades. In celebrating his life and death, we cannot turn our eyes from the shadow-side of that life, his immersion in the blind-spots and prejudices of his time. Nor can we overlook the fearful legacy of his time in all the centuries since then. How different might the Middle East be today if western Christendom had not taken up arms against the Muslim world century after century under the banner of the cross of Jesus Christ? How differently might the three great families of Abraham have developed their family life, had the Christian branch of it shown more of the penitent spirit of the younger son, and less of the censorious character of the elder brother?

In spite of the shadows, however, there is still a splendid light that shines from Richard's life. Like Francis, he lived a life of simplicity, generosity, and joy. "Is it just or right in the sight of God", he asked, "that

---

[3]   Mark 8:34.

we should eat and drink from vessels of gold and silver while Christ in his poor is crucified with hunger?"[4] His officials begged him not to be so prodigal; his charity ran the risk of running the diocese of Chichester into debt. Richard was not to be dissuaded. With his poverty came that spirit of joy, without which self-discipline becomes self-righteousness, and generosity turns to condescension. People made a pun out of his name: RICARDUS, they said, stood for *Ridens, Carus,* and *Dulcis*—laughing, dear, and sweet. Even the strait-laced Dominican Ralph Bocking, who feels obliged to say that Richard didn't laugh *heartily,* cannot disguise the fact that the people of Sussex remembered him for his laughter. St Richard echoes something of the infectious joy of St Francis.

The lights and the shadows of Richard's life invite some self-examination on our part. For one thing, we have to ask ourselves, what are the blindspots of *our* time, the things on which future generations will look back and ask with incredulity how we could think, or say, or do this or that, and still call ourselves Christians? And for another thing, we have to ask ourselves what it means for *us* to "take up the cross". If not hairshirts and acts of self-wounding piety, then what? If not taking up the sword in defence of a territorial Christendom, then what? Where in our Christian lives is to be seen what a much later Christian, Dietrich Bonhoeffer, whom we also commemorate this week, called "the *cost* of discipleship"? In the Gospel reading this morning, the Gospel writer shows us Jesus well aware of the cost of his own discipleship: his own living out the Father's will. "Now my soul is troubled. And what should I say—'Father, save me from this hour'? No, it is for this reason that I have come to this hour. Father, glorify your name."

Let me suggest one way—among many others—in which we might understand a contemporary "taking up of the cross", an identifying of ourselves with the living, suffering, and dying of Jesus; and for this we go back to words of St Richard that I have just quoted. "Is it just or right in the sight of God that we should eat and drink from vessels of gold and silver while Christ in his poor is crucified with hunger?" That was St Richard's question to the people of Sussex in his time; and it is a question

---

4   *Saint Richard of Chichester,* p. 181.

that uncomfortably addresses us still. *Christ in his poor*—that is a phrase that takes us straight back to the Lord himself:

> "I was hungry and you gave me no food, I was thirsty and you gave me nothing to drink, I was a stranger and you did not welcome me, naked and you did not give me clothing, sick and in prison and you did not visit me." ["But . . .] Lord, when was it [. . .]?" [. . .] "Just as you did not do it to one of the least of these, you did not do it to me."[5]

We have to find Christ still suffering in the pains of his brothers and sisters and serve him there. We have to ease the cross from his shoulder there. Just as Simon of Cyrene took the cross, lifting it from Christ's shoulders to ease his burden, so Christ bids us take the cross, easing the load on those who suffer, and in whose suffering Christ is still crucified. "Bear one another's burdens", writes St Paul, "and so fulfil the law of Christ."[6] The cross of human pain is not only to be carried, it is to be shared out as well; and our Christian discipleship means taking our share of the burden laid on those in whom Christ suffers.

We are spoilt for choice: the cross of hunger; the cross of Aids; the cross of terror, torture, and repression; the cross of landmines hidden in the earth from some forgotten war; the cross of age-old tribal hatreds handed down from one generation to another, blighting the lives of young people and training them to think of their neighbours as their enemies. There are so many crosses to be lifted from the shoulders of the poor. And we, so many Simons of Cyrene in the crowd, can do so little, so late, to help.

And yet here I am, self-righteous and censorious, making you and me feel vaguely uncomfortable, without that note of laughter and joy that ran through St Richard's life, even when he was being serious. And this takes us back to the Lord as well: "who for [. . .] the joy that was set before him, endured the cross, disregarding its shame, and has taken his

---

5   Matthew 25:42–5.

6   Galatians 6:2 (RSV).

seat at the right hand of the throne of God".[7] That inextricable blend of compassion and happiness, tears and laughter, cross and resurrection, lies at the heart of the life of Jesus; it is the authentic note of all his saints; it certainly characterizes St Richard, the laughing saint of Sussex; and it is the joyful spirit in which we, too, are told to take the Saviour's cross. It will do more for the world's ills than any amount of grim do-goodery. St Richard, like his Lord, knew that there was a joy that lay before him. It did not make him blind to the world's ills; rather, as with all the saints, it alerted him the more to those in need around him. But it was joy that was his motive, and laughter that drove him on; and when that laughing voice was silenced in April 1253, the people of Sussex knew that they had had a saint among them.

"Joy", wrote C. S. Lewis, "is the serious business of heaven."[8] It is to that serious business, that we, with all the saints, are called.

---

[7]   Hebrews 12:2.

[8]   C. S. Lewis, *Letters to Malcolm: Chiefly on Prayer* (London: Geoffrey Bles, 1964), p. 122.

3 0

Lancelot Andrewes[1]

Lancelot Andrewes, who lived through the reigns of Queen Elizabeth I and King James I, was the most distinguished English churchman of his time. He combined qualities of deep personal holiness and formidable intellectual power that shaped and sustained the Church of England at a formative period of its history. A profoundly spiritual man, he spent five hours a day in prayer, and left to posterity a record of his praying in his book of private devotions, the *Preces Privatae*. A gifted liturgist, he made his private chapel a model of ordered and beautiful worship, with vestments, candles, and incense. An effective controversialist, he defended the *via media* of the Church of England. A proficient linguist—15 modern languages as well as the classical ones—he was admirably qualified to direct the making of the greatest translation of the Bible into English—the King James Version of 1611. He was passionately convinced of the need to have the scriptures in what was called the vulgar tongue (the King James Version is a masterpiece: but it is our misfortune to live so far removed in time from it that its English is no longer vulgar). And finally, a master of the spoken word, Andrewes was regularly called on to preach to the Queen, and then to the King; and even James I, who liked to talk noisily during sermons, was quelled to silence. You may think that you have never heard a word of Andrewes's sermons, but if you know the poem by T. S. Eliot called the "Journey of the Magi", then you have, for the opening lines of that poem are a direct quotation from the sermon that Andrewes

---

[1] Sermon preached at mattins in Chichester Cathedral on the Third Sunday before Advent, 6 November 2005, marking the fourth centenary of the consecration of Lancelot Andrewes as bishop of Chichester on 3 November 1605.

preached before the King at Whitehall Palace on Christmas Day 1622: "A cold coming they had of it at this time of the year, just the worst time of the year to take a journey, and specially a long journey in. The ways deep, the weather sharp [. . .] 'the very dead of winter.'"[2]

For all his intimidating presence, Andrewes was not without humour. John Aubrey in his *Brief Lives* tells of a Cambridge alderman who used to fall asleep during sermons, to the great annoyance of his vicar who began to include in every sermon a denunciation of those who fell asleep when he preached. The alderman sought advice from Andrewes who suggested that he eat less before church. The alderman tried, but still fell asleep. Andrewes then suggested that he ate more, and got his sleep over and done with before church. The plan worked: the vicar prepared a terrible denunciation of those who slept in church, and the alderman sat through it wide-eyed. Andrewes was criticized for lacking seriousness: but, as Aubrey says, "he had learning and witt enough to defend himselfe".[3]

Andrewes's life has not escaped criticism in our own day either; a contemporary writer sums him up thus: "scholarly, political, passionate, agonised, in love with the English language, endlessly investigating its possibilities, worldly, saintly, serene, sensuous, courageous, craven, if not corrupt then at least compromised, deeply engaged in pastoral care, generous, loving, in public bewitched by ceremony, in private troubled by persistent guilt and self-abasement".[4] When I read those words, I was struck by the comparison with his predecessor as bishop of Chichester, St Richard; in whose life it is equally difficult to disentangle the virtues and vices of the individual from the corruptions and prejudices of the time.

---

[2]   As quoted in T. S. Eliot, *For Lancelot Andrewes: Essays on Style and Order* (London: Faber and Faber, 1970), pp. 22–3; cf. Eliot's "Journey of the Magi", in *The Complete Poems and Plays of T. S. Eliot* (London: Faber and Faber, 1969), pp. 103–4 at 103.

[3]   '*Brief Lives', Chiefly of Contemporaries, Set Down by John Aubrey, Between the Years 1669 and 1696*, ed. Andrew Clark, vol. 1 (Oxford: Clarendon Press, 1898), p. 30.

[4]   Adam Nicolson, *Power and Glory: Jacobean England and the Making of the King James Bible* (London: HarperCollins, 2003), pp. 26–7.

Lancelot Andrewes was bishop of Chichester for only four years before being moved to Ely, and finally to Winchester. While here, he lost no time in conducting a visitation of this cathedral. During his time here, Andrewes also wrote a fierce riposte to Cardinal Bellarmine, who had attacked King James I in print; a first edition copy of that book is one of a number of Andrewes's works still in the cathedral library. He died on 25 September 1626, and is buried in what is now Southwark Cathedral, in those days a collegiate church that stood next door to the bishop of Winchester's London house.

But it is not his death that we particularly remember today; rather his narrow escape from death on 5 November 1605. Two days earlier, he had been consecrated bishop of Chichester in St Paul's Cathedral, and the event was timed to enable him to take his seat in the House of Lords on 5 November when King James I came to open Parliament. The Gunpowder Plot horrified Andrewes. Each year thereafter, it was Andrewes who was called on to preach before the King on 5 November; each year, he recalled the events and rekindled the outrage that they provoked. And this is suddenly where Andrewes's life spans the centuries, and takes on a contemporary interest. Let's draw a comparison. A minority religious community deprived of both civic and religious freedom, widely suspected of disloyalty to the English crown and in league with foreign powers bent on the destruction of the English state, but in fact composed for the most part of people wanting only to live quietly and sociably and to practise their religion without offence: sounds familiar? The long years of repression and discouragement give birth to a murderous fringe of young zealots, convinced that their religion both sanctions and requires a violent solution: sounds familiar? Murder in the name of God as the quick way to do his will and get to paradise: sounds familiar? The larger peaceable part of the religious minority then convicted by public opinion of what has been done in their name by the militant fringe: sounds familiar.

Many people have pointed out the parallels between the times of the Gunpowder Plot and our own; not least in Edward Kemp's remarkable play, tellingly entitled *5/11*. But not so many people have looked to see what the Church did at that time to shape the opinions of people in response to contemporary terror. And in that, Andrewes had a significant part to play. His, in fact, was the task of articulating a public response to such an appalling attack both on human life and on the institutions of society. His was the task of giving vent to a corporate anger, but at the same time of finding some constructive channel through which it could run. How did he do it?

I had not read Andrewes's Gunpowder Sermons until I came to prepare for this one. I was unsurprised by what I found, but surprised at what I did *not* find. What is in those sermons, year after year, is a reiterated horror at the attempt on innocent life, at the method chosen, at the threat to the peace and order of society, and at the association of all these things with religion. Andrewes lived in a time which had no concept of democracy or political pluralism; the idea of a loyal opposition would seem a contradiction in terms; and Andrewes, it must be said, was one of those who believed that the safety of the commonweal lay solely in the hands of divinely appointed kings. The attempt to destroy all that struck him as not only outrageous but actually sacrilegious.

All of that is passionately expressed in his sermons. But then, I thought, there will be an unpalatable dose of "no popery" in all of this. Andrewes, as I knew, had already engaged in sharp controversy with Roman Catholic antagonists; public opinion was ever ready to burn effigies of the pope (just like the nonsense that still goes on at Lewes today). But that is what is missing from the Gunpowder Sermons. Certainly, he has a go at the Jesuits, and he takes an odd swipe at his old adversary Cardinal Bellarmine. But of persistent, strident anti-popish sentiment there is very little sign. He is, as I have said, horrified at the way in which the Gunpowder Plot was conceived in the name of God: "undertaken with a holy oath", he says, "bound with the holy sacrament [...] a sacramental treason, hallowing it with orison, oath and eucharist; this passeth all the rest".[5] You see the point of his protest: Andrewes is not saying, "That's where that particular religion gets you if you take it to its extreme"; he is saying, "How appalling to take that religion in such a way as to make it justify the very opposite of everything for which it stands."

---

5   Lancelot Andrewes, *A Sermon Preached before the King's Majesty at Whitehall, on the Fifth of November A. D. MDCVI* (Oxford: John Henry Parker, 1841), p. 269.

"Terrorism" has become one of the signs of our times. It is a bad word if we think of it as a single phenomenon, and even worse if we also connect it in our minds with Islamic militancy. There are many terrors, many terrorisms, and many different terrorists in our day; and a good deal of terror is meted out by lawfully constituted governments. But among all these crosscurrents of terror, we are particularly preoccupied at present with Islamic militancy; and as I have already suggested, there are some telling parallels between it and the fanatical fringe of the English Roman Catholic community at the start of the seventeenth century. Public opinion was very ready to lump all Roman Catholics together; even a slightly more sophisticated opinion was ready to claim that there was something about Roman Catholicism which was intrinsically subversive of public peace and order. Such prejudices have not wholly vanished from England, and live on still in Northern Ireland. English Roman Catholics long had to protest their loyalty to England, and endure the humiliation of not quite being believed. But today we see the Muslim community of England undergoing the same humiliation in just the same way: of being painfully compelled to protest their loyalty to their country, being forced to demonstrate the peaceable virtues of Islam; there is a persistent notion about that Islam is intrinsically subversive of public peace and order, and that dreams of a universal caliphate under a tyrannical Sharia law are what Islam is all about.

In his own day, Andrewes could clearly distinguish the substance of a religious tradition—however much on theological grounds he might also disagree with it—from the way in which its more fanatical adherents misrepresented it. And what he preached in public, he prayed in private. Every day, as we know from his posthumously published *Preces Privatae*, he prayed for the Church: and he began not with the Church of England, but with the Church universal. He prayed for the eastern Church and its particular needs. He prayed for what he called the western Church, and here he meant both the Roman Catholic Church and the Churches of the Reformation. He prayed for their peace, their reconciliation, and what he rather delightfully called their "adjustment". And then he prayed for the Church of his own land; knowing that its needs were quite as great as those of any other part of Christendom.

"Bring the families of the nations", we prayed in today's collect, "divided and torn apart by the ravages of sin, to be subject to [Christ's] just and gentle rule."[6] Like Lancelot Andrewes, we must preach what we first pray; and having prayed it, and preached it, then we must practise it: and hope that like Lancelot Andrewes, bishop of Chichester, we may become an instrument of peace in a troubled world.

---

[6]   *Common Worship: Services and Prayers for the Church of England* (London: Church House Publishing, 2000), p. 424.

31

The fearful saint[1]

The season of All Saints and All Souls directs our attention to those of
our brothers and sisters in Jesus Christ who have already made their
journey through this life. All Saints' Day calls to mind those who have
been conspicuous in their Christian witness; All Souls' Day those, a far
greater number, who have not been exceptional Christians, who perhaps
did not even do their best, but who owned the name of Christ and who
now, we hope and pray, rest in his peace. We could choose any one from
a million possibilities for meditation today; and I choose one—for no
other reason than that we sing his hymns (and we shall sing one of them
at the end of this sermon); and his life tells us something of the nature
of Christian discipleship.

William Cowper was a poet whose life spanned the last 70 years of
the eighteenth century.[2] Did we not still sing his hymns, he would I
suppose be rather dimly remembered as a minor poet of the period (his
best-known poem being the comic ballad "John Gilpin") and the author
of some sensitive and witty letters. Four of his hymns make him better
known: "God moves in a mysterious way", "Hark, my soul, it is the Lord",
"O for a closer walk with God", and that which we shall sing in a moment,
"Jesus, where'er thy people meet".

---

[1]   Sermon preached at mattins in Chichester Cathedral on the Fourth Sunday
      before Advent, 3 November 2002. The readings were Isaiah 66:20-3;
      Ephesians 1:11-23.

[2]   See Lord David Cecil's *The Stricken Deer or The Life of Cowper* (London:
      Constable & Co., 1929). Cowper's surname is pronounced "Cooper".

Each of them expresses a deep sense of personal trust in God. Listen to these words that he puts into the mouth of God, paraphrased from the prophet Isaiah:

> Can a woman's tender care
> cease towards the child she bare?
> Yes, she may forgetful be,
> yet will I remember thee.
>
> Mine is an unchanging love,
> higher than the heights above,
> deeper than the depths beneath,
> free and faithful, strong as death.[3]

Or again:

> So shall my walk be close with God,
> calm and serene my frame;
> so purer light shall mark the road
> that leads me to the Lamb.[4]

Yet the reality of Cowper's life was sadly different from what these words suggest. From early adulthood to the end of his life he suffered deep depression, which from time to time drove him insane. And his religion was as much the cause as the cure of his condition.

Cowper's faith was that of an eighteenth-century evangelical. The evangelical movement was a necessary reaction to much that was dry and heartless in the English religion of the time. It brought fervour and feeling and personal conviction ("enthusiasm" it was called) back into Christianity; it broke down the social barriers in which the established Church had acquiesced, and in the person of John Wesley it spoke to

---

[3] "Hark, my soul, it is the Lord", *Ancient & Modern: Hymns and Songs for Refreshing Worship* (London: Hymns Ancient & Modern, 2013), no. 654; Isaiah 49:15.

[4] "O for a closer walk with God", *Ancient & Modern*, no. 131.

the farm labourers and coal miners and factory workers of England in a voice that they had not heard before. Later, it broke down other barriers too, and William Wilberforce and others went on to campaign effectively against the slave trade. In the hymns of Charles Wesley and John Newton and Isaac Watts and William Cowper, we have a body of hymns which neither the nineteenth nor the twentieth century can match.

But it was a type of religion that carried within itself the seeds of its own corruption. When, as in Cowper's case, it was connected to the theology of John Calvin, in which the doctrine of predestination was paramount, eighteenth-century evangelicalism insisted that the "saved" would feel within themselves the assurance of salvation. For those whose hearts were strong, this was a message of hope. But those whose hearts were frail, those who suffered from a disordered emotional life, might not feel this assurance. William Cowper did not always feel this assurance. At times he did and at times he didn't. But for those who didn't feel the assurance of salvation, and yet continued to believe a Calvinist theology, there were dreadful conclusions to be drawn. No feeling, no assurance; no assurance, no salvation; no salvation, then nothing left but to be lost for ever. As Cowper's sad life wore on, the conviction that he was eternally lost to God took increasing hold upon him. He never lost his belief in God, as a modern person would probably do: that was not his sense of loss. He continued to believe that God existed, and was just, and holy, and good; but that he himself was not among God's elect.

There were periods of his life in which the darkness lifted. His faith in God came out, as it were, into the daylight; and his exquisite hymns were the fruit of that. Sometimes he lived in the half-light, with a sense of darkness not far away: we have more than a hint of that in his most famous hymn:

> God moves in a mysterious way
> his wonders to perform;
> he plants his footsteps in the sea,
> and rides upon the storm.

Ye fearful saints, fresh courage take;
the clouds ye so much dread
are big with mercy, and shall break
in blessings on your head.

His purposes will ripen fast,
unfolding every hour;
the bud may have a bitter taste,
but sweet will be the flower.[5]

Yet it was often not so for Cowper: the clouds did not break with mercy,
the bitter taste in the bud remained. Once, he overheard an old man
singing one of his own hymns as he went about his work:

O for a closer walk with God,
a calm and heavenly frame;
a light to shine upon the road
that leads me to the Lamb![6]

As he heard the words, he remembered with anguish the moment of faith
and hope in which he had written them; they gave hope to the old man,
but to Cowper they could no longer give hope. The darkness came to
him more and more frequently, and it seems that Cowper died without
finding the daylight again.

I find the story of William Cowper not only immensely sad, but also
significant. One lesson for us to learn is a truer relationship of faith and
feeling. There are, for most Christians, periods of our lives when our
feelings and our faith do not match. There are, in the old terminology
of the spiritual life, periods of dryness. There are times of doubt. There
is, so those furthest advanced in the life of prayer have told us, the dark
night of the soul. Only those who lose their lives for Christ's sake will
find them, so Christ tells us; and there is, for all of us, sooner or later, an

---

[5]   "God moves in a mysterious way", *Ancient & Modern*, no. 647.

[6]   "O for a closer walk with God".

unmaking to be done as we come closer to God.[7] Death is that unmaking
for all of us; but for all of us too, in different ways, there is an unmaking to
be done *before* death. It may be the decline of physical or mental health.
It may be the bereavement of family and friends. It may be the loss of
work, security, role, or the esteem of others. It may be the disappearance
of old certainties. A true Christian faith embraces such unmaking, such
purgation, as our necessary preparation for meeting God. It is the sign
of grace and hope and eventual resurrection. Had Cowper's faith been
rooted in a more generous and humane theology, he and his friends
might have seen his depressions and his lack of religious feelings in this
light. We cannot say that he would not have been depressed; but we *can*
say that his religion would not have reinforced his depression by telling
him that his lack of feelings meant that he was lost to God.

William Cowper has long since met his maker; long since entered into
the joyful realization that, if our hearts condemn us, God is greater than
our hearts.[8] What this fearful saint has left behind him are his hymns;
hymns of faith and serenity and hope: made all the more precious by the
doubt and sorrow that went into their making. Here are words that still,
three centuries on, help us to

> [. . .] prove the power of prayer,
> to strengthen faith and sweeten care,
> to teach our faint desires to rise,
> and bring all heaven before our eyes.[9]

---

7   Matthew 10:39; 16:25.

8   1 John 3:20.

9   "Jesus, where'er thy people meet", *Ancient & Modern*, no. 696.

David Melville[1]

I am very glad to have the opportunity to take part in the commemoration of your founder. My connection with the commemoration is that when David Melville left Durham in 1851, he moved to a parish in Worcestershire, and subsequently to the post of canon and sub-dean of Worcester Cathedral, and on his death in 1904 was buried in the cathedral cloister garth. I'm afraid I knew nothing of this until the Hatfield College Choir came to sing in Worcester last summer, and we visited Melville's grave.

As we all know, this visionary and innovative educationalist, with a passion for broadening social access to higher education, was more or less forced out of the post of master of his newly-founded "Hatfield Hall" by reactionary diocesan forces embodied in the person of the archdeacon of Durham. Writing to me recently, your present master remarked that Durham's loss was no doubt Worcester's gain. But I'm not sure about that. Melville evidently did bring much to Worcester. He was an active and conscientious parish priest, in the best energetic Victorian style. At Worcester Cathedral, he was known as a vigorous preacher and a brilliant conversationalist. He continued to campaign on the educational issues close to his heart, lobbying Gladstone among others, and helping to create the unaristocratic ethos of the new Keble College in Oxford. But I doubt that any of these opportunities gave him the platform for achieving as much by way of educational reform that would have been his, had he been allowed to remain at this college and to develop it. Durham's loss was probably everyone's loss; which makes it all the more right,

---

[1] Sermon at evensong in Hatfield College, Durham, on Friday, 29 January 2010, to commemorate the life of David Melville, first master of the college.

and all the more moving, for him to be commemorated tonight in this college—now come of age and grown up out of all recognition from the small theological society that he founded, but still bearing witness to his ideal of bringing the benefits of higher education within reach of many.

From a Christian point of view (and the life of this chapel bears witness to Melville's conviction that Christian faith and enlightened educational practice belong together), the story of David Melville prompts us to reflect on lives that are in some way or other unfinished, cut short, or do not achieve their full potential.

Physically, his life was not cut short; he lived to the age of 91, retiring only two years before his death. And it would be impertinent to say that his life, enriched by the evident affection of family and friends, was "unfinished", or in any sense a failure. But if I am right in my suspicion that he was denied the circumstances that would have enabled him to achieve yet more in the field of educational reform, how as Christians do we think about that loss: that loss of potential, that loss of achievement, that loss which was not only Durham's but everyone's? And is there something to learn about that kind of loss that sheds some light on the incompleteness of our own lives: of missed achievements, lost opportunities, disappointed hopes, frustrated ambitions?

At the heart of the Christian faith, there is a human story—a divine story but also a human story—of one whose life was most definitely cut short. The cross, the central Christian symbol, proclaims it. This person, whom Christians believe to have embodied a whole and perfect humanity, died prematurely and in apparent failure, with the hopes of his followers dashed and frustrated. And although the story goes on to tell of resurrection, we must not get there too quickly, as though the cross were a temporary setback or a minor diversion. The Christian faith feels the full weight of the real death of Jesus; and the resurrection speaks of the way in which God was able, not just to reverse the crucifixion, but to transcend it, to transform it, to give it meaning.

Here, then, is a pattern. The crucifixion of God is the worst that the world can do to God. The resurrection is the best that God can make of that worst. Within that pattern, there is room for the innumerable patterns of our own lives: all our losses, our failures, our setbacks, our disappointments; and then our successes, too, our triumphs and achievements. All are accommodated within that "worst" and that "best" which Christian faith ascribes to the death and resurrection of Jesus. However disastrous our lives may seem at times, they are never so disastrous as to be beyond the reach of the crucified Christ; just as the beauty and glory of life at its best reflects something of the risen Lord. And the creative God, who brought resurrection out of the shattered pieces of Christ's crucified life, can also bring resurrection out of the shattered fragments of our lives too.

David Melville was, it seems to me, a gracious man. That is to say, he did not let what must have been the shattering blow of his departure from Durham destroy his life. He did what he could with such opportunities as were left to him. He allowed the grace of God to work in his life, transcending frustration and disappointment. He put his Durham experience to good use and continued to campaign for better education for a greater number. And that must have demanded an enormous generosity, humility, a sense of humour, a sense of forgiveness; so maybe he became the better man because of it.

I must not turn him into a plaster saint. We read that when he was called to give evidence to the Royal Commission of 1862 that investigated the state of this university, he took the opportunity to denounce the archdeacon of Durham, whose immediate retirement was the first recommendation of the Commission. Perhaps he enjoyed his moment of retribution; at any rate, we can enjoy it for him. But then, when he returned late in life to receive an honorary doctorate of divinity, he spoke generously of those who had opposed him so many years before. That is the mark of a life in which the grace of God has begun to transcend all sense of grievance or frustration.

And our best response to that is gratitude: gratitude for that triumph over defeat and disappointment; gratitude for all that David Melville achieved in his few years as the first master of Hatfield Hall; gratitude for the men and women down the years since then who took his small beginnings and made of them something great—made this college, which is the real and lasting tribute to its founder.

"In my end is my beginning"[1]

"In my end is my beginning," wrote T. S. Eliot.[2] As we offer this mass in thanksgiving for the life and work of Chichester Theological College, and do so, perhaps in this particular way for the last time, it is good that we have returned to this chapel, which at various times in the history of the college served as the place of collegiate worship. Here, also, successive bishops upheld the college in their own prayers: William Otter, instrumental in its foundation; George Bell, who re-established it after the war under the principalship of John Moorman; Eric Kemp, so firm a defender of the college and all for which it stood. We may say that much of the life of the college was sustained here. For a while, the college was known as St Richard's College; and we are deeply mindful of being here where Richard prayed. For much of its history, the college unashamedly expressed a love for Our Lady, the angelus bell sounding across the meadows; and here is the lovely roundel of Virgin and Child, which Richard knew, and which no doubt inspired the words of his particular prayer to her.[3] So we may say: "In my end is my beginning." Here the story of Chichester Theological College comes home.

---

1   Sermon preached at a eucharist in the Bishop's Chapel at Chichester on Thursday, 18 June 2009 for former members of Chichester Theological College.

2   T. S. Eliot, "East Coker", in *Four Quartets* (*The Complete Poems and Plays of T. S. Eliot* [London: Faber and Faber, 1969], pp. 177–83 at 183).

3   "Mary, Mother of grace, Mother of mercy, protect us from the enemy now and pray for us at the hour of our death" (*Saint Richard of Chichester: The Sources for His Life*, ed. David Jones [Lewes: Sussex Record Society, 1995], p. 213).

If there is one figure in my mind today, as well as all these other luminaries ancient and modern, it is that of our first principal, Charles Marriott. Nothing gives me greater honour than that my name comes at the bottom of a list of which his name is at the top. Of the "twelve good men" whose short lives were written by Dean Burgon, whereas others were given titles such as "The Learned Divine", "The Restorer of Ancient Paths", and even "The Single-Minded Bishop", Marriott's life is entitled simply "The Man of Saintly Life".[4]

Burgon's treatment of Marriott is interesting. He described his significant contribution to the Oxford Movement, his wonderful influence in the university after Newman; but then he confessed that the story showed much promise unfulfilled. There was, for instance, no major work of scholarship. His life was cut short at 47, after years of ill-health. As Burgon said, "It is impossible to lay down the story of such a life [. . .] without something akin to disappointment."[5] But he went on to draw a distinction between his "works", which were relatively insubstantial, and his "work" which was of a different order altogether. And his "work" was to be a man of saintly life. "He lives at this day", said Burgon, "he will go on living, in the good lives of others." And so he introduced the comment which has become famous: "'If I have any good in me', (remarked Edward King, Bishop of Lincoln) 'I owe it to Charles Marriott.'"[6] Of course, it is the mark of a saint, such as Edward King was, to attribute his virtues to another; but it is also the mark of the saint not to make a misattribution in such a matter. We may take it that this "man of saintly life" did inspire sanctity in others; and besides that, no other works or achievements need count for very much.

As with the founding principal, so with the college which he helped to found. We may continue to feel disappointment over its premature dissolution; we may regret that there were not more "works" (in the plural) recorded in its honour; but its "work", at its best, was of a different order. Its "work" was to touch lives and to nourish them in holiness. Being

---

[4] John W. Burgon, *Lives of Twelve Good Men*, vol. 1 (London: John Murray, 1889), pp. 296–373.

[5] Burgon, *Lives of Twelve Good Men*, p. 370.

[6] Burgon, *Lives of Twelve Good Men*, p. 372.

an institution, run by human beings, it often failed; and sometimes it touched lives unfruitfully and even damagingly. At its best, it made good priests out of many of its students, and they in turn helped to nourish good Christians. And so the college lives today, and it will go on living, as Burgon said of Marriott, "in the good lives of others".

Chichester Theological College was born of that profound sense, which fed and was fed by the Tractarian movement, of the one, holy, catholic, and apostolic Church. If Charles Marriott had been allowed to peer down the years, two particular moments might have caught his eye: two moments when that Tractarian vision of the Church shone with peculiar splendour. One moment occurred in 1955, when Bishop George Bell, saddened by the non-participation of the Roman Catholic Church in the World Council of Churches, went to find someone who might foster an Anglican / Roman Catholic ecumenical conversation. He was recommended to the new archbishop of Milan, Giovanni Battista Montini (later Pope Paul VI); and his visit was built upon by John Moorman and others from this college, forging personal friendships with Montini which paved the way for the presence of ecumenical observers at the Second Vatican Council, the establishment of the Anglican Roman Catholic International Commission, and the foundation of the Anglican Centre in Rome.[7]

The other "moment" which would have gladdened the heart of Charles Marriott was that day in July 1942 when Vivian Redlich willingly exposed himself to arrest and death, rather than desert his congregation in Papua New Guinea at the time of the Japanese invasion. Although recently gathered testimony has revised the picture so memorably told year by year in the college "martyrology"—it seems that he may well have been murdered not by the Japanese but by Papua New Guineans eager to ingratiate themselves with the victorious side[8]—the price that

---

[7]   I treasure the memory of my own one meeting with John Moorman, in Rome, on the eve of the election of Pope John Paul II in October 1978.

[8]   See the memoir of Archbishop David Hand, *Modawa: Papua New Guinea and Me 1946-2002* (Port Moresby: privately published, 2002), p. 188: "Fr Vivian Redlich and Fr Henry Holland were not beheaded by Japanese soldiers on Buna Beach (as were other martyrs) but murdered by Orokaivans

Redlich paid for his faithfulness remains the same. An ordinary and rather unmemorable student of the college so absorbed the lessons learnt here—lessons of faithfulness, obedience, self-forgetfulness, discipline, all rooted in that Tractarian vision of the holiness of the Church—that when the time of trial arrived, he did not fail.

"In my end is my beginning", wrote Eliot in the concluding line of "East Coker". But he began the poem by reversing the line: "In my beginning is my end"; and he went on to describe how

> In succession
> Houses rise and fall, crumble, are extended,
> Are removed, destroyed, restored [...]
> Old stone to new building, old timber to new fires,
> Old fires to ashes, and ashes to the earth [...]
> Houses live and die:[9]

Most institutions have a limited lifespan, and their end is implicit in their beginning. The valuable institutions are not necessarily the ones that survive, but the ones that contribute "old stones" to "new building". In this place where, in Eliot's words again, "prayer has been valid",[10] we give thanks not just for the old stones of Chichester Theological College, but for the new building, to which in a whole variety of ways they have been put; not just for old timber, but for the new fires which they have lit and fed; not just for past lives, but for past lives that live, and will go on living, in the good lives of others.

---

to whom they had come to offer the Christian faith and teaching." He adds: "The full story must wait to be revealed to the public."

9   "East Coker", p. 177.
10   "Little Gidding", in *Four Quartets* (*Complete Poems and Plays*, pp. 191–8 at 192).

3 4

A saint in the making[1]

Forty years ago, as a young man, I came into this church. I didn't know anyone here, and I had only the vaguest conception of the liturgy that was unfolding in front of me. But what spoke to me, as it has spoken to so many thousands of others, was this building; and I remember that as a significant moment in my personal pilgrimage. And although this is not the first time that I have preached here, it is an immense privilege for me to help you mark the completion of the latest phase of the internal restoration of this church, which first spoke to me so many years ago. I do so with a sense of discharging a forty-year-old debt of gratitude. And what a splendid way to celebrate the season of All Saints, reconnecting with the figures of the saints and angels who crowd the sanctuary, surrounded (as the epistle to the Hebrews puts it) by so great a cloud of witnesses.[2]

Two years ago, the archbishop of Canterbury preached to you here and spoke of the "need to tell the stories of the Saints to remind ourselves what is possible within any Christian family". And, he went on, "within our Anglican family we need to go on telling a few stories about those who have shown us that it is possible to lead lives of Catholic holiness even in the Communion of the See of Canterbury!"[3] I should like to speak to you this morning about someone who himself spoke about holiness,

---

[1] Sermon preached at the patronal festival eucharist at All Saints', Margaret Street, London, on Sunday, 6 November 2011. The readings were 2 Esdras 2:42–8; Hebrews 12:18–24; Matthew 5:1–12.

[2] Hebrews 12:1.

[3] <http://rowanwilliams.archbishopofcanterbury.org/articles.php/856/ archbishops-sermon-at-all-saints-margaret-street-london.html>, accessed 10 January 2023.

and also practised it; someone, indeed, who preached from this pulpit: Edward King, bishop of Lincoln, who died 101 years ago—not quite a contemporary; not even someone within living memory; but someone at any rate with whom we shared the twentieth century from either end.[4]

Edward King has come as close to being formally enrolled among the saints as is possible in a Church which lacks a formal canonization system. What was so remarkable about him? Evidently he was possessed of a character and a personality that irradiated goodness, compassion, integrity, charity—indeed all the Christian virtues. He agreed with his fellow Tractarian, Henry Liddon, that "light-heartedness is at once the right and the duty of a redeemed Christian whose conscience is in fairly good order",[5] and he exemplified that redeemed light-heartedness in his own life. Light-heartedness—and light: Henry Scott Holland, a friend for many years and, like King, a professor at Oxford, wrote of him that

> it was light he carried with him—light that shone through him—
> light that flowed from him [...] He was alive with a spirit of
> good cheer which years could not damp, nor infirmities becloud.
> He thought better and better of the world every year that he
> lived. It was impossible to depress him. He loved everybody and
> everything.[6]

So, apart from everybody, whom did he love? He loved his friends— and they were many. He loved his parishioners—in a tiny Oxfordshire village. He was still corresponding with some of the farm labourers, for whom he had established a night school, half a century later. He loved his ordinands—he was principal of the newly-established Cuddesdon Theological College. It was a love not without challenge. "We were most

---

[4]   The latest biography is by Michael E. Marshall, who was vicar of All Saints', Margaret Street, when I visited all those years ago: *Edward King: Teacher, Pastor, Bishop, Saint* (Leominster: Gracewing, 2021).

[5]   George W. E. Russell, *Edward King, Sixtieth Bishop of Lincoln: A Memoir* (London: Smith, Elder & Co., 1912), p. 111.

[6]   H. Scott Holland, *A Bundle of Memories* (London: Wells Gardner, Darton & Co., 1915), pp. 48–50.

tenderly, yet most unflinchingly, compelled to place our lives before God", recalled one of his students.[7] There is the authentic note of holiness: the quality of the numinous, inspiring awe as well as love, fearful as well as attractive.

In 1885, Gladstone appointed Edward King bishop of Lincoln; but there were misgivings on the bench of bishops. King was thought to be disorganized, no kind of administrator. Worse still, he was considered untidy, and the bishop of Newcastle sent him the address of a decent tailor. But those who knew him well believed that a remarkable episcopate was about to begin. "It shall be a Bishopric of Love," wrote Scott Holland ecstatically; and so it was.[8] Stories abound of his pastoral solicitude, his encouragement of hard-pressed and worn-out parish priests, the endless trouble that he took with individuals. When a young Grimsby fisherman was condemned to hang for murder, it was King who visited the boy, confirmed him, signed an unsuccessful petition for the commutation of his sentence, and stood with him at the end upon the scaffold. A firm Anglo-Catholic, the first Anglican bishop to wear a mitre since the Reformation, he won the hearts of the people of Protestant Lincolnshire. "Nowt but an old Methody," said a Wesleyan. "It might ha' been 'the General' himself!" exclaimed a Salvationist. "Saintliness and shrewdness were equally characteristic of him," was the comment of one Lincoln dignitary; "he was, in the best and highest sense, a man of the world, without an atom of worldliness."[9]

Edward King thought about holiness—not his own, which he would not have noticed; but the *idea* of holiness, and the idea of becoming holy. The reconnection of the sacramental life of the Church to the idea of personal holiness is one of Anglo-Catholicism's great gifts to the Church of England, and King taught that as well as practised it. He was in no doubt whatever that the means of grace—scripture and sacrament, prayer and fasting and almsgiving, meditation and confession—were exactly

---

[7]   Quoted in J. Richard C. Symonds, *Alternative Saints: The Post-Reformation British People Commemorated by the Church of England* (Basingstoke: Macmillan Press, 1988), p. 221.

[8]   Russell, *Edward King*, p. 90.

[9]   Russell, *Edward King*, p. 113.

that: the means of *grace,* the methods by which God nourishes the Christian soul in sanctity.

But he was fearful of religiosity taken as a short-cut to authentic holiness. When principal of Cuddesdon, it was reported to him that one earnest young student had eaten nothing for the whole of Holy Week. On Good Friday, the student received a note from Edward King: "Dearest man, eat breakfast and come down to the lower level of yours, E. K."[10] He had the same gift as St Philip Neri of gently deflating ridiculous expressions of religion.

"I do value so highly", he wrote to one of his correspondents, "a natural growth in holiness, a humble, grateful acceptance of the circumstances God has provided for each of us, and I dread the unnatural, forced, cramped ecclesiastical holiness, which is so much more quickly produced, but is so human and poor." Again, "Go gradually, and as far as possible, naturally, taking the circumstances God gives you, and trying to serve Him in them."[11] Having said that, however, King was quite clear that the Christian life is the business of becoming holy, and that is not to be left to chance. He was quite prepared to use the startling image of "machinery" to make the point. "We know the machinery now for Saint-making, and we have got the *stuff,* only we must work and make them." But what *is* that "machinery"? "I want to see English Saints made in the old way", he went on, "by suffering and labour and diligence in little things, and the exercise of unselfish, untiring love; quiet lives lived away in holes and corners and not known to the public while alive."[12] That is exactly the "little way" of his contemporary St Thérèse of Lisieux, though I do not think that they can have known anything of each other.

So there, in summary, is the story of Edward King, English saint of the twentieth century. Edward King's "life of Catholic holiness within our Anglican family" is neither the first nor the last to have been so lived; but the significance of it lies in the coherence of his teaching about holiness, and the unconscious practice of it himself.

---

[10] W. Owen Chadwick, *The Founding of Cuddesdon* (Oxford: Oxford University Press, 1954), p. 115 n. 1.

[11] Chadwick, *Founding of Cuddesdon,* p. 115.

[12] Russell, *Edward King,* p. 48 (original emphasis).

Sometimes we talk of the saints as exemplars of what is impossible for the rest of us. "We feebly struggle, they in glory shine" indeed;[13] but that must not be the last word on the subject. The holiness of the saints beckons us towards them, urges us to practise lives of holiness ourselves; as Edward King said, "we have got the stuff for saint-making, only we must work and make them". So this All Saintstide is not just a celebration of those who are holy; it is a call to become holy ourselves. It is a call to be renewed in prayer, in reading the scriptures, in devotion to the eucharist, in the use of solitude and silence, in that simplifying of our bodily life that we call fasting, in that unstinting generosity to others that we call almsgiving. It is a call to practise the beatitudes: to be poor in spirit, to be merciful, to be pure in heart, to be peacemakers, to hunger and thirst after righteousness. As we marvel at the sight of the blessed, gathered around the altar of this church, we are looking, not at other people's calling, but at our own.

---

[13]   William Walsham How, "For all the saints who from their labours rest", *Ancient & Modern: Hymns and Songs for Refreshing Worship* (London: Hymns Ancient & Modern, 2013), no. 296.

3 5

"In thy light shall we see light"[1]

Light is an image frequently used in education. A person who is educated and liberally minded is described as "enlightened". The age of critical scholarship, scientific discovery, and rational philosophy was called the "Enlightenment". We speak of "shedding light" on a matter when we seek to teach, to explain, to inform. The image of light is almost always a positive one; and it always speaks to us of the improvement, the enlargement, the enhancement of our lives. It is therefore not surprising that in seeking an appropriate phrase for her tombstone, the friends and relatives of Alice Ottley chose a quotation to do with light. But Alice Ottley, and her collaborator, William Butler, believed not only in education, but in *Christian* education. It was an avowedly Christian school for girls which they founded.

A word in passing about William Butler. He was part of the Oxford or Tractarian movement in the middle years of the nineteenth century, that movement which sought to renew the Church of England in its

---

[1]   Sermon preached at evensong in Worcester Cathedral on Sunday, 23 September 2012, commemorating the centenary of the death of Alice Ottley on 18 September 1912. In 1883, together with William Butler, canon of Worcester, she founded a school for girls in the city. For 124 years, the school, eventually named after its founder, played a significant part in the educational and spiritual life of Worcester. In 2007, the Alice Ottley School merged with its neighbour, the Royal Grammar School, and the school continues to cherish the legacy of Alice Ottley. Her tombstone in Astwood Cemetery in Worcester carries the inscription "In thy light shall we see light": words from Psalm 36 (BCP), preceded in that psalm by the words, "For with thee is the well of life."

faith, its worship, its learning, its love of beauty, its sense of history, and its awareness of being, not an insular "state" Church, but part of the great tradition of Catholic Christianity down the ages. These principles William Butler put into practice during a long incumbency of the parish of Wantage in Oxfordshire; from Wantage he came to Worcester in 1880, where he spent five years as a residentiary canon; in 1885 he went to be dean of Lincoln, dying nine years later. In their shared passion for education, William Butler and Alice Ottley were kindred spirits. In Wantage, he founded the Convent of St Mary the Virgin, and through it the famous St Mary's School, which, like Alice Ottley School, merged with a neighbouring school as recently as 2007. Like Alice Ottley, William Butler believed in the "light" which education brings.

But for them both, as I say, true education meant *Christian* education; and that was a contentious matter then, as it remains today. In fact, for the whole of Christian history, Christians have occupied different places between two poles in their attitude to learning. On the one hand, there has been a suspicion of any learning, or any culture, which is not explicitly rooted in the Bible. This has made for narrowness, intolerance, and a general denial of the good things of this world. As long ago as the third century, the Christian teacher Tertullian was demanding to know what "Athens had to do with Jerusalem", by which he meant that Christians, whose faith was symbolized by Jerusalem, had no business with the classical culture represented by Athens.[2] But at the same time, there were others, equally influential, such as Clement of Alexandria, who saw all knowledge, all learning, all quest for truth, as an aspect of our search for God, and who thought of Plato as foreshadowing Christ, just as Moses foreshadows Christ.[3] And Tertullian and Clement have both had their followers in every Christian century since then.

---

[2]   *De Praescriptione Haereticorum* (7), in *Tertullian on the Testimony of the Soul and on the 'Prescription' of Heretics*, tr. T. Herbert Bindley (London: SPCK, 1914), p. 45.

[3]   *Stromata* (1.5), in *The Writings of Clement of Alexandria: Volume 1*, tr. William L. Wilson, Ante-Nicene Christian Library 4 (Edinburgh: T&T Clark, 1867), p. 366.

Alice Ottley and William Butler were inheritors of the tradition of generous appreciation of learning and culture. For them, there was no contradiction between the light that we seek through science, through art, through learning of every kind, and the Light which is God himself. They knew the words of Psalm 36, verse 9: "For with thee is the well of life; and in thy light shall we see light." While their school curriculum would no doubt today strike us as limited, it was nonetheless founded on a belief that a Christian needs an informed and an enlarged mind if he or she is to serve their creator to the best of their ability. It is not surprising to find that Alice Ottley belonged to those thoughtful Christian circles who were *not* scandalized or scared by the theories propounded by Charles Darwin, and who saw no contradiction between evolving species and a creative intention.

Tragically, these unnecessary controversies have not yet faded from the scene. The Church of England, through its diocesan schools, and also through such independent schools as cherish their Christian foundations, must continue to stand for a form of education which is unafraid to explore, unafraid to question, unafraid to embrace new insights, confident that all the light that we find in following such paths is ultimately subsumed into the Light which is God himself. "For with thee is the well of life; and in thy light shall we see light." And for those who embrace that generous vision of Christian education, the name of Alice Ottley will continue to be a beacon of light.

July 1914[1]

The last week of July 1914 was an eventful one for a young man called Herbert Cox. His wife Janet was expecting their first child. At the same time, two of Herbert's sisters were travelling on the continent with their father Job. They were marking Job's retirement from the post of superintendent engineer of the Parks Department of Birmingham City Council, whose parks are to this day adorned by the bandstands which Job Cox designed. Letters home from Job and his daughters during that month of July gave no sign of the gathering clouds, more evident to those reading the morning papers in England than to those reading the same papers two days later in Lausanne. Moreover, Job, having pre-booked the entire holiday through Mr Lunn's travel agency, was known to be travelling without any cash. In the event, after many adventures and much changing of trains, several days after war had been declared, Job and his daughters found their way home to Selly Park. In the meantime, on 27 July, the very last day of that pre-war epoch before the continent of Europe descended into war, Janet Cox was safely delivered of a daughter. I tell this story because Job Cox was my great-grandfather, Herbert and Janet Cox my grandparents, and the child born on that last day of peace in Europe was my mother. Tomorrow would have been her hundredth birthday.[2]

---

[1] Sermon preached at the opening service of the Three Choirs Festival in Worcester Cathedral on Saturday, 26 July 2014 (the feast of Anne and Joachim, parents of the Blessed Virgin Mary). The readings were Isaiah 49:13–19; Philippians 4:4–9.

[2] Extraordinarily, my predecessor as dean of Worcester at the time, William Moore Ede, was also in Switzerland on the day that war broke out, ironically attending a peace conference.

But I tell the story for other reasons as well. First, it reminds us that the events whose centenary we mark at this time were not so long ago: in the span of my family, a generation and a half. This is still our world and our time. Second, it reminds us how vast upheavals in history can take us unawares. There were just 37 days from the assassination in Sarajevo to Great Britain's declaration of war, and no one foresaw that the one would lead to the other: less time than it took a Birmingham widower and his unmarried daughters to take a trip to the Swiss lakes. And third, it also reminds us that when vast historical upheavals do happen, life still goes on: domestic arrangements have to be made, children are born, signs of new life and new hope recur, small hints of peace keep breaking out.

The occurrence of this Three Choirs Festival with the centenary of the First World War inevitably means that the programme of words and music over the next few days reflects a Great War theme. Music and war are old companions; music has stirred the courage of those going into battle, accompanied the triumph of victory, lifted the spirits of those facing defeat, and given voice to the grief of those who mourn. We shall hear all of that this week, whether it be the weaving of Wilfred Owen's poems into the mass of the dead in Britten's *War Requiem*, Walton's soundtrack for the film *Henry V*, the music of the Royal Marines Band, Elgar's setting of Laurence Binyon's poem "For the Fallen", or the festival commission of the setting of lines by Edward Thomas and others by the German composer Torsten Rasch.

The mention of the festival commission reminds us that the purpose of the First World War centenary is not to stoke the fires of ancient hostility, but rather to seek a language for reconciliation and friendship; and that, too, is a gift that the arts can give us. This cathedral enjoys a friendship with the cathedral of Magdeburg in central Germany; and our good friend Bishop Ilse Junkermann of Magdeburg, in sending us her greetings today, describes the war memorial housed in her cathedral. It is a sculpture made in the 1920s by the expressionist artist Ernst Barlach. He was commissioned to make something to salute those who died for God, Kaiser, and Fatherland. But he made something that spoke rather of the futility and waste of war. In the 1930s, it fell under Nazi disapproval and was taken away; in the 1950s, it was returned, and in the 1980s, it became the place where prayers were offered for those who struggled under the disintegrating communist regime of East Germany. In such a way does art become a focus for reflection, a room for hopes and dreams, and a call to action. As Wilfred Owen famously wrote: "My subject is war and the pity of war. The poetry is in the pity [. . .] These elegies are [. . .] in no sense consolatory. All a poet can do today is to warn."[3] The medium may be poetry or sculpture or drama or music; but the art is there to disturb and to warn. It is in that spirit that we commemorate in words and music the outbreak of the war that was supposed to end war, but has brought us, a century on, to the conflicts of Ukraine, Syria, Iraq, Gaza, and so much more. We find ourselves still upon the darkling plain of Matthew Arnold's poem:

> Swept with confused alarms of struggle and flight,
> Where ignorant armies clash by night.[4]

And we must ask ourselves how many of the wars of the present time are perpetuating ancient hostilities which the Great War did nothing to resolve.

Well, a solemn reflection; and if I ended there, it would signal a sad week, we wouldn't quite be capturing the spirit of a festival, and the beer tent would stand empty. My opening story, however, told how, under the gathering clouds of war, my great-grandfather snatched a holiday in Switzerland after a career of building bandstands; and then lifted a glass to toast my mother's birthday. Jollity and *joie de vivre* and determination to survive are part of the human response to dreadful events; and the humour of the trenches and the air raid shelters is also what we must remember. "They gave me this name like their nature, /" wrote Woodbine

---

3   Quoted by Jon H. Stallworthy, *Wilfred Owen* (Oxford: Oxford University Press, 1977), p. 266. The lines occur in the draft of a preface to a collection of poems which Owen was planning in the summer of 1918, and are described by Stallworthy as "perhaps the most famous literary manifesto of the twentieth century". Owen was killed at the front on 4 November 1918, seven days before the armistice.

4   "Dover Beach", in Matthew Arnold, *Poetical Works* (London: Oxford University Press, 1950), pp. 210–12 at 212.

Willie, Geoffrey Studdert Kennedy of Worcester, "Compacted of laughter and tears, / A sweet that was born of the bitter, / A joke that was torn from the years."[5] The prophet Isaiah in the first reading this morning painted a picture of places made waste by war, but bade the skies sing for joy and the mountains break out into music, because one day God would bring comfort to his people. The apostle Paul in the second reading told his readers to rejoice, for the God of peace would be with them, and urged them to contemplate beautiful things; Paul wrote most likely from a prison cell from which he went to his death. And the poet Matthew Arnold, uncannily capturing the atmosphere of the summer of 1914 though he wrote half a century before, recalls his companion in the poem to the virtues of personal affection and fidelity.

There is a balance to be captured here: between turning a blind eye to the horror of the world on the one hand, and being so absorbed in the horror that we overlook the small signs of ordinary life, the songs, the jokes, the gestures of friendship, and the irrepressibility of the natural world, which enable us to carry on being human. The arts, I think, are one way in which we discover the balance between the two. We find the balance struck, for instance, in Sebastian Faulks's novel of the Great War, *Birdsong*. We find it in Edward Thomas's exquisite poem located not far away in Adlestrop, published in 1917 but dated back to the summer of 1914, in which, again, birdsong is made the supreme metaphor of faith and hope. We shall find it again and again in the singing that we shall hear this week.

At the heart of the Christian faith is the story of God made real in a human life, lived in Palestine, meshed into ordinary human relationships, as today's commemoration of the forebears of Mary, the mother of Jesus, reminds us. And it becomes the story of God exposing himself to the worst in this world that one human being can do to another (the story traced out, for instance, in Haydn's *Seven Last Words from the Cross*). And then it becomes the story of life and hope, of forgiveness and reconciliation, of laughter and festivity, as the crucified Lord becomes the risen Lord. Christians take this story of redemption as the central theme

---

[5] "Woodbine Willie", in *The Unutterable Beauty: The Collected Poetry of G. A. Studdert Kennedy* (London: Hodder & Stoughton, 1929), p. 1.

of the whole human story, seeing in the cross of Jesus the passion of all humanity, and seeing in his resurrection the hope that defeats the very worst that this world can do. The story of the suffering God, who is also the rising and forgiving God, as Geoffrey Studdert Kennedy discovered in his ministry to troops on the Western Front, is in the end the only story that can encompass all the fractured experiences of so terrible a thing as war. It is the story that explains this cathedral, all our cathedrals, our daily worship, and the majestic architecture and glorious music with which we clothe our Christian faith. It is the story which is the thread that runs through this festival, taking its cue from so sombre a theme, but meeting it with beauty, with festivity, with joy.

3 7

True peace[1]

It is an honour to be with you today, as you mark the centenary of the end of the First World War; and I come with the greetings of the bishop and people of the church of Worcester. It is even more of an honour, and a humbling one, for an Englishman to be asked to speak to you on this occasion.

Let me tell you what these past four years of remembering have meant for us in Britain. We have remembered a war in which a generation of the young perished. Every village memorial in England records many more names from the war of 1914 to 1918 than from the war of 1939 to 1945. We have remembered the waste of war. It was a mechanized war in which old ideas of military glory gave way before the appalling fact of mass destruction. The remembering of the centenary of this war has been sombre and heart-searching, and the word victory has been hardly spoken.

The first-century historian Tacitus was the first writer to describe the effects of war in both your country and mine. He wrote one book on how the Romans succeeded in conquering Britain, and another book on how they failed to conquer Germany. Tacitus tells us that one of the British chieftains said of the Romans: "they make a desolation and they call it peace".[2] Those words could be said about the First World War. That war

---

[1] Sermon preached in Magdeburg Cathedral on Sunday, 11 November 2018 at a service to mark the centenary of the end of the First World War. The readings were Jeremiah 6:6–10,13–16; Ephesians 2:13–20.

[2] "Ubi solitudinem faciunt, pacem appellant" (*Agricola* [30], in Tacitus, *Agricola, Germania, Dialogus*, Loeb Classical Library 35, 2nd edn, tr. Maurice Hutton, Robert M. Ogilvie, Eric H. Warmington, William Peterson and

led to a peace, but it was a peace which was a "desolation". Those who won that war imposed a peace on those who lost. It was a peace which solved nothing, but which sowed the seeds of bitterness and despair which in turn bore terrible fruit a generation later. The commemoration this weekend of the eightieth anniversary of Kristallnacht reminds us of what grew and flourished in that "desolation" which followed the First World War.

Such a peace is not peace as the Bible understands it. Peace, in the biblical sense, is a strong and positive thing: peace includes safety and security and wellbeing. There can be no true peace where there is injustice or exploitation or humiliation; no true peace where the strong take advantage of the weak, or the rich take advantage of the poor. We are reminded of the words of the prophet Jeremiah: "From the least to the greatest of them, everyone is greedy for unjust gain; and from prophet to priest, everyone deals falsely. They have treated the wound of my people carelessly, saying, 'Peace, peace', when there is no peace."

As Christians, we believe that there can be no peace worthy of the name which does not embody a humanitarian reaching out to the world's poor, an embracing of the equality of women and men, a commitment to the idea of a global family in which all must help each other, and a radical hospitality to the stranger from whichever land he or she may come. Nor can there be a true peace which does not include treating the earth itself with reverence and care, and conserving its resources. Yet who can look at the world today and not think that all these marks of true peace are once again under threat? We see gates shutting, walls being built, borders closing. There is too little peace in our world today, and too much "desolation".

The biblical vision of peace is not only positive; it is personal. In Paul's letter to the Ephesians we read, "he is our peace". True peace is embodied in the person of Jesus Christ. His body was torn apart on the cross, but is still the place where a divided world can find its unity. Christians have received the gift of Christ's peace, and are then entrusted with the gift of

---

Michael Winterbottom [Cambridge, MA: Harvard University Press, 1970], p. 81).

his peace to others. It is a special commission to the Church of Christ to be a peacemaking body in the world.

In the aftermath of the Second World War, there was a movement towards a deeper Christian unity, which bore fruit, for example, in the foundation of the World Council of Churches. The great Bishop George Bell of Chichester, friend of Dietrich Bonhoeffer, was a leading figure in that movement. Only if Christians spoke with one voice, he argued, could they bear witness to Christ's peace in a divided world. At the same time, the great European project was born (not without Christian inspiration): the vision of a continent at peace, which remains the vision of the European Union. This vision, as we know, is under threat today. I come from a country which has chosen to leave the European Union (in my view a lamentable decision). But whatever my country does in the next few months and years, there is a consensus among all the churches in Britain that we must work all the harder to preserve and protect the links that still bind us together. In this, all the churches of Europe (and the Church of England is proud of its identity as a European Church) have their part to play, entrusted with the gift of Christ's peace to an increasingly divided continent. On this centenary of the end of the First World War, it is for each one of us to receive again the gift of Christ's peace, and to offer it to others.

Quintessential England[1]

This county, Mr Chairman, which you and your fellow councillors have the privilege of serving as our elected representatives—this county of Worcestershire is often described as "quintessentially English". Of course, every county makes its unique contribution to what we mean by England; and there is much about England that we do not find in Worcestershire, not least the sea (though our well-publicized floods do their best to make up for that). All the same, we know what people mean when they talk of Worcestershire in that way: the magnificent ring of hills, the rich agricultural landscape of the south of the county, the rivers and canals and the industrial heritage associated with them and the edges of the Black Country; the villages, small towns, this so-very-typical cathedral city; the castles and churches and this cathedral itself where so much of England's history has been reflected and indeed enacted. It is a county about which quintessentially English poets from William Langland in his *Piers Plowman* to A. E. Housman in his "Bredon Hill" have rhapsodized. It is a county which those quintessentially English composers Elgar and Vaughan Williams have invoked in their music. It is a county about which that most English of prime ministers, Stanley Baldwin, whose ashes lie here beneath the floor of the nave, was always eloquent. J. R. R. Tolkien said that there was more of Worcestershire in his imaginary "Shire" than any other county.

The danger of this (perhaps rather complacent) way of thinking about Worcestershire, or indeed any other part of England, is that we make it the vehicle for whatever we think that England should be like.

---

[1]   Sermon preached at the county civic service in Worcester Cathedral on Sunday, 1 March 2020. The readings were Jeremiah 18:1–11; Luke 18:9–14.

We are tempted to impose our notions of Englishness on the landscape. "England" is an increasingly sensitive and important subject, and our notions of what it is to be English are a very pressing concern. The separation of the United Kingdom from the European Union has left us, as we all know, in a deeply divided state; and that divisiveness cuts in more than one direction. We are feeling the strain of this on the different constituent parts of the United Kingdom; and in whatever way the United Kingdom evolves (or fails to evolve) to meet this strain, the issue of the future of England is likely to become as pressing as the growing debates about the futures of Scotland and Ireland and Wales. More than ever, we need to notice the way in which we think and speak about England.

There have been many calls for unity and reconciliation in our national life in recent months, and rightly so; we cannot live or flourish in a state of division. You, Mr Chairman, have very appropriately made "unity" the theme of this service today. But the question is, on what is that national unity to be built? And if we think specifically about England for a moment, where is our sense of English identity to be found?

In the minds of some people, it seems, our future consists in getting back to some point in the past when (we are told) all was well. And this is the particular risk in celebrating Englishness, for that so very quickly turns into nostalgia for the past; a past, moreover, that very likely never happened. The question that we should ask is whether there is some quality in our celebration of Englishness, in our sense of the English character, which points us forwards and not backwards; something which gives hope for the future and not just longing for the past?

I believe that there is. And to illustrate what I mean, let me use the example of England's greatest gift to the world: its language. The peculiar glory of the English language is its hospitableness, its power of absorption, its capacity for accommodation. Onto the stock of Old English have been grafted words from Latin, French, Norse, German, Arabic, Indian, Spanish and the languages of the Caribbean. This has given English not only an enormous vocabulary but a suppleness, a variety, a capacity for shades of meaning which outrun most other languages.

And the English language has this power of absorption, this hospitableness to external influences, this capacity for accommodation, because that has also been the history of the English people. Words from elsewhere did not arrive on the wind; they arrived on the lips and in the minds of successive races which have made their home on this island. Vikings and Normans followed on the heels of Saxons; and then waves of immigrants and refugees—Huguenots from France, Jews from central Europe, Asians and West Africans and Eastern Europeans, all enriching the land and culture and language and people of England in a way that is thoroughly, traditionally, and quintessentially English. That is profoundly hopeful for the future of England, provided that we keep our doors and our hearts open to such enrichment. That is the only foundation for our future national unity, for it is the only way to keep faith with our historic talent for hospitality, our characteristic capacity for absorption and accommodation.

The readings that we have heard in this service—from the prophet Jeremiah in the Old Testament and the Gospel of Luke in the New Testament—are those usually read in church on this first Sunday of Lent. Both speak to us of the importance of "repentance", which is one of the spiritual disciplines of Lent. Repentance means "thinking again". It means reflecting on our lives and seeing where we fall short. It means trying to do something about it and seeking the mercy of God. In the reading from St Luke's Gospel, the story is about two men; one very pious and full of it, not seeing the need to change; the other not very pious, but humble about himself, willing to change, and grateful for God's mercy. The reading from Jeremiah translates that same story into a story about the community, the kingdom. Just as in the case of individuals, so in the case of communities, there is the need from time to time for reflection, for self-examination, for seeing where we are falling short, for trying to do something about it, and seeking the mercy of God as we do so. Neighbourhoods, cities, counties, nations, all need their moments of reflection, their opportunities for repentance, for "thinking again".

For centuries, this cathedral has been the sacred place where the common life of this county has been acknowledged, celebrated, reflected upon, and offered up for God's mercy and grace and guidance and protection. It has also been the sacred place to which people from every background and race and tradition have come, pilgrims from distant places who have found here a hospitable welcome and whose lives have left their mark upon the very stones of this building. As once again we lift up the life of our county in this place, let us pray that we may be true to our historic talent for hospitality. Let us pray that our unity may be that of reconciled diversity and not that of exclusion and introversion. Let us pray that, in that sense, Worcestershire may indeed be "quintessential England".

39

Francis Brett Young[1]

My parents did not own many novels, but among the ones that they did was *Doctor Bradley Remembers*. What *I* remember is the not-exactly-sensational title, and the far-from-enticing plain navy-blue binding of what was probably the first Heinemann edition; and if I ever opened it, which I doubt, I would have found the 700 pages of print off-putting. I might, however, have been intrigued by the endpapers, for I loved maps (then and now), and it would not have taken me long, even as a young boy, to work out that those endpapers depicted a strange world, a blend of fact and fiction, a map of the West Midlands which was partly that of any other atlas, but also partly the author's imagination. This was not the world in which I was brought up, but it was my parents' world, both of them born in Birmingham; Birmingham was much talked about (though hardly ever visited) in my childhood years.

Arriving 12 years ago to live and work in the diocese of Worcester brought some new discoveries. The first was Worcestershire itself and those parts of the Black Country that lie within the diocese. The second was Birmingham, which I now have reason to visit quite often. The third was my own family tree, with unsuspected Worcestershire branches, including nineteenth-century horse-dealers in Evesham and agricultural labourers in Fladbury. And the fourth was the memorial to the author of *Doctor Bradley Remembers*, and many other books, here in the north transept of the cathedral.

---

[1] Sermon preached at evensong in Worcester Cathedral on Sunday, 17 March 2019, commemorating the fortieth anniversary of the Francis Brett Young Society, and the sixty-fifth anniversary of the death of Young and of the interment of his ashes in the north transept.

So began an exploration of that world of Worcestershire, Shropshire, Birmingham, and the Black Country evoked by Francis Brett Young in his books; an exploration carried out, so to speak, in three dimensions—on the ground, by living and working in this part of the country; through the books themselves; and through my own family history, my parents' reminiscences of life in Birmingham in the twenties and thirties, and the discovery of remoter forebears, some of whom certainly lived that harsh rural life which Francis Brett Young describes so well.

Why do we love these books? For the infinite care that he takes to build up his characters, their lives, their loves; and the world that they inhabit, their land, their city, their village. The books are long; too long for many readers today, accustomed to more instant excitement. There are many long novels published today, but often they are long because of the intricacy of the plot, whereas Francis Brett Young's books are long because he invites you to explore those characters and their world with the same patient care and fascination as he feels for them.

We love his books for their closely observed changes of social life. His is not some unchanging world, the eternal sights and sounds of England of which his friend Stanley Baldwin (whose ashes also lie in this place) wrote so romantically.[2] His is always a society just slipping out of its inherited ways, challenged by change, his characters struggling to survive and struggling to adapt to new and often unwelcome times. Nowhere does he do this better than in the books about his own profession as a doctor. What a social history of medical practice in the last decades of the nineteenth century and the first decades of the twentieth is to be found in *My Brother Jonathan* and *Doctor Bradley Remembers*! And if we need reminding of the fact (and we do), these books tell us what it meant to have no National Health Service, and a warning of what we face if we throw it away.

There were some professions which Francis did not love, and one of them is my own, at any rate in some of its manifestations; but I forgive him that, because I know the sillinesses of clerical life even better than he did. Though he shrank from what he called "mystical religion", by which

2   Stanley Baldwin, *On England and Other Addresses* (London: Philip Allan & Co., 1926), p. 7.

I think he meant any sort of explicit or enthusiastic religious belief or practice, he honoured what he took to be the central teachings of Christ, and we honour that in him. And both he and some of his characters sought out choral evensong in this cathedral.

The Island, that long cycle of poems which celebrates our national history through a particular Severn-side lens, bore a double dedication: to his wife Jessica, and to what he calls his other "unwavering love", England. He regarded *The Island* as his greatest achievement, and it has many fine passages, including those which Andrew Downes has set to music. The Churchillian rhetoric of its closing lines, however, which no doubt Francis meant as a personal testament, reads less well today. At a time when "our earthly rulers falter" (as Chesterton put it), we need to write about our native land in more guarded, more nuanced, more reticent ways.[3] It is not that Francis was uncritically patriotic. His ambivalence towards the Boer War is well known, and his evocation of Boer history and culture in *They Seek a Country* and *City of Gold* is both moving and immensely informative.

And it is not that I advocate no patriotism, no love of England, at all. Indeed, I think that recapturing a love of England, rescuing ourselves both from national self-deprecation, on the one hand, and from a bombastic nostalgia, on the other, may be one of our pressing tasks in the years ahead. But recounting our past victories will not achieve that. To me, it is Francis Brett Young's novels, more than his poetry, which point us to the recovery of a true and humble love of England. That close and patient and loving attention to the people and the places that have made us, the world of our parents and our grandparents and our great-grandparents; the cities and the towns and the villages that they inhabited; the harsh lives of both the urban and the rural poor; the ambitions, anxieties, social uncertainties, and titanic hard work of the new professional classes; all, rich and poor alike, prey to the effects of war and incurable disease with their legacy of loss and bereavement: this is the world out of which our world was fashioned. Such stories tell us how we came to be, and we love

---

[3]   G. K. Chesterton, "O God of earth and altar" (*Ancient & Modern: Hymns and Songs for Refreshing Worship* [London: Hymns Ancient & Modern, 2013], no. 582).

the people whose blood runs in our veins. Francis Brett Young is far from being the only chronicler of that world, that England, and he is far from the greatest. Hardy did it, and all the great Victorian novelists before him; but Francis Brett Young made a solid and enduring contribution to that chronicle of England, and rooted it here in the West Midlands, and for that we honour him today.

> And when they asked him where he would lie, he bethought him
> Of our church of St Mary at Worcester, saying, 'I commend
> My body and soul to God, and to St Wulstan.'
> So we buried him here.[4]

---

[4] Francis Brett Young, *The Island* (London: William Heinemann, 1944), p. 128. The words were printed on the front of the order of service for the interment of Young's ashes in Worcester Cathedral on 3 July 1954. In *The Island*, the lines refer to the burial of King John in the quire of Worcester Cathedral, as requested in John's will, written shortly before his death and preserved in the cathedral library.

40

Known to God[1]

I begin with a personal recollection. It happened in 2004, when I was invited to preach at a commemorative service in Normandy to mark the sixtieth anniversary of D-Day. It was one of dozens, perhaps hundreds, of such services held that weekend in Normandy; this one in the small seaside village where I am fortunate enough to have a small flat. But my recollection is not so much of the service, though that was memorable enough, with people from Britain, the United States, Canada—and Germany—taking part. My particular recollection is of crossing the Channel on the previous Friday, on a ferry ship which was, apart from me, full of veterans and their families. As the ship approached that part of the Normandy coast which in D-Day terminology is called Sword Beach, the veterans all gathered by the ship's rail to gaze at the approaching shoreline. For some of them, perhaps, it was the first time that they had seen it since that June morning, when they sailed out of the night towards the enemy guns. There was a profound silence on board. None of the rest of us could feel what they felt, but we could guess: they were remembering the fear of that moment; they were remembering that they had survived the day, and lived another 60 years; they were remembering their friends who hadn't.

At the end of this service, we will hear the familiar words of John Maxwell Edmonds, commemorating the Battle of Kohima in India fought in April 1944:

---

[1] Sermon preached at evensong in Worcester Cathedral on Trinity Sunday, 16 June 2019, marking the seventy-fifth anniversary of the D-Day landings. The readings were Exodus 3:1–15; John 3:1–17.

When you go home, tell them of us and say
For your tomorrow, we gave our today.[2]

Or as another poet, Charles Causley, put it in his poem "At the British
War Cemetery, Bayeux", where he imagines the dead saying to the living:

All we ask
Is the one gift you cannot give.[3]

They lost their life; and we cannot give it them back. They lost their
"today" for the sake of our "tomorrow", and every "tomorrow" in the
75 years since that June morning has been different and better because
of it. Those who had lived under tyranny were set free of it; those who
had clung to their freedom against all the odds were assured of it. Three
generations have grown up in western Europe without war; and western
Europe had not been without war for a thousand years before that. The
events of that June morning, and the terrible months that followed it,
and the eventual armistice in the following year, gave birth to one great
conviction, embodied in 1951 in the formation of the European Coal
and Steel Community, that the nations of western Europe would make
another European war, in the words of one of its architects, "not only
unthinkable, but materially impossible".[4] For nearly 70 years, that has
held good; but that conviction, and the commitment of European nations
to each other, is something that sadly can no longer be taken for granted.

---

[2]   The epitaph carved on the memorial of the 2nd British Division in the
      cemetery at Kohima has become world famous as the Kohima Epitaph. The
      verse is attributed to John Maxwell Edmonds (1875–1958), and is thought
      to have been inspired by the epitaph written by Simonides to honour the
      Spartans who fell at the Battle of Thermopylae in 480 BC.

[3]   Charles S. Causley, "At the British War Cemetery, Bayeux", in *The New Oxford
      Book of War Poetry*, ed. Jon H. Stallworthy (Oxford: Oxford University Press,
      2014), p. 338.

[4]   The Schuman Declaration of May 1950; see <https://european-union.europa.
      eu/principles-countries-history/history-eu/1945–59/schuman-declaration-
      may-1950_en>, accessed 10 January 2023.

That little seaside village, where I preached my sermon in 2004, endured the terror of enemy occupation, as did every other community in Occupied France. My best guess as to what that meant for so small a village comes from the experience of one part of my family, who lived just a few miles from that Normandy coast, on Jersey. One of my mother's cousins, living on the family farm throughout the war, kept a diary; a remarkable document that chronicles the day-to-day life of the farm with the strange and terrifying experience of the occupation. Entries such as that of 1 July 1943: "Listened [on our secret wireless set] to a wonderful speech by Churchill last night. We look forward to being released soon. Everyone hopes it will be this year. Margaret and Dorothy did not come today, as we wanted to finish picking the blackcurrants." Or 9 June 1944: "One feels very solemn at the thought of the great battle going on so very close to us—only a narrow strip of sea between us and the Cherbourg peninsula. I planted ageratum in the avenue and begonias in the back border." And how heart-breaking the realization in the weeks following D-Day that while France was being liberated, the Channel Islands would have to wait for the day of final surrender: "14 July. [We] no longer expect the Americans. [But many people] have already eaten their iron rations, especially the tin of sardines."[5]

So our remembrance today encompasses not only the service-men and service-women who fought and died, and the service-men and service-women who fought and lived, but the countless other people who lived their lives under terrifying conditions, and made the best of it, and hoped for better times to come. Their fidelity and endurance also had a part to play in the reconstruction of the post-war world, rebuilding families and neighbourhoods and communities, which is as important as the rebuilding of continents and nations.

In his first broadcast to the nation as prime minister on 19 May 1940, Winston Churchill concluded his speech by saying, "Today is Trinity Sunday. Centuries ago words were written to be a call and a spur to the

---

5   Nan Le Ruez, *Jersey Occupation Diary: Her Story of the German Occupation, 1940–45* (St Helier: Seaflower Books, 1994), pp. 130, 192, and 202.

faithful servants of Truth and Justice."[6] Well, today is Trinity Sunday, the great Christian celebration of God who loves us as our Father, and stands beside us as our Lord Jesus Christ, and who empowers us as the Holy Spirit. The readings to which we have listened are those appointed for Trinity Sunday. The first, from the book of Exodus, told of God's revelation of himself to Moses in the burning bush, saying to Moses, "I have heard [the cry of my people who are in Egypt . . .] I know their sufferings, and I have come down to deliver them." God is the God of freedom, God is the one who longs to liberate us from all that holds us in thrall. And in the second reading, where the truth about Jesus is gradually dawning on Nicodemus, we read that "God so loved the world that he gave his only Son." God so loved the world: God is the God of love, who holds every one of his children in his hands. How telling are the graves of those soldiers whom no one could identify. Their gravestones say simply "Known to God". When all else is stripped away from us, everything that can identify us to one another, we are still known to God.

Keith Douglas was a poet, and a soldier who served with the Sherwood Forest Yeomanry. He was killed on 9 June (the same day as my aunt was writing in her diary about the great battle across the sea) as his regiment advanced towards Bayeux. He was 24. In a remarkable poem, too long to read in full, he speaks of the stripping away of our identity in death:

> Remember me when I am dead
> and simplify me when I'm dead.[7]

Death is the last great simplification of our lives, when all that matters is that we are "known to God". And so to the God whom we celebrate today, Father, Son, and Holy Spirit, we commend ourselves, our loved ones, all who have lived for us and all who have died for us; that in that enfolding presence we may know ourselves to be known, and loved, and simplified, and set free.

---

6   <https://winstonchurchill.org/resources/speeches/1940-the-finest-hour/be-ye-men-of-valour/>, accessed 10 January 2023.

7   Keith C. Douglas, "Simplify me when I'm dead", in Simon Featherstone, *War Poetry: An Introductory Reader* (London and New York: Routledge, 1995), p. 203.

George Bell[1]

The hymn that we sang at the beginning of this service is one that I chose some months ago, not knowing that it would be in the news in the past week—not so much the hymn as the man who wrote it, George Bell. Having sung the hymn "Christ is the King", it is a good moment, on this feast of Christ the King, to talk about its author.

George Bell was one of the most significant Church leaders of the twentieth century, anywhere in the world. He was dean of Canterbury from 1925 to 1929, and bishop of Chichester from 1929 to 1958. I'm not going to pepper this sermon with dates, but those dates will help you to place him in his own time. He died on 3 October 1958, and his name is the most recent one added to the Church of England calendar. A statue of him is to be erected on the west front of Canterbury Cathedral.

I'll say more about his achievements in a moment, but why has he been in the news in the past week? Because, some years ago, an allegation was made that he had, many years before, abused a child. The allegation was taken seriously, as it should have been; it was investigated, as it should have been, but very clumsily and carelessly, as it should not have been. A conclusion was very quickly reached, and an apology and compensation offered, but a later independent review carried out by a leading QC, Lord Carlile, judged the investigation to have been disastrously flawed. Nonetheless, it was still publicly maintained that a "significant cloud" hung over the name of George Bell—until last week, that is, when the

---

[1]   Sermon preached at the eucharist in Worcester Cathedral on Sunday, 21 November 2021, the Feast of Christ the King. The readings were Daniel 7:9,10,13,14; Revelation 1:4b–8; John 18:33–7.

archbishop of Canterbury retracted those words. The statue of Bell is still to be put up in Canterbury.

A sermon is not the place to negotiate the dangerous waters of historic allegations, retrospective investigations, posthumous apologies, and the presumption of innocence for the dead as well as for the living. A sermon *is* the place to celebrate the saints of God, and to draw inspiration from their lives; and I count myself among those hugely relieved to be able once again to speak of the heroic virtues of Bishop Bell.[2]

So back to Bell himself, and why, 63 years after his death, he is still important. Think of some of the things which we count as precious in our Anglican heritage—Anglicanism at its very best: a commitment to worship; a commitment to learning; a commitment to history; a commitment to social justice; a commitment to speaking the truth to those in positions of power; a commitment to being tolerant towards those of other churches and other faiths; a commitment to the power of the arts to communicate meaning when ordinary words fail.

George Bell embodied all those things to an exemplary degree. Who spoke up for refugees from Nazi Germany whom the British government foolishly interned as enemy aliens? Who spoke out against the British government's policy of fire-bombing German cities, even in the final stages of the war? Who campaigned against those who demanded that the people of post-war Germany be left to starve? Who insisted that if the churches were to have any voice in the post-war world, it must be a united voice, and so helped to found the World Council of Churches? Who had the vision of communicating the Christian message through art, and poetry, and drama—commissioning paintings from sources as diverse as the German refugee Hans Feibusch and the Bloomsbury Group, and engaging T. S. Eliot to write the most famous of his plays, *Murder in the Cathedral*? Who invited Mahatma Gandhi to stay in his house in Chichester at a time when Churchill was calling Gandhi a "half-naked fakir"? Who made friends with the prophetic German theologian Dietrich Bonhoeffer, and who was it to whom Bonhoeffer sent his final

---

[2]   Not that I stopped observing his name on 3 October; in 2019, I was in Rome, and had the privilege of commemorating Bishop Bell when I presided at the eucharist in the Anglican Centre on that date.

message to the world, while he was being led to the scaffold for his part in the plot to assassinate Hitler?[3] The answer is that it was the short, dumpy, mild-mannered, softly-spoken bishop of Chichester, George Bell—a pastoral bishop in Sussex, as I can testify from the priests I knew, whom he had ordained, and the laypeople I knew, whom he had confirmed.

When I had the privilege of being the canon librarian at Chichester Cathedral, one of the prize possessions in my care was Bishop Bell's visitors' book. There, page after page, in fading ink, was the rollcall of those who enjoyed his hospitality and came under his influence: writers, artists, theologians, philosophers, politicians—the Establishment and the emphatically non-Establishment. The only guest who left no signature was the goat which Gandhi took with him everywhere for the sake of her milk. The goat was tethered on the palace lawn.

A profoundly observant commentator of the Church of that time wrote, in 1967: "If Christian faith survives in the twenty-first century, Bonhoeffer, by his writings and by his faithfulness unto death, may well be judged one of [those] who made its survival possible. Among his mentors, and his closest friends, was George Bell."[4] That gives Bell his place in history.

Bishop Bell did not court controversy, he was not a temperamentally combative person, he simply and painstakingly tried to speak the truth.

---

[3]   The message from Bonhoeffer was conveyed to Bell via a British prisoner of war, Payne Best, in April 1945. Payne Best's account is that Bonhoeffer said to him: "This is the end—for me the beginning of life", and then asked him to convey a message to Bell if Payne Best should ever reach home. Bell's own recollection of the message conveyed by Payne Best was: "Tell him that for me this is the end but also the beginning. With him I believe in the principle of our Universal Christian brotherhood which rises above all national interests, and that our victory is certain" (Eberhard Bethge, *Dietrich Bonhoeffer: A Biography* [London: Collins, 1970], p. 830 n. 54). The following morning, 9 April, at Flossenbürg Concentration Camp, Bonhoeffer was hanged for his part in the 1944 plot against Hitler. Hitler himself committed suicide on 30 April, and the German government surrendered on 8 May.

[4]   Donald M. MacKinnon, *The Stripping of the Altars* (London: Collins, 1969), p. 84.

Of course, he was not in physical danger, as Bonhoeffer was, or Gandhi. Nonetheless, what he did required moral courage to a high degree, which I think did not come to him easily; for instance, to make a speech in a packed House of Lords, knowing that not one person there agreed with him; or being told by the dean of Chichester that he would not be welcome to preach in the cathedral on Remembrance Day. There is always a price to pay when unwelcome truths are told to those in positions of power.

And here I think of the Gospel reading for this feast of Christ the King. Pontius Pilate wanted an answer to his question: did Jesus claim to be a king, the sort of king to threaten the stability of the Roman order? Jesus replies sadly, perhaps wistfully. What is the point of a philosophical discussion with a Roman bully who's only concerned about the safety of his own position? "Look", he says, "I haven't come to fight you. I've only come . . . to tell the truth. Those who care about the truth will listen to what I am saying." Do you remember Pilate's reply? According to the evangelist, "Pilate said to him, 'What is truth?' After he had said this, he went out."[5] And do you remember Bacon's famous gloss on that verse? "'What is truth?' said jesting Pilate, and would not stay for an answer."[6]

Pilate sneered at truth-telling, not realizing that it is more dangerous than all the armed rebellions and insurrections in the world. "I am [. . .] the truth," said Jesus.[7] Truth was what he embodied, what he was, what he is. And down the centuries, faithful followers of Jesus have been, and done, the same, speaking truth to those in positions of power: Peter and Paul before Caesar, Hilda at the Synod of Whitby, our own Wulfstan before the Bristol slave-traders, Catherine of Siena before the pope, Joan of Arc before the English, Thomas More before Cromwell, Dietrich Bonhoeffer before the Gestapo, Janani Luwum before Idi Amin, Oscar Romero and Jean Donovan before the death squads of El Salvador; so, too, within a different religious tradition, Gandhi. Truth-telling at a price: of such is the kingdom of heaven; so, too, Bishop Bell.

---

[5]   John 18:38 (RSV).

[6]   Francis Bacon, *Essays, or Counsels, Civil and Moral* (London: Folio Society, 2002), p. 3.

[7]   John 14:6.

When St Paul wrote to the Corinthians about "truthful speech", he made clear the kind of seedbed in which truthful speech is cultivated: "in honour and dishonour, in ill repute and good repute. We are treated as impostors, and yet are true."[8] Being truthful is tough; none of us finds it easy. We joke, we gossip, we gloss, we exaggerate, we skirt around it, we prevaricate, we deal in rumours, sometimes we slide into slander, sometimes we just lie. Truthfulness is born of a spiritual discipline which I, for one, feel that I have scarcely begun to learn. But others have done better, and their truthfulness has renewed the face of the earth. Faced by the austere example of the saints, we can do better too.

> O magnify the Lord, and raise
> anthems of joy and holy praise
> for Christ's brave saints of ancient days.
> *Alleluia.*[9]

---

[8]   2 Corinthians 6:7–8.

[9]   George Bell, "Christ is the King! O friends rejoice", *Ancient & Modern: Hymns and Songs for Refreshing Worship* (London: Hymns Ancient & Modern, 2013), no. 486.

4 2

Gathering the fragments[1]

Jesus said to his disciples, "Gather up the fragments that remain, that nothing be lost." Why does the fourth evangelist lay such emphasis on the gathering up of the fragments after the feeding of the 5,000? The other Gospel writers tell of the extraordinary quantity of bread left over, and invite us to see in that a sign of the generosity, "the sheer prodigality of God".[2] But only St John is careful to say that nothing was *lost*; and why should that be? The commentators are divided. For some it means that the precious gifts of God are to be guarded, not to fall into the wrong hands. But then the Lord would surely have done better not to feed the 5,000 in the first place. No, the command to gather up the fragments that nothing be lost has echoes later in the Gospel: first, when Jesus twice says that of those whom the Father has given him he has lost not one; and also when the high priest prophetically says that it is the task of the messiah to gather into one the scattered children of God.[3] In other words, the fragments of bread on the hillside that Jesus tells the disciples to collect symbolize all those whom God has given him, the children of God who in themselves are lost and scattered and fragmented, but whom it is the purpose of the Lord to gather into one, leaving none behind.

---

[1] Sermon preached at evensong in Worcester Cathedral on Saturday, 28 April 2007, on my installation as the forty-sixth dean. The readings were Isaiah 43:1,2,4–7; John 6:1–13.

[2] To use a phrase that I recall from the installation sermon of Eric Heaton as dean of Durham on 1 May 1974 (where it referred to that which cathedrals themselves express).

[3] John 6:39; 17:12 (cf. 18:9); 11:52.

We only know what the Church is by means of great scriptural images: the Church as the body of Christ, the Church as the ark of salvation, the Church as the fold of the Good Shepherd, and so on. Each of these has a truth to tell, but each by itself is incomplete. Left to themselves, the images that I have just mentioned can give the idea that the Church is, or is supposed to be, a place of perfect unity, clarity, and absolute security. But *this* image says something else. Here the Church is in itself fragmented; the children of God are those who are dispersed and scattered; and while it is certainly the purpose of the Lord (and of those whom he calls to share in his apostolic task) to gather the Church into unity, it is fragmentation which is the Church's starting point and usual condition. And in giving us this image, St John of course echoes the words of the prophet Isaiah that we have also heard in this service: the promise of the Lord to gather his people from north and south and east and west, everyone whom he calls by his name, whom he formed and fashioned for his glory.

I don't know much about computers, but I do know that my computer has a function called "de-fragmentation". Bits of computer memory, so I understand, which become scattered and dispersed, and so impede the computer's effectiveness, are gathered up and put in order, so that the computer works more smoothly. And this is not the same as building the computer in the first place; nor is it the same as repairing the computer when it breaks down; de-fragmentation is a constant and normal task of gathering up the fragments that remain, that nothing be lost.

And in just the same way, the task of de-fragmenting the Church is a constantly repeated one; which means that some current criticism of the Church, and in particular of the Anglican Communion, is beside the point. That criticism begins from the assumption that the Church is, or is supposed to be, or claims to be, a place of unity; and therefore (so that criticism goes on), if the leaders of the Church (and in particular our great archbishop) are engaged in a very public task of putting the Church back together again, that must at best be crisis management, is probably a papering over of unbridgeable divisions, and is at worst a cynical attempt to perpetuate an institution that has outlived its use. No: the de-fragmenting of the Church is the constant and repeated and normal ministry of the Lord to his people, uniting their "scattered companies" (to use that phrase from our first hymn)[4] so that of those whom God has given him Christ may lose not one. There *is* a scandal of disunity in the Church, but it is not that the scattered children of God need repeatedly to be gathered into one; rather it is that when Christ comes among us for that purpose, we are so resistant to his gracious de-fragmenting. The Church's response to her Lord is too often, "Computer says no".[5]

The de-fragmenting of the Church is not an end in itself. The gathering into one of the scattered children of God is a task that embraces the Church but reaches far beyond it. The only purpose in de-fragmenting the Church is that the Church in turn may contribute to the de-fragmenting of society and to the gathering up of *all* God's children; gathering them up not so much *into* the Church as into their full potential as God's children and a full enjoyment of his love.

And cathedrals, I believe, have a part to play in this. Cathedrals are, or should be, well placed to contribute to the constant de-fragmenting of the diocesan family; if that is *not* the case, then it is hard to see what is meant by the cathedral as the diocesan mother church. Admittedly, the role of a cathedral within its own diocese can be a bit of a puzzle, both to the resident cathedral community and to the rest of the diocesan family; and perhaps the defining and redefining of the cathedral's diocesan role is itself a de-fragmenting task.

Cathedrals, with their conspicuous presence on the landscape and in the history of their city and county, can also contribute to the de-fragmenting of society; though again it must be admitted that cathedrals have not always been perceived in this way, and at times have been exclusive and oppressive institutions, the very guardians of disunity and fragmentation. I might add, with the utmost respect for the ancient oaths that I have just sworn, that deans have sometimes spent too much time preserving their tenements, and given less attention to the quality of life lived in them.

---

[4]   George Bell, 'Christ is the King! O friends rejoice', *Ancient & Modern: Hymns and Songs for Refreshing Worship* (London: Hymns Ancient & Modern, 2013), no. 486.

[5]   To use a catchphrase from the TV comedy *Little Britain*.

But we may take courage and inspiration here from the Benedictine foundations of this place. The monastic rule, for which this church was first built, was a path of discipleship designed not only to bring unity and order into the lives of the monks who practised it, but also to touch the lives of all who came near it. St Benedict famously said that every guest was to be received with the reverence due to Christ himself:[6] and that rule, generously and imaginatively applied, would itself do much to de-fragment our world. The very shape of this building, reaching out north, south, east, and west, and gathered into the upward thrust of the great tower, is a striking image of Christ's gathering and uniting mission.

Tomorrow is the Lord's Day, and many of us will celebrate the Lord's Supper, either here or elsewhere. That pre-eminent sign of the Church constantly gathered and re-gathered from fragmentation into unity, may recall for us a prayer which has come down to us probably from the first century:

> As the grain once scattered in the fields
> and the grapes once dispersed on the hillside
> are now reunited on this table in bread and wine,
> so, Lord, may your whole Church soon be gathered together
> from the corners of the earth
> into your kingdom.[7]

May this Cathedral Church of Christ and the Blessed Mary the Virgin of Worcester, always be the instrument of that kingdom, to gather the scattered children of God into its unity and peace.

---

[6] Chapter 53: *The Rule of St Benedict in Latin and English with Notes*, ed. Timothy Fry (Collegeville, MN: Liturgical Press, 1981), pp. 254–9 at 254–5.

[7] *Common Worship: Services and Prayers for the Church of England* (London: Church House Publishing, 2000), p. 292.

Camels, needles, and rich people[1]

It is said that those who become hugely rich overnight can endure feelings of guilt and even suffer serious psychological damage. Some of these unfortunate people may turn to counsellors who (it is good to know) are able to relieve them of their guilt and, by way of a bonus, relieve them of large fees, thus reducing the amount of wealth about which they need to feel guilty. We may take it that these counsellors, engaged as they are in such a useful service to society, do not feel guilty about growing rich on the guilt of others. So everyone comes away feeling better.

Our Lord had a simpler way with the super-rich who worried about their wealth, as we have just heard. He told them to give it away and follow him. And in case they felt that this was a touch drastic, he said that the rich had no more chance of getting into the kingdom of heaven than a camel of squeezing through the eye of a needle. It just can't be done, so the wealth had better go, and go quickly. The man in Mark's story (Matthew calls him a young man and Luke a ruler, so we call him the "rich young ruler") knew that there was something missing from his life, but when faced with the truth about himself he could not take it; he went away, we are told, sorrowful and with his face fallen, "for he had many possessions". Evidently it wasn't the message that he was expecting; and no more were the disciples who witnessed the scene. And when Jesus went on to make his remark about camels, needles, and rich people, they were (we are told) "perplexed" and "greatly astounded" and said, "Then who *can* be saved?"

---

[1] Sermon preached at the eucharist in Chichester Cathedral on Sunday, 15 October 2000 (Proper 23). The readings were Amos 5:6,7,10–15; Hebrews 4:12–16; Mark 10:17–31.

It was an idea, you see, rooted in the culture of the time that wealth was a sign of God's favour. Parts of the Old Testament can be read in this way—though not the prophets, certainly not the prophet Amos, who as we have heard this morning castigated the rich for oppressing the poor, and lambasted the powerful for denying justice to the weak, and roundly told them that the judgement of God hung over them. Jesus repeats the message of Amos and warns of the spiritual danger of riches; though he was not the only one of his day to do so; indeed, his remark about camels and needles echoes or is echoed by a rabbinic saying to the same effect, only in *that* saying, the camel becomes an elephant. Incidentally, this may help us to put out of our minds what perhaps we learnt in Sunday School, that the "eye of a needle" was a *rather* narrow gate in the wall of Jerusalem through which a camel might find it *rather* hard to pass. The eye of a needle means the eye of a needle, and a camel means a camel, and an elephant means an elephant; and camels and elephants find it more than "rather hard" to get through the eyes of needles.[2]

But what is Jesus really saying about wealth?—that it *disqualifies* us from the kingdom of heaven; or only that it is not, in itself, a passport to heaven, or indeed to any sort of happiness? It is clear that in the case of the rich young ruler, Jesus could see that *his* wealth was getting in the way of his becoming a disciple; he had to get rid of the one before he could become the other. But Jesus had other friends and followers who were people of property and some wealth—Lazarus, who presided over a hospitable home; Zacchaeus, who gave away half (but only half) of his fortune; Joseph of Arimathea, who had made a fine tomb for himself; the unknown man who owned the house in Jerusalem with the large upper room; and so on. And the first Christians, after their brief experiment with communism, included many more of such people: Christians with houses, Christians with money, Christians (even) with slaves.

Perhaps the key to the teaching of Jesus about wealth is to be found in St Luke's Gospel, where we read the parable of the "rich fool" who built himself barns and yet bigger barns to store his goods, but forgot

---

[2]   See, for instance, Morna D. Hooker, *The Gospel According to St Mark* (London: A & C Black, 1991), pp. 242–3.

that he could take none of them with him.[3] "You cannot serve God and mammon," says Jesus; or again, in St Matthew's Gospel, he says, "Do not lay up for yourselves treasures on earth, where moth and rust consume and where thieves break in and steal, but lay up for yourselves treasure in heaven [. . .] For where your treasure is, there will your heart be also."[4] That, in effect, was the challenge that he flung down to the rich young ruler in this morning's Gospel, for he could see that his heart was with his treasure, and his treasure was located very much in this world. It was *unsafe* for the young man to retain his riches, whereas others who had learned the lesson of sharing their wealth generously and open-handedly with others, who had learned (so to speak) to let their hearts go out of it, so that others might share it with them—for them it was *less unsafe* to remain rich.

There *is* a vocation to Christian poverty: the Lord followed it himself, and called the twelve and others of his immediate following to that way of life. St Paul and others in the next generation discovered the truth of "having nothing, and yet possessing everything".[5] Monks and nuns and friars and missionaries and workers among the poor in every generation since then have borne witness to the same Christian calling.

And there *is* a vocation, not to Christian wealthiness, but rather to the Christian *stewardship* of wealth; but what warnings there are in the gospel to those who follow that way!—to *have* mammon, but not to *serve* it; to *have* treasure on earth but not to have your *heart* in it; to *have* money, but to renounce the *love* of it, which is the root of all evil;[6] to *be* rich, but to escape the condemnations which the prophets hurl upon those rich who fail in the fearful responsibilities which wealth brings with it; to spend money (and to save money) for the good of human society, but not to hoard it, not to see it as one's private possession upon which the needy can have no claim.

"Whoso hath this world's good, and seeth his brother have need, and shutteth up his compassion from him, how dwelleth the love of God

---

3   Luke 12:16–21.

4   Luke 16:13; Matthew 6:19–21 (RSV).

5   2 Corinthians 6:10.

6   1 Timothy 6:10.

in him?" asks St John in his first epistle.[7] That is one of the offertory
sentences in the Prayer Book order for holy communion, by which the
congregation is reminded that they have no right to the Lord's table
unless they come with some practical token of their concern for others.

Now the giving of charity to others is a difficult business, and
sometimes poses hard questions about the best way to go about it. The
government, we learn, may try to persuade us not to give to beggars in
the street; and there may be wisdom in that; it is, at any rate, not a clear-
cut question one way or the other. But will we divert the money that we
might have given on the spot to the appropriate organizations, so that the
disadvantaged may benefit in a more structured and systematic way? Will
the voluntary aid agencies, which have suffered as well as gained from
the National Lottery, see a revival of that generous giving to charity, at
which as a nation we were once quite good, but in recent years much less
so? Or, as a different route to the same end, will we embrace the raising
of taxes that government may invest more in the eradication of poverty
here and in other parts of the world?

At our worst, the possession and responsibility of wealth can be
the cause, as it was for the rich fool in the parable, of spiritual death;
a preoccupation with the cares of this world that cut us off from the
kingdom of God. At our best, wealth can be an instrument of good, the
potential for a generosity that does good to giver and receiver alike. And
when we are neither at our worst nor at our best, then the cares of wealth
can be at least an irritation that can drive us to look for more lasting
values. That was the path on which the young man in this morning's
Gospel began so promisingly, but sadly lacked the courage to follow
through.

The seventeenth-century priest and poet George Herbert wrote a
poem about the irritating value of the world's riches, and how they send
us in search of a less fragile fortune. The poem is called "The Pulley", and
it echoes the famous words of St Augustine that our hearts are restless

---

7   1 John 3:17 (AV), as given in the BCP.

till they find their rest in God; words which in turn are echoed in the collect for today.[8]

> When God at first made man,
> Having a glasse of blessings standing by;
> Let us (said he) poure on him all we can:
> Let the world's riches, which dispersed lie,
> Contract into a span.

> So strength first made a way;
> Then beautie flow'd, then wisdome, honour, pleasure:
> When almost all was out, God made a stay,
> Perceiving that alone of all his treasure
> Rest in the bottome lay.

> For if I should (said he)
> Bestow this jewell also on my creature,
> He would adore my gifts in stead of me,
> And rest in Nature, not the God of Nature:
> So both should losers be.

> Yet let him keep the rest,
> But keep them with repining restlesnesse:
> Let him be rich and wearie, that at least,
> If goodnesse leade him not, yet wearinesse
> May tosse him to my breast.[9]

---

[8]   Augustine, *Confessions* (1.1), tr. Henry Chadwick (Oxford: Oxford University Press, 2001), p. 3; *Common Worship: Services and Prayers for the Church of England* (London: Church House Publishing, 2000), p. 418.

[9]   *The Works of George Herbert*, ed. Francis E. Hutchinson (Oxford: Clarendon Press, 1941), pp. 159–60.

4 4

Corinthian Christianity[1]

When public figures say foolish things (as, sad to say, does happen on rare occasions), a stock excuse is to claim that they were quoted out of context. Nine times out of ten, when the remark is fitted back into its context, it is still foolish, but such an excuse is obviously less painful than the simple admission, "I am a fool."

But foolish remarks are not the only kind that can be taken out of context; the same can happen to wise and beautiful remarks. We should bear this in mind every time that we read the thirteenth chapter of St Paul's first epistle to the Corinthians, as we have done this morning. Everyone loves this passage, this passage in praise of love. We choose it for weddings and funerals, and rightly so. But we read it, as we have done this morning, without reading the twelfth and the fourteenth chapters as well—or, indeed, the whole epistle. And while there is so much in it that unfailingly makes an impact on us, which we rightly prize as wise and beautiful, there is also so much of its meaning, so much of its depth, which is quite lost unless we read the whole epistle.

So what is the context? Very briefly, St Paul had been having trouble with the church at Corinth; all sorts of trouble, as one can infer from what he writes in both his first and his second letters to the Corinthians. The heart of the trouble seems to have been this. The Corinthian Christians (or more probably an influential elite within the congregation) believed that they had already received all the spiritual gifts inherent in the kingdom of God. They thought of themselves as spiritual athletes,

---

[1]   Sermon preached at the eucharist in Worcester Cathedral on the Fourth Sunday of Epiphany, 31 January 2016. The readings were Ezekiel 43:27—44:4; 1 Corinthians 13; Luke 2:22–40.

religious champions, theological Olympians. They had nothing more to learn; they had reached the end of their spiritual journey; they had arrived. They seem to have exercised extraordinary charismatic gifts. They spoke in tongues and didn't mind that others found that excluding. Above all, they prided themselves on what they called "the knowledge"— rather like London taxi-drivers, except that, for the Corinthians, this was a spiritual knowledge, a depth of spiritual insight which, they believed, meant that they knew all that there was to be known about the mystery of God.

Much of this can be pieced together from the first eleven chapters, as Paul deals with the fall-out of this deeply mistaken mentality. In Chapter 12, he deals more directly with the spiritual (or, as we would say, charismatic) gifts on which the elite of the Corinthian congregation prided themselves: profound spiritual knowledge, deep godly wisdom, glorious gigantic leaps of faith, acts of healing, voices of prophecy, discerning of spirits, speaking in tongues.

St Paul's way of dealing with these is fourfold. First, he reminds his readers that these are gifts from God, not personal achievements. God has given them for a purpose, for the building up of the body of Christ, and not for personal aggrandisement. Second, he insists that these gifts are complementary, not competitive. It is pointless for the Corinthians to rate one gift above another, because every gift is needed within the body. Third, he tells them (at any rate, later in the epistle) that his own spiritual experience is rather more impressive than theirs. He has the decency to apologize for boasting, but he finds it necessary to take them down a few pegs. And fourth, he tells them (and this is the cliff-hanger with which Chapter 12 ends) that there is a still more excellent way. And that is what, in Greek, Paul calls *agapē*; what is traditionally translated into English as "charity", but in more recent versions as "love".

Neither English word is very good: "love" is too vague, it has too many meanings; and "charity", once a rich and splendid word meaning sacrificial and unselfish love, has acquired a modern meaning which is all to do with donating money. But "love" is the word in the version read this morning; it will have to do.

And so St Paul begins Chapter 13. "If I speak in the tongues of mortals and of angels", he says, "but do not have love, I am a noisy gong or a clanging cymbal." The barb is a double one. Speaking in the tongues of mortals and of angels is exactly that in which the Corinthians took such pride. That's one barb. Well, says Paul, if it's done without love, you're no more than a noisy gong or a clanging cymbal. That's the second barb. Why? Because Corinth was well known for the manufacture of noisy gongs and clanging cymbals. If you wanted to send a gift labelled "a present from Corinth", it would be a noisy gong or a clanging cymbal; like a stick of rock from Brighton, or a miniature Eiffel Tower from Paris. If you're doing all this fine spiritual stuff without love, says St Paul, it's as tacky as a stick of rock or a Corinthian gong.

And so he goes on. He runs through the whole list of what the Corinthians thought was their spiritual speciality—prophetic powers, understanding mysteries, faith to remove mountains—none of it any good at all without love.

What is love? Paul tells us: and maybe that middle passage is the one that we love best: the passage beginning, "Love is patient; love is kind". It's not that we are very good at love; but we know that we should be, and we would like to be, and that is why God made us. Paul's definition of *agapē* tells us what the English word "charity" once meant: "It does not insist on its own way; it is not irritable or resentful; it does not rejoice in wrongdoing, but rejoices in the truth. It bears all things, believes all things, hopes all things, endures all things."

"Love", says Paul, "never ends." Prophecies, tongues, knowledge—all those spiritual gifts of which the Corinthians thought so much—they all have a shelf life. But not love.

And then Paul embarks on what may seem like a digression, but it isn't really. He goes on to talk about knowledge. Knowledge, you remember, was what the Corinthians prized above all else; a deep spiritual knowledge, they thought it was, knowing God directly; knowing all that there was to be known. No, says St Paul, it's not like that. We are but children in the knowledge of God; and our words about God are childish, and our reasoning about God is childish. You Corinthians think that you have seen into the depths of the mystery of God, but you haven't; you've hardly started. What we see of God is like catching a glimpse of something at the back of the mirror: oblique, tantalizing, back-to-front; just like the parables of Jesus. So all the knowledge that we ever have in this life, Paul tells the Corinthians, is partial, provisional, preliminary.

Last week we celebrated the feast of St Thomas Aquinas. Aquinas wrote vast magisterial books about the mystery of God, but at the end of his life, he said that they reminded him of so much straw.[2] That's the humility of someone who knows that they don't know much.

I called this a digression, because Paul seems to have wandered off his main subject, which is love. But it isn't a digression at all. The theme of love is there all along. When that day comes, he says, "I will know fully, even as I have been fully known." There is one who knows me, he says; and that, my dear Corinthians, is far more important than all the things that you think you know. There is one who knows, and sees right through me, knows all my boasting and my foolishness and silly spiritual pride, but he sees me and he knows me with the eyes of love, and that is why I still exist. And one day, he will open my eyes so that I will see him, and I will see myself as he sees me (what purgatory that will be, but what paradise as well), and in that exchange of love between my maker and myself, I will truly have arrived—which is more, my dear Corinthians, says St Paul, than you have done; and which is the reason that God's love lasts for ever.

The Church always reads this passage as Lent approaches. It's not difficult to think why. Lent is the season for looking into ourselves, noticing those Corinthian elements in ourselves, the things in which we take pride, and asking ourselves whether these things are done with or without love. And if the answer were to be "without", well then, our Christianity would be like theirs, tacky, like a stick of rock or a Corinthian gong.

---

[2] Quoted, for instance, by G. K. Chesterton, in *St Thomas Aquinas* (London: Hodder & Stoughton, 1943), p. 113.

God is faithful[1]

There is a tailor in, let us say, Panama, whom I will call Mr Pendel, who once a year sends me an advertisement to say that for a few days in the following month, he will be available at a prestigious hotel in central London, and that if I care to present myself he will take my measurements for a suit at a price which I will not be able to resist.[2] I have, for the past 20 years, resisted; but nonetheless, I applaud Mr Pendel's tactics. There is just that much extra incentive to offer myself to his tape measure, knowing that the opportunity will only be there for a few days; and that, who knows, next year Mr Pendel may have retired, or will be dead, or will not write to me, and I shall have irretrievably missed the chance of appearing in his pinstripe worsted. Mr Pendel, his letter subtly implies, does not really need my custom; he's doing me a favour by being in London at all; but I on the other hand (so his letter quietly suggests) badly need Mr Pendel with his tape measure and his scissors.

We might think that there's something of Mr Pendel about God in the reading from Isaiah this morning. "Seek the Lord while he may be found, call upon him while he is near." There is some pressure in those words. And there is more pressure in what comes next: "'For my thoughts are not your thoughts, nor are your ways my ways,' says the Lord." The Lord has other matters on his mind; we are not his sole concern; and if we seek him some other time, it may not be convenient, he may not be available.

---

[1]   Sermon at the eucharist at St Stephen's House, Oxford, on the Third Sunday of Lent, 7 March 2010. The readings were Isaiah 55:1-9; 1 Corinthians 10:1-13; Luke 13:1-9.

[2]   I have borrowed the names from John le Carré, *The Tailor of Panama* (London: Hodder & Stoughton, 1996).

But that of course would be absurd; God does not fly in from elsewhere, and fly out again; if he is accessible to us at all, then that is not limited by time or circumstance, let alone by divine whim; he is the God of love and compassion, and therefore must be available . . . whenever we want him.

But that's not quite right either. If God is not a bespoke tailor with a precious timetable, neither is he a shop assistant, humbly at our disposal whenever we choose to stop by. "Can I help you?" says the shop assistant. "No thank you, I'm just browsing," we instinctively reply; summoning him only when we've decided what we want. Is that the nature of our relationship with God: browsing, and only calling him over when we are ready to make use of him?

Perhaps the truth of the matter lies in the reading from the first epistle to the Corinthians. "God is faithful", we read, "and he will not let you be tested beyond your strength, but with the testing he will also provide the way out so that you may be able to endure it." "God is faithful": that is the point. We must not read that whole sentence in such a way that we hurry over those first three words. His not allowing us to be tested beyond our strength, his providing a way of escape so that we may be able to endure it: those are vital and saving truths, but they stem from what comes first: "God is faithful". It is because God is faithful that he is neither like Mr Pendel with his hint of take-it-or-leave-it; nor like an obsequious shop assistant, only too happy to oblige whenever it suits us; no, he is faithful, he is constant, and in that faithfulness, that constancy, there is the call to us to be faithful, to be constant, in return.

Inscribed on the bell of another theological college, which it would be tactless to mention here, are words from the first epistle to the Thessalonians: *pistos ho kalōn*, "he who calls [you] is faithful."[3] It is, you see, a theme of St Paul. "God is faithful." "He who calls you is faithful." There is a faithfulness in his calling, and a calling in his faithfulness; he calls us, he summons us, to reflect his faithfulness back to him.

Where is the faithful God in this morning's Gospel reading?

> At that very time there were some present who told Jesus about the Galileans whose blood Pilate had mingled with their

---

[3]   1 Thessalonians 5:24.

sacrifices. He asked them, "Do you think that because these Galileans suffered in this way they were worse sinners than all other Galileans? No, I tell you; but unless you repent, you will all perish as they did. Or those eighteen who were killed when the tower of Siloam fell on them—do you think that they were worse offenders than all the others living in Jerusalem? No, I tell you; but unless you repent, you will all perish just as they did."

Two apparently recent disasters: an atrocity carried out by Pontius Pilate, and the accidental collapse of a building; in both of which innocent people died. *Were* they innocent?—that was the question. The theology which the book of Job had criticized centuries before was still alive and well: these people died, therefore they must have deserved it. It is a theology *still* alive and well; witness the callous remarks of certain American evangelists following the earthquake in Haiti. It is a theology alive and well, and it gives Professor Dawkins and his friends plenty of ammunition; but Jesus disowns it. Were they worse than the people who did not die? No. That is his emphatic answer. But he has something to say in addition; and this tells us something about the faithfulness of God. "Unless you repent", says Jesus, "you will all perish just as they did." His words, of course, were spoken into a specific situation: the situation of first-century Jerusalem, bubbling with rumours of insurrection, and rabble-rousers claiming that a rebellion against the might of Rome was bound to succeed because, as they would say, "God is faithful." God had promised a throne to David, and that meant that Caesar must be toppled from his, and that meant that an armed revolt was guaranteed success—guaranteed by the faithfulness of God. "No", says Jesus, "there is no divine guarantee, God will not sign you a blank revolutionary cheque. Unless you think again—unless you *repent* of this folly—you will come to grief. You will die on the edge of the sword, or under the collapsing walls of Jerusalem, and that will be something that you have entirely brought upon yourselves; for the faithfulness of God is not of that nature."

God does not meekly underwrite our projects. That is something that *we* have to learn, quite as much as the people of Jerusalem. Here again we need to hear the words of the Lord in Isaiah: "my thoughts are not your thoughts, nor are your ways my ways". God's thoughts were very different from those of the people of Jerusalem, with their thoughts of armed rebellion. God was faithful to Jerusalem, but he was faithful with a faithfulness which was also a calling: a calling to repent, a calling to think again, a calling to submit their thoughts to his thoughts, and their ways to his ways.

There is, I believe, a particular temptation to those called to serve God in the sacred ministry of the Church, to believe that his thoughts are always our thoughts, and his ways our ways. It is often rooted in a defective idea of vocation, which puts too much emphasis upon the inward personal sense of being called, and not enough on the external confirmation of that call by the mind of the Church. So God's vocation becomes "my vocation", my precious gift from God, which he has, so it would seem from the way in which some people talk, entirely handed over to those who have received it. It is very surprising to me to learn what some deacons and priests (and bishops too, for all I know) count as part of their calling: a calling to this or that large and successful parish in a prosperous part of the country, or a calling to this or that Oxbridge chaplaincy, or a calling to canonries or appointments by the Archbishops' Council. Whenever I assist in the appointment of a priest to a living, I long to hear that they feel called to the dull, day-in-day-out, repetitive routine of pastoral ministry, the doing of the same things again and again (but always trying to do them well), the calling to spend and be spent in the service of God without much regard to career-planning or professional development. Sometimes priests do speak in that way, but not always. I once interviewed a priest for a post, and he told me that God had called him to be a leader. When I asked him, as I always do, what books he read, he had to think for a bit and then he said that he had read an interesting book comparing the leadership styles of Winston Churchill and Adolf Hitler. I never did find out which of the two styles he thought was going to be of more use to him in his parochial ministry, but I doubt that it was God's thought that he should be like either of them. The fact is that God does not hand over his vocation; his vocation never becomes "my vocation", as if it belonged to me; it remains *his* vocation, *his* calling, and his thoughts are not always our thoughts; the ways in which he leads you and me are his ways, not ours. But he who calls us is faithful.

4 6

Memory[1]

One of the pleasures of getting older (there are just a few) is that one's memory gets larger—not of course one's memory of where one left one's keys, or what the unreadable squiggle in one's diary for tomorrow morning might mean (one's memory for such matters becomes more and not less elusive); but one has *more* of a past; and at least bits of one's past are worth remembering. For me, this chapel is a place of memories. I see the much-loved Sir Richard Southern in the presidential stall; I see a revered tutor and chaplain, Eric Heaton; I see the present prime minister, a little younger than I, often in this chapel; I see a recent under-secretary-general of the United Nations, then an unassuming student just fled from Idi Amin's brutal regime in Uganda. Some of those who have helped to shape the story of our times also have memories of this place.

Memory has intrigued writers both ancient and modern. Marcel Proust explored the association of events, places, and people that might be evoked by a single sight or sound or taste or smell. It is the commonplace character of some of these associations that makes his great work so compelling; for he holds up a mirror to our own "lost time" and shows us the cavernous extent of our memories if we chose to explore them with an equal thoroughness.[2] For A. E. Housman on the other hand (a member of this college, who probably *didn't* retain fond

---

[1]   Sermon preached at evensong at St John's College, Oxford, on Sunday, 29 October 2006.

[2]   Marcel Proust, *In Search of Lost Time*, tr. Charles K. Scott Moncrieff, Terence K. Kilmartin and Dennis J. Enright, 4 vols (London: Everyman Publishers, 2001).

memories of this chapel), it was the inaccessibility of our memories that gives to his verse its peculiar poignancy:

> What are those blue remembered hills,
> What spires, what farms are those?

> That is the land of lost content
> I see it shining plain,
> The happy highways where I went
> And cannot come again.[3]

Wordsworth searched his memory for those "intimations of immortality" that proved for him that

> Our birth is but a sleep and a forgetting:
> The soul that rises with us, our life's Star,
> Hath had elsewhere its setting,
> And cometh from afar:[4]

The human soul, he tells us, comes from God, "trailing clouds of glory", and our deepest intuitions are but fragments of our memories of heaven; memories that die as the child grows up and eventually "fade into the light of common day".

Spiritual writers have explored the idea of memory as well; often heirs of the same Platonist tradition as their secular counterparts. For St Augustine, memory was a palace of many rooms; but not somewhere in which to wander nostalgically; rather somewhere to visit for the serious purpose of tracing out just how much God had shaped one's life without one's realizing it.[5] He was for ever struck by the idea that God was at work

---

[3] A. E. Housman, *A Shropshire Lad* (40), in *The Collected Poems of A. E. Housman* (London: Jonathan Cape, 1939), p. 58.

[4] "Ode", in William Wordsworth, *Selected Poems* (London: Everyman's Library, 1975), pp. 331–6 at 332.

[5] Augustine, *Confessions* (10.8), tr. Henry Chadwick (Oxford: Oxford University Press, 2001), p. 185.

in his life long before he knew it: "Late have I loved you, beauty so old and so new."[6] Though he had come to God late in life, God had come to him from before the beginning of his existence, and his existence only made sense when at long last he found his way to God. "You have made us for yourself," he wrote in his *Confessions*, "and our heart is restless until it rests in you."[7] Retracing the steps of his life through his memory, he could begin to see God's gentle tug always upon him, the gracious shaping of events and circumstances that eventually tumbled him tired and defeated into God's hands.

But what of the memories that are more painful to the touch; the mistakes, the follies, the missed opportunities, the things that one's ambition once vaulted at—but the memory of which is now just an embarrassment; the damage one has done to oneself, and worse, to others? It is harder to trace the hand of God in those memories, and there is no pleasure in recalling them. The wisdom of the day is that such things should be left alone. Move on. Don't dwell on the past. Get on with your life. Well, there's common sense in that as far as it goes; but sometimes the past will not be shrugged off so simply. Then the wisdom of the day is to hand over the past to the professionals: the psychotherapist, or at any rate the professional counsellor, is the one to sort it out. And there's a common sense there too: I would be the last to deny the value of psychotherapy for the healing of a deeply painful memory. But perhaps between the common sense of shrugging off the past, and the common sense of handing it over to the professional physician, there is a middling wisdom; a dealing with the past ourselves; and maybe the Christian tradition here can lend a hand.

"Repentance" is what it is called in the Gospels; and, like many Christian words, it is one that has acquired a bad name. If the word conjures up nothing but breast beating or making oneself out to be worse than one is, then forget the word but hold on to what it really means: repentance (in the Greek, *metanoia*) is a thinking through of things all over again; almost a re-imagination of the past. It is to acknowledge one's responsibility for what one has done or failed to do, without

---

6   Augustine, *Confessions* (10.27), p. 201.

7   Augustine, *Confessions* (1.1), p. 3.

self-punishment but also without excuse; it is an attempt at honesty. But repentance is all of this, not carried out in a vacuum, but in a certain context; and the context is God. Because I believe that God knows me, I believe that it is worth attempting to know myself as well. Because I believe that God accepts me, I believe that I can learn to accept myself as well. And if, in the past, I have damaged not only myself but (as is very likely) other people too, then because both they and I are held in God's love, then it is possible for me to hope to be forgiven. Even if, in practical terms, reconciliation is now impossible, it is possible for me still to pray for those whom I have hurt, as well as for those who have hurt me. It is even conceivable that somewhere in the mystery of the love of God, those whom I have hurt remember me, and have forgiven me, and pray for me. The idea of God lets shafts of hope filter through even the most intractably painful memories.

For the Christian, God is the context for this facing of the past in its shameful and painful aspect; for God is the one who has plumbed the depth of human shame and pain. That is what we remember and rejoice in, when we speak of Christ upon the cross. That is why, as T. S. Eliot said, "we call this Friday good".[8]

I recall a time of my life when all was bad; and I took myself, bruised and self-pitiful, into retreat at a monastery; the classic sort of running away, you might think. But the guest master of the monastery, who could have known nothing of what I was feeling, met me at the monastery door and took my suitcase and led me to the chapel and sat me down. "I will leave you here for a while", he said, "and then I will come and take you to your room. In the meantime, look at the crucifix above the altar, and remember, *the worst has already happened.*" That was the beginning, for me, of facing up to my difficulties and not running from them. Knowing that the worst has already happened, and that it has happened to God, and that God has borne it, taken it, carried it, absorbed it, and by his infinite forgiveness redeemed it; that is what enables us to face the past. His fingers can probe even the most painful bits of memory and bring his peace to bear upon them.

---

8   T. S. Eliot, "East Coker", in *Four Quartets* (*The Complete Poems and Plays of T. S. Eliot* [London: Faber and Faber, 1969], pp. 177–83 at 182).

In the *Divine Comedy* of Dante Alighieri, Dante pictures himself travelling through hell and purgatory and heaven in search of love and God and redemption. In purgatory, he imagines himself experiencing, not punishment, but what that word properly signifies, a painful but still joyful purification of the past. He then pictures himself as having reached the garden of Eden, his lost innocence restored. Housman would have called it the land of lost content; but this is a land to which, unlike Housman, Dante believed he *could* come again. There he was bathed, he tells us, in two rivers. The first was the river Lethe, which Dante had borrowed of course from classical mythology. It is the river of oblivion, which to the pagan mind was part of the promise of death, the opportunity to forget. But Dante then introduced a second river into Eden: it was his own poetic invention and he called it Eunoë, or "good remembrance".[9] The waters of good remembrance restore the memory of the past but in such a way that it can be received simply as a gift and a healing. The past is now seen for what it most truly is, the place in which God has been for ever acting providentially. Our mistakes, our follies, our missed opportunities, even our deepest sins prove to have creative possibilities in them from which God can still bring peace and healing into the present moment.

What Dante evoked poetically, the person who prays begins to prove by way of personal experience. At the foot of the cross, one comes to know that the worst has happened; and that the one upon the cross can turn even our damaged memories into matters of good remembrance. The "blue remembered hills" become a landscape transfigured by God; and the past no longer a source of pain.

---

[9]   Dante Alighieri, *Purgatory* (28), in *The Divine Comedy*, tr. Geoffrey L. Bickersteth (Oxford: Basil Blackwell, 1972), pp. 465–73.

Angels[1]

"I would like to buy an angel," I said to the shopkeeper. It's not what I usually ask for in shops. I do not tour supermarkets looking for angels, hunting for a discount on seraphim, or hoping to buy one of the cherubim and getting the other one free. But this was not an ordinary shop: the sign on the pavement offered crystals, and tarot cards, and reiki, and . . . angels. So I went in to have a look.

There were no angels. There were little models of angels made of glass. There were cards that had angelic messages on them, such as "Now is the moment to embrace your heart's desire" and "Follow the guidance of your soul to discover your inner truth" and other such none-too-specific pieces of advice. There was the opportunity of a fifteen-minute consultation with an angel, at a cost of £15, but I rather imagined that the conclusion would be the same sort of message as on the cards. I came away without an angel.

People do believe in angels. Many people who have no conventional religion, or no connection with the Church, put their faith in angels. Look in any mainstream bookshop. Someone I know who is a professed atheist and a devoted reader of Professor Dawkins believes in angels, and in the capacity of angels to guide and guard her life. Angels are one element of traditional Christianity which survives in the minds of people even though they have abandoned—or never had—anything else to do with the Christian faith—whether the Church, or Jesus Christ, or even God. The odd thing is that there are also many Christians, who do believe in

---

[1] Sermon preached at evensong in Westminster Abbey on Sunday, 28 September 2014, the Eve of St Michael and All Angels. The readings were 2 Kings 6:8–17; Matthew 18:1–6,10.

God, and in Jesus Christ, and who belong to the Church, for whom angels play a very unimportant part in their faith, if at all.

Today we celebrate the feast of Michaelmas; the Church's annual celebration of St Michael and All Angels. The angels are there in our liturgy: they were there in the psalms and hymns and readings and anthem this afternoon; and every time we celebrate the eucharist we say that we do so "with angels and archangels and with all the company of heaven".[2] The Christian tradition is full of angels, whether we think of the paintings of the Middle Ages and the Renaissance, the figures in many a stained-glass window, or Jacob Epstein's great sculpture of St Michael on the walls of Coventry Cathedral. And the figure of the angel can still surprisingly speak to a contemporary and secular culture: has there been so popular an installation of public art in recent years as Sir Antony Gormley's "Angel of the North"? There is something of a puzzle about an inherited Christian belief which has gone dead for many Christians today, but is apparently alive and well for many others, for whom it is Christianity itself that has gone dead.

If there are two ways in which a belief in angels functioned for many Christians in the past, and still functions for many but not all Christians today, and many others who are not Christians at all, we have only to look at this afternoon's two readings. In the first reading, from the books of the Kings, the prophet Elisha and his servant find themselves in a city besieged overnight by an enemy army, a terrifying situation. But Elisha can see with a prophet's eye, and he enables his servant to see as well, that beyond the besieging army is another one, a more powerful one: "the mountain was full of horses and chariots of fire." If only you have the eyes to see (this story is saying to us), then even the most desperate and menacing of human situations are subject to yet greater forces for good—which is a comforting idea, even though it often doesn't feel like it.

And in the second reading, from St Matthew's Gospel, Jesus himself speaks of every child having their own guardian angel who "continually sees the face of my Father in heaven"—which again is a comforting thought, even though, when terrible things happen to children, we may wonder what this means.

---

[2]   From the communion service in the *Book of Common Prayer.*

And that, perhaps, is the issue. There are those, some of them Christians and some of them not Christians, who are comforted and reassured at the thought of a kindly unseen world that redresses the balance from the terrors and confusions of the world that we see every day; and there are those, some of them Christians and some of them not Christians, who are offended by the very idea of finding comfort in an unseen world, when this world cries out for action.

There is truth on both sides. And if that sounds like a Church of England thing to say, let me call upon two of the four evangelists, St Luke and St John. St Luke's Gospel is filled with angels. Gabriel announces the birth of Christ; the heavenly host sings over the stable; an angel strengthens him in the garden of Gethsemane; angels attend the sepulchre at his resurrection. And in St Luke's continuing narrative (that we call the Acts of the Apostles) angels reappear: at the ascension, and in the life of the early Church. And through all of this (St Luke seems to be saying), when Christ walked the earth, the veil between earth and heaven was very thin; the glory of heaven kept breaking in, the kingdom of God was but a hairsbreadth away, everywhere there was a whisper of angelic presences.

St John's Gospel, on the other hand, is almost wholly devoid of angels. None at Christ's birth; none in his ministry; at one point some people think that they hear an angel's voice but others say that it was only thunder. Only at the resurrection are there angels to speak to Mary Magdalene, but she is too confused in her distress to take in either them or the risen Christ himself. In effect, St John tells his story without any angelic intervention. Now St John profoundly believed that when Christ walked the earth, almighty God was present and heaven had come very close: but whereas for St Luke that divine presence is dispersed and scattered among a hundred angelic presences, for St John it is in one place only—in the life and mind and heart and body of Jesus Christ.

The Church receives and celebrates both Gospels—indeed, all four Gospels—and many centuries ago, the Church rejected the idea that the Gospels should be synthesized or sewn together or somehow mixed and blended. Each of the Gospel writers' way of telling the story of Jesus has its own particular perspective, its own authority and authenticity. So for those who respond to the idea of angelic presences, they have the encouragement of St Luke to see the everyday world quivering with the divine presence. And for those for whom that is a dead idea, they have the reassurance of St John that it is in Christ alone that we find the very presence and power and word of God, made flesh in this world.

Each of the four Gospels has its own particular perspective and its own authority and authenticity. But if there is one point at which the perspective of St Luke and the perspective of St John coincide, it is in the conversation between Jesus and Nathanael, which closes the first chapter of St John's Gospel.[3] This conversation refers back to an episode in the Old Testament when the patriarch Jacob, wandering homeless in the wilderness, dreams one night of a ladder set up between earth and heaven, allowing the angels of God to travel between the two. The dream was so real when Jacob woke up that he knew that he had been in the house of God and at the gate of heaven: one of those places where the divine world breaks into our own.[4] Jesus says to Nathanael that if he follows him, he too will have Jacob's vision; he too will find himself at the place where heaven and earth converge; he too will see the angels of God ascending and descending upon . . . and then Jesus says "the Son of Man"—which is his way of referring to himself. Jesus himself is the ladder set up between earth and heaven, Jesus the point of intersection where the angels find their way to earth and back. St Luke is right: heaven is very close and the angelic presences are all about us. But so is St John: it is only in Jesus that heaven breaks into our earthly world.

---

[3]   John 1:47–51.

[4]   Genesis 28:10–17.

4 8

Living for ever, dying tomorrow[1]

On 16 November 1240, Edmund of Abingdon, archbishop of Canterbury, died while travelling through Burgundy on his way to Rome. His body was carried to the lovely Cistercian abbey of Pontigny, where his shrine may be seen to this day. Edmund was a famous scholar and teacher, one of the first great masters of this university, and his memory is perpetuated in the name of St Edmund Hall. A contemplative by nature, he was reluctantly called to great office in Church and state for which he was not particularly suited, and of which he did not always hide his distaste. On an earlier visit to Rome, he was summoned to a meeting with the pope after the hour of compline. In no uncertain terms, he told the pope what he thought of his misplaced priorities. The pope laughed at him and told him that he should have been a monk. "Yes, I should," replied Edmund, and added words to the effect that "then I shouldn't have to bother with you." Canonized seven years after his death, Edmund was both loved and revered in his generation. His contemporaries said of him that "he studied as if he would live for ever, and lived as if he would die tomorrow"; and I take that maxim as the theme for our meditation this morning.[2]

---

[1] Sermon at the eucharist in Pusey House, Oxford, on the Second Sunday before Advent, 16 November 2003. The readings were Daniel 12:1–3; Hebrews 10:11–14,18; Mark 13:24–32.

[2] Michael R. Newbolt, *Edmund Rich: Archbishop and Saint* (London: SPCK, 1928), p. 44. The words do not appear in the contemporary life by Matthew Paris (*The Life of St Edmund*, tr. and ed. C. Hugh Lawrence, Stroud: Alan Sutton Publishing, 1996). Whatever their provenance, they sum up the spirit of St Edmund.

Every serious reflection on the nature of human existence must reckon with the paradox contained in those words. We have (as Shakespeare put it) "immortal longings".[3] I do not necessarily mean longings for immortality, but rather the sense that the noblest human undertakings outrun any single lifespan. The mediaeval cathedrals, most of them, were built by those who knew that only their grandchildren would see their life's work completed. For ourselves, in idealistic mood, we want to save the planet, we want to do our bit for the world, we want to leave something behind us, we want to write that novel or paint that picture or compose that music that even posterity will still judge to be great. We have longings which cannot be satisfied in a lifetime; and those are our best desires, and the world would be poorer if we did not have them.

St Edmund, we are told, "studied as if he would live for ever"; and there we hear an echo of that heady twelfth-century renaissance, when both men and women were intoxicated by the classics, by theology, by the sheer joy of learning. There is a note of youthfulness there, and maybe those who achieve great things are the ones who have never quite grown up, never quite lost hold of those immortal longings. There is something diminished about a person who has settled only for manageable goals, who has tempered their aspirations to no more than a lifespan. Wordsworth mourned the loss of the "visionary gleam" of youth, the "intimations of immortality" that with adulthood "fade into the light of common day".[4]

There is, however, the other side of the paradox, which is the fact of death. St Edmund not only "studied as if he would live for ever": he also "lived as if he would die tomorrow". Youth relegates the thought of death to the distant horizon; and middle age, not wanting to count the years, tries to push it still further back. Ours is a culture particularly reluctant to speak of it, and we have largely forgotten traditional and healthy ways of mourning the dead. The Church in this country has colluded with this, offering funerals from which the coffin is often banished as

---

[3]   William Shakespeare, *Antony and Cleopatra* (5.2.317), in *Complete Works*, ed. A. Jonathan Bate and Eric Rasmussen (Basingstoke: Macmillan, 2007), pp. 2158–239 at 2236.

[4]   "Ode", in William Wordsworth, *Selected Poems* (London: Everyman's Library, 1975), pp. 331–6 at 332–3.

unsightly and upsetting, with hackneyed readings which announce that "death is nothing at all".[5] Even to speak of death, as I do now, would be called morbid by many people. But the Christian tradition is more robust than that. Living in the face of death, acknowledging the fact of it, and reflecting from time to time that death may come tomorrow, or today, and what meaning does that give to my life now—that is not morbid, it is simply rational. "Redeem thy mis-spent time that's past", wrote Bishop Ken in his morning hymn, "and live this day as if thy last": that is the practical and unembarrassed voice of the Christian centuries.[6]

How can the two sides of this unmanageable paradox be grasped? How could St Edmund hold onto that childlike sense of immortal possibilities, and yet meditate daily on his own mortality? It is the Christian faith that offers the framework of thought within which the paradox can be held. If human beings have intimations of immortality, if we are at our best when we are doing things of which we shall never enjoy the fruits, and shaping for the better a posterity that we shall never live to see, then either we have been badly designed, doomed to certain disappointment, or else death does not have the last word.

The idea of resurrection is not built into the human outlook; it is a specific idea that emerged within a definite culture, at a particular time and place. This morning's reading from the book of Daniel is one of the earliest expressions of it: "Of those who lie sleeping in the dust of the earth many will awake, some to everlasting life, some to shame and everlasting disgrace."[7] Even in the time of Christ, the idea of resurrection was still controversial, as we can tell from the debates between the Sadducees and Pharisees. Jesus, a Pharisee in this as in some other respects, proclaimed

---

5   The words, often used at funerals and memorial services, occur in "The King of Terrors", a sermon preached by Henry Scott Holland in St Paul's Cathedral on Sunday, 15 May 1910, following the death of King Edward VII; see <https://en.wikisource.org/wiki/The_King_of_Terrors>, accessed 10 January 2023. The paragraph in which the words occur does not represent the message of the sermon as a whole.

6   "Awake, my soul", *Ancient & Modern: Hymns and Songs for Refreshing Worship* (London: Hymns Ancient & Modern, 2013), no. 1.

7   Daniel 12:2 (Jerusalem Bible).

the idea of resurrection; and then, on the third day, he went on to enact it. It was the central theme of the early Christian message. Our intimations of immortality do not prove the resurrection true, but if it *is* true that Christ rose from the dead, then our deepest human longings can be satisfied. We can, like St Edmund, like all the saints, like children, live as if we shall live for ever: because in Christ that is our future.

Yet death is real, and the Christian doctrine of the resurrection is predicated on the fact of it—the shock, the reality, and the grief of it. The ultimate certainty and the penultimate unpredictability of death remain matters that our culture invites us to ignore but which the Christian tradition strongly recommends us to consider.

Even those early intimations of immortality in the book of Daniel knew that before the rising to new life came a time of great distress; and the theme is taken up in the reading from St Mark that we heard proclaimed as today's Gospel. Speaking as the storm clouds gather about him, the Lord tells of great distress to come, of the certainty of the final victory of the Son of Man, but also of the unpredictability of its timing: "as for that day or hour, nobody knows it, neither the angels of heaven, nor the Son; no one but the Father."[8] Not knowing the timescale of things was part of the mortal nature that the Son of God took upon himself; like us, there were matters about which he had to be agnostic. We cannot know the day and hour of our personal destiny; it escapes our plans, and so we pretend that it will never happen.

The Christian doctrine of the resurrection, on the other hand, takes in the reality of both Christ's death and ours; it arises from his taking of our mortal nature, his real dying, and his harrowing of hell. Death is *not* "nothing at all"; it is the great enemy of human existence, but through the death and resurrection of Jesus, it can become our friend. St Francis, Edmund's younger contemporary by a year or two, called bodily death his "sister"; and sisters can be both dear and awkward companions.

There is, of course, one way of misunderstanding the Christian tradition at this point: and it is a jibe made against Christians from time to time. We are thought to be people so in love with the afterlife that we welcome death as the way to it, and so out of love with this world

---

8   Mark 13:32 (Jerusalem Bible).

that we don't mind leaving it behind. But that convenient simplifying of the Christian religion won't work at all. The life of this world; the life of the earth, and of the body, of flesh and blood and brain; of human society and culture; of learning, science and art—that is the world of God's creating, the world within which Our Lord took flesh; a world to be loved and relished, and a world that we should grieve to lose. The Lord's weeping at the grave of his friend is of critical importance in a Christian understanding of death.[9] Death cannot be smoothed out by making the world no loss.

No: Christians are called to be people in love with this life, people living, working, studying, loving, making, exploring, learning as if they would live for ever—so much so that it is a grief to die; and yet we are also called to be people for whom even the certitude of death, which we unwaveringly acknowledge, is overarched by the still greater certitude of resurrection. So we *should* study, like St Edmund, and live and love and work as if we would live for ever; for in Christ we shall—and each day is his gift for us to enjoy in the intensity of the present moment. And we *should* live as if we might die tomorrow; for we know that one morning of our lives will be the last, and if we live with Christ, we should be ready to die with him.

When Edmund of Abingdon died, on this day all those centuries ago, he asked for a crucifix and kissed the wounded side of Christ (indeed, we are told that he licked and sucked it, to the astonishment of those around him) and quoted from the prophet Isaiah: "With joy you will draw water from the wells of the Saviour."[10] Though the style of doing it might not be ours, his way of dying was all of a piece with his way of living. He placed his own death within the scope of Christ's death; and in that he found cause for joy. He had studied as if he would live for ever; and lived as if he would die tomorrow; and when death came in search of him, he was ready to lose his life, joyful in the expectation of finding it.

---

[9]   John 11:35.

[10] Paris, *Life of St Edmund*, p. 155; Isaiah 12:3 (Vulgate): "haurietis aquas in gaudio de fontibus salvatoris" (*Biblia Sacra Iuxta Vulgatam Versionem* [Stuttgart: Deutsche Bibelgesellschaft, 1969], p. 1109).

4 9

Alleluia is our song[1]

It was a short journey from Jerusalem to Emmaus, but it was a journey packed with purpose and meaning. Some journeys are like that. They don't have to be long for a lot to happen. And today we also have in mind another journey, a short one—far too short—but still packed with purpose and meaning: Denise's journey. And like the journey of the disciples on the road to Emmaus, Denise's journey was one of hope, joy, pain, longing, questioning, discovering, and arriving.

Denise's journey began 51 years ago in Pennsylvania, the youngest of a large family, a family described in one of her obituaries as "rambunctious". (I did have to look up "rambunctious" in the Oxford Dictionary, and I found it there, though it says in brackets, "chiefly North American". It means, as far as I can tell, "rambunctious".) And then her journey brought Denise to England, and a love of all things English, and an English home and family.

Some of you have been Denise's companions for all or much of that journey; most of us knew her only during one stage or another; all of us have shared with her at least a few miles of the road. And all of us, during the last year, have been to some degree caught up in the hope, the joy, the pain, the longing, the questioning, the discovering and the arriving that have marked her short journey: the journey which ended, like the one to Emmaus, on Easter Sunday afternoon, breaking bread at home with the risen Jesus.

If all of us have shared part of that road with Denise, none of us have done so more closely, more lovingly, or more intensely than her husband

---

[1] Sermon preached at the funeral eucharist of Denise Inge in Worcester Cathedral on Tuesday, 6 May 2014. Denise had died on Easter Day, 20 April. The readings were Song of Solomon 8:6,7; Luke 24:13–35.

and their children. If Denise longed to live, it was to be wife to John and mother to their children. And during these recent months, the rest of us have shared their hopes and fears; and now we offer them our helpless but still deeply felt love.

Denise was an Easter Christian. When diagnosed with cancer, she said, "Whatever happens, alleluia is our song." But she had learnt the truth of that long before her illness. Years earlier, she had discovered the joyful mysticism of Thomas Traherne, and became a respected authority on him: that seventeenth-century priest and poet of the Herefordshire countryside whose voice of desire and freedom, happiness and holiness, was lost for so long, but is now (thanks in large part to Denise) so widely heard again. Traherne wrote that

> Your enjoyment of the world is never right, till every morning you awake in Heaven; see yourself in your Father's Palace; and look upon the skies, the earth, and the air as Celestial Joys [...] You never enjoy the world aright, till the Sea itself floweth in your veins, till you are clothed with the heavens, and crowned with the stars.[2]

In Traherne, Denise discovered, not just a subject, but a kindred spirit, a fellow Easter Christian. And tomorrow Denise will be laid to rest in a country churchyard, in Traherne's Herefordshire, in the earth and under the sky which they both understood so well.

Nonetheless, Denise felt a little constrained by being known as the authority on Traherne. She found another subject: bones, and the places where they are buried. That she should move from the sunlit mysticism of Traherne to the dark shadows of the ossuary came as a surprise to some; though not if you happened to know that the bishop of Worcester and his family are required to live above a mediaeval charnel-house. Denise began to study the subject partly to come to terms with the neighbours downstairs.

Again, Denise's chosen subject was for her more than a subject. The tour of bones was for her an exploration of the fears and shadows in

---

2   Thomas Traherne, *Centuries*, 1.28,29 (London: Faith Press, 1960, p. 14).

which we shrink from our mortality. And before her book was done, her illness came, and she found that she was examining her own mortality. The charnel-houses, she says, stirred her to "life-enriching responses".[3] She was surprised to find that preparing to live and preparing to die were the same thing. She remained an Easter Christian in all that she thought and did.

And when her illness came, she found—and remained firm in—her conviction of the healing power of the risen Christ. Whatever happened, alleluia was to be the song. And we prayed for her; more than that, in a truly extraordinary way, John and Denise gathered us into their praying. The prayers in this cathedral and at her parish church of All Saints have been but the tiny centre of an enormous web of praying that has been worldwide, emailed and blogged and connected in all the ways in which news can be shared and words exchanged. John, you have led people in prayer in the past few months, far more than perhaps you know; and many, in their affection and anxiety for you and for Denise, have prayed in ways in which they have not done before.

And Denise has died. Like the sorrowing disciples on the road to Emmaus, we are left saying, "We had hoped . . . we had hoped." But here we need to remember, or learn, that we can only become Easter Christians by being first Maundy Thursday Christians and Good Friday Christians. The stranger who accompanies the disciples on the road to Emmaus gently reminds them of the *whole* story of the one whose death they mourn. *He* had longed to be spared pain and death, that's the Maundy Thursday part, the Gethsemane part; but he was not spared, that's the Good Friday part, the Calvary part; and yet at the end of the road, the disciples find that the one walking beside them is indeed their friend, and he is alive; and that the end of the story—the Easter part—is the resurrection and the life. Jesus is seated at the right hand of God, but only having endured the cross, despising its shame.

Traherne's contemporary, the Puritan leader Richard Baxter, curate of Kidderminster in this diocese, wrote in one of his poems:

---

3   Denise Inge, *A Tour of Bones: Facing Fear and Looking for Life* (London: Bloomsbury, 2014), p. 187.

Christ leads me through no darker rooms
than he went through before;
he [or she] that into God's kingdom comes
must enter by this door.[4]

It is not that we must take our fair share of bad things for good things
to happen; nor that life in this world is so bad that we can only hope
for good things hereafter (no student of Traherne could think that); but
rather it is that we who hope to follow Jesus begin to find the pattern
of his life worked into ours. Our pain becomes part of his passion, our
longings part of his prayer, and the horizon of our lives is lit up by his
resurrection. And we find, too, what Denise so deeply believed and felt,
that Christ is not only the one whom we hope to follow, but is also the
one who is our companion on the road, who walks beside us, who shares
with us his bread, and who is with us at our journey's end.

Three months ago, during that gracious respite of her disease, John
and Denise with many others from this diocese made a pilgrimage to the
Holy Land. You have all seen the picture of Denise and John standing,
hand in hand, trousers rolled up, shin-deep in the River Jordan, looking
for all the world like a pair of children on holiday—which they were.
Denise's smile proclaims the faith of one who is not afraid of the journey's
end. If she felt, as she told us, no more than a bundle of bones wrapped
in thin skin, then her wide and loving heart is plain for all to see. And
when, just a few weeks later, the time came for Denise to tread the verge
of Jordan once again, no one needed to bid her anxious fears subside. She
knew that the death of death and hell's destruction would land her safe
on Canaan's side. She knew (and those who were with her on Easter Day
can testify that she knew) that many waters cannot quench love, neither
can the floods drown it. She had come to know that God takes the dry
bones of our mortality, and he clothes us with the heavens, and he makes
the sea race in our veins, and he crowns us with the stars. Denise, you
are right: whatever happens, alleluia is our song.

---

4   "Lord, it belongs not to my care", *Ancient & Modern: Hymns and Songs for
     Refreshing Worship* (London: Hymns Ancient & Modern, 2013), no. 306.

The Queen is dead, long live the King[1]

The Queen is dead. Long live the King. Those time-honoured sentences, which nowhere form part of the formalities of the succession, nonetheless capture the moment in which we find ourselves. They are a constitutional statement: that the throne is never vacant, that we are never for one moment without a head of state, that beneath all the turbulence of political activity, we have ways of affirming the deep continuity of our national life. They are also an emotional statement. The Queen is dead. Our beloved monarch, monarch for the whole of the lives of so many of us, has gone. It is a time of family bereavement and national mourning. But her successor is there. A new reign has begun. And our lips form those ancient but still unfamiliar words: Long live the *King*.

The scriptures say much about kings, and that is the theme of the readings this morning. The book of Proverbs is a celebration of wisdom, and wisdom here is more than what we usually take it to mean, more than a merely personal quality. Wisdom, in the Old Testament, is one of the primary qualities of God, the principle by which God brought the world into being and continues to uphold it. "By me", speaks the voice of wisdom in this reading, "kings reign, and rulers decree what is just"—words which were alluded to in yesterday's proclamation of the King's accession. And although not all kings are wise, nor are all rulers just, nonetheless the power and authority by which they rule derives from

---

[1]   Sermon preached at the eucharist in Worcester Cathedral on Sunday, 11 September 2022, following the death of Queen Elizabeth II and the accession of King Charles III. The readings were Proverbs 8:1–16; Revelation 21:22—22:4; Luke 22:24–30.

the wisdom that sits at the right hand of God, and the wisdom of God is the standard by which they are judged. The Revelation of St John paints a picture of the heavenly city, God's own kingdom. Here, the nations walk in God's light, and the kings of the earth bring their glory and lay it at the feet of the one who is Lord of lords and King of kings. So the book of Revelation reinforces the message of the book of Proverbs, that earthly kings have a higher allegiance than themselves, and are judged by the benchmark of God's wisdom.

And so we come to the Gospel of St Luke, where Jesus says that the kings of the earth may lord it over their subjects, but he will show the world a better way: "the greatest among you must become like the youngest", he says, "and the leader like one who serves. For [...] I am among you as one who serves."

Jesus is the Servant-King. For him, true kingliness lies in emptying himself and taking the form of a servant and being obedient to the point of death. True kingliness lies in laying aside his garments, and girding himself with a towel, and washing his disciples' feet. So our three readings convey the same message that the true king is one who reigns by the wisdom of God; the true king lays his glory at the feet of the King of kings; the true king does not lord it over his subjects but follows the pattern of the Son of Man who came not to be served but to serve.

We give thanks today for the life of our Queen, in whom these truly sovereign qualities were present to an exemplary degree. That wisdom marked the way in which she reigned for 70 years is not in doubt. That she offered her allegiance, by way of personal commitment and personal conviction, to the King of kings, was a matter of which she made no secret. That her unswerving aspiration, and her unfailing achievement, was that of a life of service, was evident to the end. Characteristically, the last photograph, from last Tuesday, was of her doing her constitutional duty. Equally characteristic was the smile with which she did so.

Each of us has our particular memories of the Queen. My one meeting with her, as some of you know, was on the occasion of her visit to this cathedral in the year of her diamond jubilee. On her arrival, as we paused before the event began, there were a few moments of conversation, of which my main recollection is that she apologized for arriving late. "We're always late," she said, as if with just a bit more effort she could learn to be punctual. I remember saying, absurdly, that it didn't matter. I also treasure the thought that, within the last fortnight of her life, I received the notification that she had approved my retirement as from next year. I don't suppose that she gave it a great deal of thought, but it's important to me. My successor, of course, will be appointed by King Charles.

And so we pray for our new King. There is no doubt that his aspiration is to follow in the footsteps of his mother in all the sovereign qualities that I have just mentioned; that was clear in his moving and impressive broadcast on Friday evening, and again at the accession council yesterday morning. He prays for the wisdom to reign well. He acknowledges his own Christian faith, nurtured in the Church of England. He pledges himself to the same life of service, throughout (as he said) the remaining time that God grants him. Long live the King.

Living queens and living kings hold up to us an image of majesty. It is an ancient image, encrusted by the memories of many times and many places, many countries and many cultures; the reflection of individuals out of history and figures out of legend. The image of kingship remains, even in a world in which actual monarchy has become quite rare, one of extraordinary power. So when Jesus tells his disciples, as he does at the end of the Gospel reading, that he gives them a kingdom, he is saying something of enormous significance:

> You are those who have stood by me in my trials; and I confer on
> you, just as my Father has conferred on me, a kingdom, so that
> you may eat and drink at my table in my kingdom, and you will
> sit on thrones judging the twelve tribes of Israel.

He taught them to see kingship embodied in service. He taught them that service has a regal quality, a royal dignity, a kingly splendour. To be the servant of the King of kings is to be a king or queen, seated at the table of God in the kingdom of God, like the kings of the earth who bring their glory to the holy city. And what Jesus said to his disciples in the Gospel story, he says to us today. To be the servant and follower and disciple and friend of the King of heaven is to be kings and queens ourselves. He confers on us a kingdom.

Each of us is called to live our lives in the light of God's wisdom. Each of us is called to lay what glory we have at the feet of the King of kings. Each of us is called to serve, even as the one who came among us came as one who serves. And insofar as we dedicate our lives to him, he makes kings and queens of us all.

On the purpose of preachers and preaching

Stephen G. Cottrell

What is a sermon for? In scripture, I think that we can identify three kinds of preaching. First, there is the bare-knuckle, backstreet (if you'll forgive the aggressive imagery) proclamation of the basic heart of the gospel which is what today we might call evangelistic preaching and what in the New Testament is called *kerygma*. Then there is teaching, what the New Testament calls *didache*. Third, there is the upbuilding, encouragement, envisioning and inspiring of the congregation which the New Testament calls *paraclesis*. The tricky word *paraclete*, which Jesus used to describe the Holy Spirit in John's Gospel, is actually quite untranslatable into English.[1] Hence English translations of the New Testament come up with different terms, such as "friend", "comforter", "counsellor", and "helper". The New Jerusalem Bible ducks the issue altogether by just saying "paraclete". However, it is this third way of preaching which is, I think, what most ministers should be doing on most Sunday mornings, even if they haven't quite realized it.

Don't misunderstand me: there is still a vital and important place for kerygmatic preaching in the Church today; it's just that it won't usually be done in church buildings on Sunday mornings. It's the kind of proclamation of the message and sharing of the story at which we need to be better, but it will happen in two-minute reflections on local radio, questions and answers with sixth-formers, a breakfast meeting with local business leaders, or evangelistic events in the parish. We don't need to be preaching the basic message of the gospel Sunday morning

---

[1]   John 14:16.

after Sunday morning—though we will need to do it regularly, since it is foolish to imagine that just because people are sitting in church, they have been converted. And it is even more foolish to imagine that even if you have been converted, you don't need to be converted again. In this sense, none of us is ever fully evangelized. Every day—and certainly every Sunday—we need the message of the gospel to transform our lives.

Yet it is my hunch that even if most preachers aren't preaching evangelistic sermons on Sunday morning, what they imagine they are doing is teaching. Now again, don't misunderstand me: of course there is an important element of teaching in every sermon; but I don't believe that this is the main purpose of the sermon on a Sunday morning. After all, we know from every other experience of helping people to learn, that one person standing up and delivering a monologue—however witty and compelling—is not the best way of teaching. As some have put it: the fact that you've said it, doesn't mean that people have heard it. If you want to teach, then your first concern must be to create a learning environment, and this requires a context in which people can ask questions and some real engagement and conversation can take place (hence the success of courses such as Alpha, Emmaus and Pilgrim, which both proclaim and teach the Christian faith in a context of fellowship, conversation and dialogue). Teaching will usually include input from the front; but it must be more than that. So the sermon on a Sunday morning can't simply be teaching.

This is where the helpful concept of *paraclesis* comes in. The sermon is the place where, yes, the gospel is proclaimed, and yes, some teaching will take place—insofar as some information will be imparted—but the main purpose of the sermon will be to tell a story and paint a picture of what life in Christ can be, relating it directly to the challenges and circumstances of that particular congregation in that particular place in that particular time; flowing from the source and wellspring of life in Christ which is the weekly diet of scripture on which the sermon is based; and leading and preparing people for their participation around the table, where they will receive the word which is the living bread from heaven, Jesus himself.

This kind of preaching is both art and craft (it is vitally important that preachers learn the craft of public speaking and the tricks of the trade that go with it) and is a category of speaking, encouraging and commending which is different from but related to proclamation and teaching. It will inspire and motivate. Yet it will also carefully apply the lessons and insights from scripture into the context of that congregation's everyday life and everyday faith.

My concern, if I might be so presumptuous, is that many preachers haven't quite worked out that this is the purpose of the sermon as part of the worship and liturgical assembly of the Church, flowing from the scriptures and leading to the altar, and then—vitally—out from the altar into the world, so that the faith which we celebrate and explore on Sunday shapes and informs the lives that we lead on Monday, relating the life of faith to our missionary discipleship in the world each day.

These kinds of sermons will have the Bible in one hand and—as it were—the newspaper (or is it the iPad) in the other. The needs of the world and the news of the world will be interrogated and understood through the lens of faith. Such sermons will often touch on deep issues of life and death, the things with which all of us must live and through which we must navigate our way. The immediate issues of the local neighbourhood will be addressed. So will the biggest global concerns. We will learn to be like Christ. We will seek to have Christ's mind.

Such preaching should be beautiful. It will sometimes make us laugh. It will often make us cry. St Jerome wrote that "When you are teaching in church, try not to seek applause but lamentation. Let the tears of your hearers be your glory."[2] Just as stand-up comics nowadays get their laughs not by telling jokes, but by telling stories, so we will paint a picture and tell a story about what life looks like, lived in relationship with God each day, and how we face its challenges and receive its delights. As the stand-up comic tells stories about life, shows us how absurd life is, and makes us laugh, so the preacher tells stories about life, shows us how holy it can be, and leads us to worship and to lament that the world is not as it is meant to be.

Someone once said that they didn't remember sermons, they remembered preachers. This is a hugely significant observation. We may

---

2   Jerome, *Letter* 52.8, translated in Robert R. Atwell (ed.), *Celebrating the Saints*, 4th edn (Norwich: Canterbury Press, 2016), p. 378.

remember the sermon itself for a few hours, and possibly even a few days, while most of us will remember very few sermons for much longer than this. Yet I can remember the preachers who delivered them. Somehow, they themselves became the living embodiment of the words that they were sharing about how to live and understand the Christian faith. We remember how it felt when they spoke to us, even if we now forget the words themselves. They were able to put into words things that made sense to us. They gave us a vision of what it means to live the Christian life and follow Jesus. The Holy Spirit used their words to enable us to persevere and continue in the Christian faith and lead us to the living Word, which is Christ himself.

This also means that the gift of the preacher flows from and is rooted in their own life in Christ, their own submission to the will of God, their own deep reading of the scriptures and their watchfulness in prayer. Nothing is more important than this for Spirit-filled preaching, which builds people up as the body of Christ. As Lancelot Andrewes, the seventeenth-century bishop of Winchester, wrote:

> Let the preacher labour to be heard intelligently, willingly, obediently. And let him not doubt, that he will accomplish this rather by the piety of his prayers, than the eloquence of his speech. By praying for himself, and those whom he is to address, let him be their beadsman, before their teacher; and approaching God with devotion, let him first raise to Him a thirsting heart, before he speaks of Him with his tongue; that He may speak what he hath been taught, and pour out what hath been poured in.[3]

As I remember all the preachers whom I have heard over the years, there are a particular handful whose preaching has made an impact in my life and whose words, for me, so evidently flowed from their life in Christ. One of them is Peter Atkinson. I don't think that I've heard him preach for over 30 years, but on all kinds of occasions during that time I have found myself saying that he is, in my view, the best preacher in the Church of

---

3   *The Private Devotions of Lancelot Andrewes*, tr. John H. Newman and John M. Neale (London: H. R. Allenson, undated), pp. 275–6.

England. I've enjoyed reading these sermons of his, because they contain such pastoral wisdom and exemplify preaching as *paraclesis*. As I recall the sermons that I actually heard him deliver when we were colleagues in Chichester many years ago, it is the impact of the sermon on my life and how it felt and what it did to me that I remember. In other words, it helped me to live the Christian life. It is what most sermons are for.

Further reading

Further material by Peter Atkinson on themes from the sermons can be found as follows:

For more on **cathedrals**, see "Cathedrals at Prayer", in Stephen Platten (ed.), *Holy Ground: Cathedrals in the Twenty-First Century* (Durham: Sacristy Press, 2017), pp. 123–37.

For more on **friendship**, see *Friendship and the Body of Christ* (London: SPCK, 2004).

For more on **poetry**, see "Poets in Wartime: A Study of Geoffrey Studdert Kennedy and Geoffrey Dearmer", in Michael W. Brierley and Georgina A. Byrne (eds), *Life after Tragedy: Essays on Faith and the First World War Evoked by Geoffrey Studdert Kennedy* (Eugene, OR: Cascade Books, 2017), pp. 54–74.

For more on **scripture**, see *The Lion Encyclopedia of the Bible* (Oxford: Lion Hudson, 2009, translated into Arabic, Chinese, Czech, Dutch, French, Georgian, German, Indonesian, Polish, Romanian, and Spanish).

For more on **Shakespeare**, see "Spiritual Studies", in Evelyn Gajowski (ed.), *The Arden Research Handbook of Contemporary Shakespeare Criticism* (London and New York: Bloomsbury Publishing, 2021), pp. 222–32.

For more on **prayer and spiritual discipline**, see "Martin Thornton", in Michael W. Brierley and Stephen Burns (eds), *British Anglican Spiritual Writers of the Twentieth Century: 1963–2004* (Leiden: Brill, forthcoming).

For more on **collections of sermons**, see the review of Michael F. Perham, *One Unfolding Story*; David M. Hoyle, *A Year of Grace*; Alan B. Wilkinson, *Reflections for the Unfolding Year*; and Robert M. C. Jeffery, *The Kingdom of God Is Like a Yoghurt Plant*, *Modern Believing* 61 (2020), pp. 191–4.